Microsoft Office 2000

E CDC
Book 12

Guide & Assignments

Mary Wade

Kayser's Computing

KAYSER'S COMPUTING
Tourist House
41 Grand Parade
Cork
kaysers@indigo.ie   www.kayserscomputing.com
Mary Wade 2002

Screen shots reprinted with permission from Microsoft Corporation

Preface

This Microsoft Office 2000 Guide and Assignments Book explains concisely with precise diagrams the salient features of Word, Excel, PowerPoint and Access. The efficient management of documents, files and folders, is fully illustrated. Clear theoretical definitions of the computer world are included as well as a comprehensive guide on browsing and e-mail on the Internet. The guide's systematic structure combined with graded exercises throughout should ensure the competence of any vigiliant student.

Students at Kayser's Computing - an ECDL and City & Guilds Centre in Cork - use this guide and approve its practicality.

This guide is intended for novice and intermediate users of Microsoft Office and the Internet.

Any comments or queries to be sent to: kaysers@indigo.ie

Mary Wade

To my wonderful son, Willie, with all my love

Contents

Guide & Assignments for

Contents

Contents

Computer Theory

Types of Computers

Mainframe:

- Mainframes costing anything between £200,000 and several million pounds are used where there is a need for a computer that can cope with very high volume of transactions.
- Banks, insurance companies, and the government would be typical users.
- Mainframes are used to hold vast databases of information, which can be accessed quickly and updated by large numbers of users at the same time and support a large number of peripherals.
- Have a very large storage capacity.
- The mainframe's power is due to the phenomenal speed of the processor and the large size of the main memory.

PC:

- Acronym for **Personal Computer**
- Is a complete self-contained system
- Personal Computer costing about £1,000 is a computer generally for the use of one person at a time.
- The PC contains a single microprocessor and will be restricted in terms of both speed and storage capacity.
- The main uses of PCs are as desk-top business computers used for word-processing, small business accounts, and financial planning, or as home computers.
- Capable of stand-alone or networked use - it is possible to link PCs together to form a network that can share storage facilities, printers, or files of information.
- PCs generally cost about £1000 for a standard model.

Laptop computers:

- A microcomputer that is portable and has its own integral screen and keyboard.
- Laptops are currently about the size of a ream of A4 paper and may require electric power or have their own rechargeable batteries.
- May be bought for £1,500 plus, have limited storage capacity, their speed would be comparable to a PC - 64MB RAM would be fairly standard.

Dumb Terminal:

- A dumb terminal is an input and output device with no processing power of its own and consists of a keyboard, display screen and a communication link to a mainframe computer.

Intelligent terminal:

- An intelligent terminal is a terminal which retains a program and allows processing of data to be carried out without further access to the host computer

Hardware

The *physical* components that make up a computer system are referred to as hardware. The hardware of a typical personal computer would include a screen (known as a visual display unit or VDU), a keyboard, a printer, and the case containing the computer itself (also referred to as the processor). Generally, all computer systems include these basic components, although the specifications will vary depending on how big the systems are and what they will be used for.

Software (Application Software - see below)

Operating System: The most important systems software is the operating system. Operating systems include DOS, OS/2, Windows 3.1, 95, 98 and 2000. Having tested the presence and functioning of its components: keyboard, mouse etc, the operating system is automatically loaded when the computer is switched on. If it fails to load, the computer will not work. It translates the commands received from the applications software: word processing programs, spreadsheets etc into instructions specific to the hardware: the processor, hard disks, video system, network cards etc.

The number of functions that an operating system performs is dependent on the size and power of the computer - the operations of a powerful mainframe with many users cannot be compared to the operating system of a PC with one user; however many of the activities will be the same:
> Booting up the system, controlling input and output devices, managing the transmission of data between application software, storage device and RAM. Distributing RAM, controlling input and output devices, allowing/preventing access to authorised/unauthorised users.

System software: also includes programs which are known as *drivers*. Certain printers, for example, require separate drivers, compatible with the current operating system, to be installed before the printer will work.

Data - 3 Stages: Input, Processing, Output

Input: Data is input into the computer by, for example, typing on a keyboard or using a scanning device such as a bar-code reader in a supermarket

Processing: Once the data is input, it is processed in the "brains" of the computer - the central processing unit (CPU)

- The central processing unit is the little chip in personal computers that controls everything. It is where the basic calculating is done that translates data into files

  Output: Once the data has been processed, information can be distributed to users.

  There are *two* types of output: *soft* copy and *hard* copy
- **Soft copy** is information that is seen on a monitor - It is temporary: once the monitor is turned off or new information is required, the old information vanishes.
- **Hard copy** is output printed in a touchable form such as on paper or microfilm.

Electronic Commerce

Electronic Commerce or e-Commerce - a generic term for all forms of business transactions on the Internet. The potential of a facility to advertise and sell ones 'product' via a web site to mass audiences has limitless appeal.

- The seven most popular buys on-line are: Books, CDs, Travel, music, electronics, computer hardware and clothing. To date, books sales on-line have shown phenomenal growth - Amazon.com has been the trail blazer in this regard. Buyers can shop around for the best deals - many goods can be bought from competitive internet sites much cheaper than from a store. CDs from America can be bought for half the local price; however, delivery cost, which could be anything from courier services to standard airmail, could be considerable. Goods are sold to the highest bidders through auctions on-line - caution is advised as you could end up paying much more than the goods are worth.
- Look out for specialist web sites; Amazon.com, already mentioned, the Web's best known bookstore, now has a British subsidiary: Amazon.co.uk. Lastminute.com specialise not only in cheap travel but also in occasional purchases like cars or mobile phones.
- Shopping on-line using a credit card is relatively safe. However, it is advisable to use e-commerce sites that keep your card details on a secure server so you don't have to send them each time you make a purchase. Ensure that your browser is set up for secure connections to the internet. A padlock displaying on the status bar of the program when you connect to a secure server indicates that your data is secure.

Requirements for connecting a Computer to the Internet

- A computer with a fast processor, 32MB of RAM, up to 100 MB of free hard disk
- A Modem - the most commonly used and cheapest method of connecting to the Internet is by installing a modem and dialing via the standard telephone network.
- A Telephone line
- An Internet Service Provider (ISP). Your modem via the telephone line will link you to the Internet through the computer system of the service provider
- Connection Software: provided by the Service Provider to enable you to establish a connection through their company to the Internet

Application Software

- This term generally applies to program written for a particular purpose such as:

Word Processing:

A program specifically developed for the typing and production of letters, report and documents. Text may be keyed in and saved on disk. Unlike a typewriter, text can be recalled from disk and modified. Word processing software provides features for: Spell Checking, emboldening, italicising, deleting, moving or copying text. Text can be found and replaced with alternative text, font type and size can be changed, headers and footers can be added and tables and columns of text can be created. Using a mail merge facility, standard documents can be created and merged with variables from another file - end result appears as an original for each set of data merged.

Spreadsheets:

The most commonly used spreadsheet today is Excel. A new document in a spreadsheet known as a workbook consists of 3 default worksheet pages.

Workbooks: In Microsoft Excel, a workbook is the file in which you work and store your data. Because each workbook can contain many worksheets, named respectively: Sheet1, Sheet2 and Sheet3, you can organize various kinds of related information in a single file.

Worksheets: Use worksheets to list and analyze data. You can enter and edit data on several worksheets simultaneously and perform calculations based on data from multiple worksheets. When you create a chart, you can place the chart on the worksheet with its related data or on a separate chart sheet.

Sheet tabs: The names of the sheets appear on tabs at the bottom of the workbook window. To move from sheet to sheet, click the sheet tabs. (See Excel section)

- Each spreadsheet consists of columns down and rows across. The intersection where a column down meets a row across is called a **cell**. By default, text is left-aligned and numbers are right-aligned

- Text can be entered as headings or labels for rows, columns or groups of cells. Spreadsheets largely are used for calculations from a simple addition to a complicated formulae. The graph feature has a wide range of options used for comparisons of data.

Databases:

A database is a collection of information that's related to a particular subject or purpose, such as keeping track of customer orders.

- Using Microsoft Access, the most popular database application in use today, you can manage all your information from a single database file.

- Within the file, divide your data into separate areas called tables; view, add, and update table data by using forms; find and retrieve just the data you want by using queries; and analyze or print data in a specific layout by using reports.

- **Tables:** To store your data, create one table for each type of information that you have. To bring the data from multiple tables together in a query, form, report, or data access page, define relationships between the tables.

- **Queries:** To find and retrieve data that meets specified conditions including data from multiple tables, create a query. A query can also update or delete multiple records at the same time, and perform predefined or custom calculations on your data.

- **Forms:** To easily view, enter, and change data directly in a table, create a form. When you open a form, Microsoft Access retrieves the data from one or more tables, and displays it on the screen with the layout you choose in the Form Wizard, or a layout that you create from scratch.

- **Reports:** To analyze your data or present it a certain way in print, create a report. For example, you might print one report that groups data and calculates totals, and another report with different data formatted for printing mailing labels.

Presentation Software:

The most commonly Presentation Software used today is **PowerPoint**. Also known as presentation graphics, a type of business program for creating highly visual presentations including charts, graphs, text, sound and even videos

- You can create on-screen presentations, web pages for web use, coloured and black and white overheads, coloured and black and white paper printouts, 35 mm slides, audience handouts or speaker notes. As you work, you can choose from **5 Views**: Slide, Outline, Notes, Slide Sorter or Slide Show View.

- You have a choice of using the pre-designed presentations with suggested content prepared by professionals or creating your own presentations from the start if you know what you want to say.

- A design can be selected to add the look you want to your presentation. Add as many slides as you need; choose an Auto layout that best matches the information you want on each slide - this will take care of alignment and placement of text and objects on your slides.

DeskTop Publishing (DTP):

A program for producing professional-quality reports, booklets and magazines on a computer and peripherals. A DTP system usually consists of a computer, a mouse, a laser printer and associated software (integrated word processing, graphics and page-making programs). A scanner can be used for reproducing photographs and other artwork.

- Text and graphics can be made up into magazine-type layout with a variety of type faces and headings.

- Powerful DTP packages such as QuarkXPress and Corel's Ventura allow precise control of typefaces, placement of illustrations, indexing etc.

- Microsoft's Publisher provides pre-designed templates for a wide range of documents: newsletters, cards, banners, flyers, brochures, calendars, advertisements - these templates can be modified or the user can create from scratch. Text boxes embodying the full range of WP enhancement features are used for the inputting of text. Long textual documents can be created in a word processing software and easily imported into a text box within Microsoft Publisher.

- Text boxes can be linked so that any overflow of text in one box can be accommodated in another within a page or between pages. A datasheet frame is used for the inputting of columns and rows of data similar to a spreadsheet. Clip Art can be added to a page. Drawings created in specialized drawing packages can be imported into picture boxes. Similarly, pictures can be scanned and saved in a drawing package and easily imported.

Memory Measurement

- **Bit:** Short for Binary Digit - the smallest unit of data that the computer can handle. Data is represented by **on** and **off** states of the computer's electronic circuitry. The binary digit for on is 0 and off is 1.
- **Character:** Combination of bits (0s and 1s) are used to represent characters: letters, digits and special symbols like: $, % etc.
- **Byte:** A fixed number of adjacent bits that represent a character are called a byte - this is the amount of memory needed to store one character such as a letter or a number. Eight bits are used to represent a character
- **Field:** A collection of related characters - see Section on databases: Access.
- **Record:** A collection of fields that relate to a single unit is a record.
- **File:** A grouping of related records, such as student records.
- **Kilobytes:** is equal to 1,024 bytes or characters (KB).
- **Megabytes:** is equal to 1,024 kilobytes (approx one million bytes - abbreviated to: MB)
- **Gigabytes:** is equal to one billion bytes (abbreviated to: GB).

Computer Power

The power of a computer processing data into information is dictated by:
- CPU Speed
- The amount of RAM
- Cache memory
- Hard disk size
- Clock speed

Central Processing Unit (CPU)

- The Central Processing Unit (CPU) is the central part of the computer system consisting of the control unit, the arithmetic/logic unit and main memory - all function together as a unit.
- When data and programs enter the CPU via an **input** device such as a keyboard, they are held for processing in memory: **RAM** - see below:

Random Access Memory (RAM):

- RAM is **temporary** fast memory
- Handles your work since you last saved it
- RAM is **volatile** and data is lost when the power to the computer is turned off.
- Saving your work moves it **permanently** from RAM to disk
- The processed data in memory can be transferred to an **output** device: secondary memory. Typical output devices are Printers: print results on paper; Visual Display Units: project results on screen; or Tape and Disk drives: produce machine-readable magnetic results.
- RAM is what we mean when we refer to main memory or primary storage
- Term random access comes from the fact that data can be stored/retrieved at random
- Microcomputers come with varying amounts of RAM - the standard today is 64MB.
- Additional RAM chips can be added by installing a memory-expansion card. More RAM you have, the faster the computer operates, and the better the software performs.

Cache memory

- Pronounced "cash," cache memory is a special high-speed memory area that the CPU can access quickly.
- Cache memory is used in computers with very fast CPUs, so that these CPUs don't have to wait for data to be delivered from RAM.
- The most frequently used instructions are kept in the cache memory so the CPU can look there first. This allows the CPU to run faster because it doesn't have to take time to swap instructions in and out of RAM.
- Large, complex programs benefit the most from having a cache memory available.

Hard Disks

- Hard disks enable large amounts of data to be stored, accessed, and read at very high speeds.
- The hard disk consists of magnetic storage plates encased in a hard disk drive which is enclosed in the case of a computer.
- It is the computer's main storage device holding the files for the operating system plus the program and data files.

The System Clock

- Every microprocessor contains a system clock. The system clock controls how fast all the operations within a computer take place.
- Processing speeds are expressed in megahertz (MHz)

ROM (Read-only memory)

- A memory that holds data or special instructions for computer operations, such as starting the computer or putting characters on the screen.
- Unlike RAM, which is constantly being written on and erased, ROM, also known as firmware, cannot be altered by the computer or programmer - the actual content of ROM is fixed at the time of its manufacture.

Other Forms of Memory

- The performance of microcomputers can be enhanced further by adding other forms of memory, as follows:

Video memory:

- Video memory or video RAM (VRAM) chips are used to store display images for monitor.
- The amount of video memory determines how fast images appear and how many colours are available.
- Video memory chips essential when running programs that display a lot of graphics.

Input devices

- Within computer terminology, the word 'input' refers to anything that goes into a computer for processing from whatever source, mechanical or human. Inputting methods have evolved dramatically over the years from the earlier use of keyboard, punched cards, and paper tape. Input methods include:

The keyboard:

- The keyboard is still the most widely used input device, but it is also the most inefficient in terms of its speed of input.

The mouse:

- The mouse is a pointing device in which movements of the mouse are linked to movements of a cursor on a VDU screen. The cursor travels around the screen in response to the action of the user moving the mouse around the desk.
- A mouse-driven computer enables a user to select a desired option by 'pointing' the cursor at an icon and pressing a button on the mouse to select it.
- To select an option from a menu, the user will once more point the cursor at the required item and press a button on the mouse.

Touch screens (Touch pads):

- Touch screens, like the mouse, are designed to avoid the use of a computer keyboard when using menu-driven software.
- In order to select from a menu of choices displayed on a touch screen, the user will simply touch the appropriate icon or other reference on the screen. This action will be sensed by the computer, and the option chosen will be acted upon.

Joystick:

- An input device for a microcomputer. The stick as it moves (usually in one of eight directions) is able to control the movement of a shape on the screen.
- Sometimes there are two joysticks enabling a screen game to be played by two players.

Tracker ball (track ball):

- Another pointing device with a large ball which you rotate to move the mouse cursor; commonly found on notebook computers as a flat surface is not required for its operation.
- To use a tracker ball, you simply move the ball in the required direction using your fingers. Buttons are used as you do with a mouse.

Voice input:

- It is possible to program a computer to respond to voice commands.
- Most of the present voice-recognition systems need to be 'trained' to cope with a particular voice, and they must be retrained if the user gets a cold or has a sore throat.

Document readers:

- Document-based data can be read by humans as well as by machines.
- Document readers are used where there is a need to be able to process large volumes of similar documents, like cheques or gas bills, quickly.
- Examples of use are in the automated processing of cheques, the computer marking of multiple-choice answer sheets, and the reading of large volumes of credit-card payment slips.

Optical character recognition (OCR):

- This is a system that enables information to be automatically 'read' from a printed document. Modern OCR scanners can recognise typed and neatly handwritten material.
- OCR is used by organisations like the gas, electricity, and credit-card companies, all of whom need to process large numbers of similar documents in a short space of time.

Optical mark recognition (OMR):

- This is a simpler optical system that is designed to detect the presence of pencil marks made on a pre-printed document.
- Optical mark recognition (OMR) is used in areas where the data to be collected has a set number of options - applications include multiple-choice examinations, market research, stock control, and employees' time-sheets.
- Speed of input of OMR systems can be anything up to 200 documents a minute.

Magnetic-ink character recognition (MICR):

- The system of magnetic-ink character recognition was originally developed in the United States to enable the fast and efficient clearing of cheques.
- For MICR, the characters are printed in a special ink that can be magnetised to give off a unique magnetic field that enables each character to be read.
- MICR is used by the banks as a way of speeding up the cheque-clearing system - input speeds can be anything up to 2000 cheques a minute.

Bar-code readers:

- Bar codes are an arrangement of vertical bars and spaces that can be read by an optical scanner and used as a means of identifying products or stock items.
- Bar codes can be seen on most products purchased in supermarkets, inside library books (to control book issues), and on such items as freezers and computers.
- In supermarkets, each product carries a unique bar code that can be used both to calculate the size of the bill at the point-of-sale (POS) terminals (or check-outs) and for stock control.
- The system operates from a central computer which controls the POS terminals' scanners as the bar code is read on each item.
- When shoppers goes through a check-out, each item is passed over the scanner which reads the bar code and refers to the central computer for the description and price.
- This information is relayed to the check-out, where it is displayed on a customer panel and printed on the receipt. At the same time, the stock level for the item purchased will be reduced, providing management with up-to-date stock information and enabling more efficient stock control and ordering.

Light Pens:

- A device used in conjunction with special hardware and software that shines light on to a VDU screen to indicate a choice from a menu or to input a location in graphics work.
- In libraries, the bar codes are read by using a light-pen or wand.
- Input speeds are limited by the user, but data can be read in from a bar code at around 1.4 cm per second.

Card readers

- A card reader is a device that reads information held in the form of a magnetic stripe on a plastic card.
- Applications include cheque guarantee cards, credit cards, ATM (cash-dispenser) cards, magnetic keys, and identity cards.
- The magnetic stripe on the back of the card may hold the personal details of the owner and, with the necessary secret number, will allow access to restricted computing facilities, secure locations, credit facilities, or a bank account.
- Card readers are becoming more common as retail outlets install them to electronically capture sales information on goods purchased with credit and debit cards.

Graphics input:

- There are several ways of inputting a graphical image to a computer, three of which - the graphics pad, the image scanner, and the video scanner - are outlined below.

Graphics pads:

- A graphics pad or tablet can be used to input a graphic image to a computer in two ways: with a stylus or with a cursor.
- Freehand images may be input by drawing with the stylus on the 'bed' of the pad, below which a complex grid of wires is able to sense the position of the stylus and feed this into the computer.
- Existing drawings may be traced by the stylus on to the bed; alternatively, they may be input by using a cursor similar to a mouse.
- The cursor is positioned in turn over the key points on the drawing and one of the buttons on it is pressed.
- The computer records these points and joins them together as necessary to define the complete image.
- When used to input existing drawings, graphics pads may also be called digitisers.
- They are used by architects to design buildings, by map makers in cartography, and as part of complex CAD systems in mechanical and electrical engineering.

Image scanners:

- The image scanner is used as a means of capturing an existing two-dimensional image - a drawing or a photograph that could not be input using a graphics pad..
- Image scanners divide a picture into a matrix of millions of tiny dots each of which is stored in a file in the computer.
- It is then possible to use this file with an existing text file in order to combine pictures with text as in a newspaper.

Video scanners:

- The video scanner uses a video camera to capture an image for processing either of an existing two-dimensional picture or of a three-dimensional object.
- Video scanners will generally offer a higher resolution than image scanners

Computer Output

Computer output can take the form of a display on a screen, a print-out, or transfer of information on to a magnetic tape or disk. Most output falls into one of two categories: hard copy or soft copy. Output in a permanent or printed form is called hard copy, whereas output displayed on a screen or in audio form is called soft copy.

Soft-copy output:

- Information that is output as soft copy will either be displayed visually on a screen or else be in audio form, as in speech or music.

Visual output:

- The most common form of soft-copy output is information displayed on a screen or cathode-ray tube (CRT).
- CRTs can display information in either colour or monochrome.
- A CRT is the major component in a number of devices, notably the visual display unit (VDU), and the monitor.
- The VDU enables the user to input information to a computer by using a keyboard, mouse, or touch screen facilities and to view output on a CRT.
- A computer monitor is a high-quality CRT that is used solely for viewing output and has no other devices attached.
- Two factors limit the use of the CRT: its weight and amount of power it consumes.
- Portable computers. which must be light and be able to operate from batteries. have thus been forced to use an alternative type of display.
- Liquid-crystal displays (LCDs). similar to those found on some digital watches. are both light and economical enough to be widely used for portable computers.

Audio output:

- Audio output covers the range from the simple 'beep' to full speech synthesis.
- Speech synthesis is the production of a sound corresponding to spoken words and it is of great use where a user is unable to look at a CRT or is occupied with another task.

Hard-copy output:

- Hard copy can be defined as computer output that is in a permanent form.
- Hard copy is usually in the form of a paper print-out, although computer put on microfilm or microfiche may also be considered a form of hard copy.
- Paper print-out may be produced either on separate sheets or on continuous stationery taking the form of folded and perforated lengths of paper

Printers

There are two categories of printers:

Matrix printers:

- All matrix printers produce text and graphics images as a series of individual dots.
- To produce text of a higher quality, it is necessary to use a larger number of dots in the same area.

Dot-matrix printers:

- The dot-matrix printer is widely used as a micro-computer peripheral.
- It gets its name from the way in which a number of needles in the print head are used to print text as a series of dots using a carbon ribbon.
- The speed at which a dot-matrix printer is able to operate depends on which typeface is being printed.
- Typical speeds for a dot-matrix printer may range between 40 and 500c.p.s. according to the print quality.

Ink-jet printers:

- The ink-jet printer forms characters by projecting ink at high speed from a number of small ink nozzles on to paper, and for this reason it is termed a non-impact printer.
- Characters are produced from dots in the same way as by the dot-matrix printer.
- The major advantage over a dot-matrix printer is the very low level of noise of the ink-jet printer in operation, due to the fact that printing does not involve any impact other than that of the ink upon the paper.

Thermal printers:

- Thermal printers use heat to transfer the image from the print head to the paper.
- Text and images are made up from a series of dots, in common with other matrix printers, but with this process the print head may be either a fixed array of thermal elements that stretches across the entire width of the paper or a moving print head.

Laser printers:

- The laser printer shares the same image-printer technology as the photocopier.
- The print image is produced by a laser beam which scans across the print drum line for line as the print cylinder rotates.

Daisy-wheel printers:

- The daisy wheel from which this printer takes its name is a flat disc with a number of stalks, or 'petals', radiating from its centre, each of which has a character at its tip.
- In use, the daisy wheel rotates at high speed and the 'petals' are pushed on to a ribbon which in turn transfers the characters to the paper.

Line printer:

- The line printer gets its name from the way in which it prints a line of text at a time.
- There are two types of line printer - the chain printer and the drum printer - and, although they operate slightly differently, they produce similar results.
- The main feature of line printers is their speed, the fastest machines printing text at around 5000 lines per minute (l.p.m.). This is achieved by hitting the paper against the character and printer ribbon, rather than vice versa as with most other printers.

Graph plotters:

- The graph plotter is a specialist device that is designed to produce high-quality pictures and designs.
- Unlike matrix printers, a graph plotter reproduces the human action of drawing by using a pen.
- Graph plotters are widely used by architects and designers of all kinds.
- There are two types of graph plotter - flatbed and drum.

Computer output on microfilm or microfiche (COM):

- As an alternative to printed output, another form of hard copy is computer output on microfilm or microfiche
- COM is the recording of what would otherwise be printed output direct in reduced form on to either rolls or sheets of photographic film.

Peripherals

A Peripheral is any device that is connected to and controlled by a computer but external to the CPU etc. Examples of "peripheral Storage" are discussed below:

Primary and Secondary Storage:

The term primary storage (main memory) refers to RAM - discussed above

Secondary storage (or auxiliary storage):

- Secondary storage is any storage device designed to retain data and instructions (programs) in a relatively permanent form.
- Secondary storage is non-volatile, meaning that saved data and instructions remain intact when the computer is turned off.

Computer Speakers:

- These speakers have the same function as hi-fi music speakers used in home stereo systems.
- They differ however from conventional speakers in that they are self-amplified and magnetically shielded.
- Most speakers are AC powered and have separate volume and tone controls.

Magnetic disk and tape input:

- A magnetic disk is a computer storage device that looks rather like an LP record that has the same magnetic coating as an audio cassette tape.
- Information is recorded on to and read from the surface of the disk in much the same way as a domestic cassette tape-recorder is used to record and play back music
- Magnetic tape is the computer equivalent of the reel-to-reel tapes found on professional tape recorders.
- Magnetic disks and tape are both widely used for the storage of computerised information.
- In applications where large volumes of data have to be processed, it is usually a more efficient use of central-computer time if data is input on to a magnetic tape or disk before processing.
- This is because data can be transferred from a magnetic disk or tape far faster than it can be input from any other device.
- Speeds of input from magnetic tape or disk are termed data transfer rates
- Even though the keyboard is the slowest means of input, because it is familiar and relatively easy to operate it is the most widely used input device.

Diskettes:

- A diskette, or floppy disk stores data and programs as magnetized spots.
- The disk is contained in a plastic case to protect it from being touched by human hands.
- Diskettes are sometimes called "floppy" because the disk within the envelope or case is flexible, not rigid.
- A floppy disk measures 3.5" across. It comes inside a hard plastic jacket, so that no additional protective envelope is needed.

Optical media:

CD-ROM (compact disk, read only memory):

- The CD-ROM is not used for storage of documents, which require regular updating, because the medium cannot be written to by a CD-ROM drive; it is read only.
- However, the CD-ROM is widely used for reference material and training purposes, its huge capacity making it ideal for the storage of all forms of image, including video sequences, which take large amounts of storage space.
- The speed of CD-ROM drives is regularly being improved, although its access time cannot yet match those of magnetic hard drives.
- Software is generally supplied on CD-ROM, so the CD-ROM drive is now standard equipment on computers.

CO-R (recordable compact disk):

- The cost of CD-writers has fallen to an extent that even small organisations can afford to record their own CDs, perhaps in multi-media form, for training purposes.
- In such cases, the authoring process requires knowledge and skill in the use of suitable software if the multi-media aspects of CD-ROM storage are to be exploited.
- A specialist company, with equipment to produce a glass master, normally carries out the production of multiple copies.
- Using a CD-writer to produce multiple copies is a relatively slow and expensive process and does not guarantee that every copy is identical to the original and error free.

Microform:

- As a celluloid medium, microform can store documentary information with textual and graphical content.
- The structure of the microform can be either microfilm (a continuous reel) or microfiche (a grid pattern)
- Microform reduces storage space requirements by approximately 95% of that required by paper documentation.

Zip Disk/Zip Drive:

- A removable disk manufactured by Iomega with capacity of 100MB.
- Can be internal or external

Systems-software utilities:

- Utilities are programs that are designed to assist with the routine tasks of running a computer system.
- Examples of common utilities are programs to copy or delete files, rename files, and format new disks.
- Utilities like text editors (used to write and amend programs) and debuggers (used for finding errors in programs) may also be available to assist in the writing and debugging of computer programs.

Repetitive strain injury (RSI):

Repetitive strain injury also known as repetitive motion injury and cumulative trauma disorder is the name given to a number of injuries resulting from fast, repetitive work:

- RSI causes neck, wrist, hand, and arm pain.
- RSI problems can result from prolonged computer keyboard use
- An RSI called carpal tunnel syndrome is particularly common among people who use computers and certain types of scanners intensively. This syndrome involves damage to nerves and tendons in the hands.

RSI Causes:

RSI is basically caused by four factors:

- **Repetition and duration:** Prolonged, constant, and repetitious movements such as typing irritate tendons and nerve casings, causing them to swell.
- **Force:** The harder you hit the the keys, the more likely you are to suffer injury
- **Joint angle:** Flexing, raising, or twisting hands to reach the keys constricts the carpal tunnel (pinches the medial nerve running through the wrist).
- **Prolonged constrained posture:** Holding any position without moving puts excessive strain on muscles and tendons.
- For some victims, the pain of carpal tunnel syndrome is so intense that they cannot open doors or shake hands.
- Left untreated, this syndrome can cause atrophied muscles and permanent nerve damage.

To avoid RSI:

- Take frequent short rest breaks instead of infrequent long ones.
- Get plenty of sleep and exercise, maintain appropriate weight, sit up straight, and learn stress-management techniques.

Graphical User Interface: (GUI)

- GUI incorporates four elements: windows, icons, menus and a pointing device
- Programs such as the Apple Macintosh Finder or Microsoft Windows use a computerised desktop as the interface between the user and the operating system Pictures or icons are used to represent such items as disks, files and programs. A GUI has pull-down menus that allow the user to select from a predefined list of command choices. A GUI uses a mouse to allow the user to point at and select the items or commands that are required.
- GUI is easy to use -the icons are self-explanatory; a lot of similarity between basic functions of all Windows-based software

Data Protection Act

In response to the perceived threat of computers to personal privacy, Legislation was passed: The Data Protection Act of 1984 - to safeguard the privacy of the individual:

- This Act was enacted by the UK to comply with the Council of Europe Convention
- This legislation protects personal data handled in computers
- The aim of the legislation is to control the immense potential for misuse of information that arises when personal data is stored in computers
- Once the data has been transcribed from paper files into a form that is easily readable and accessibly by computers, it is an inexpensive and easy task for the data to be extracted from one record and correlated with personal data concerning the same person from another file - resulting in a combination of information that is considered to be an infringement of privacy.

The Data Protection Act makes the following requirements of organisations that maintain personal records on computers:

- To declare and/or register the use for which the data is stored
- To provide the data subject with a right of access to data concerning himself on their computer
- To maintain a prescribed minimum level of electronic and physical security in their computer installations
- Not to transmit personal data to any organisation that does not have similar controls over misuse of data
- In Europe, a convention concerning misuses of data was signed by all member countries of the Council of Europe
- The OECDS has also drafted a convention of similar effects

Data Security

- A system of data security must make information available to those authorised to receive without undue delay or inefficiency.
- It must keep information secret from those not so authorised in such a way that the cost of unauthorised disclosure would exceed the value of the information to the illegitimate recipient
- This system may involve physical security (safes, locks entry cards) for access to disks and passwords and also the technique of cryptography and authentication.

Health and Safety: computer work environment

- Prolonged use of computers can cause eyestrain, muscular strain, changes in colour perception, back and neck pain, stomach aches, and nausea.
- To reduce such physical problems, it is recommended that the time spent at a VDU be reduced to a maximum of two hours per day of continuous screen work.
- It is recommended that periodic rest breaks be granted
- Steps should be taken to reduce or alleviate glare produced by overhead fluorescent lighting - glare reduction screens should be available as required by the employee.
- The computer screen should be adjustable to the extent that it can be swiveled and tilted in accordance with the user's requirements.
- The keyboard should be separate and adjustable, with numeric keypads and function keys, so that the user can adjust as appropriate - keyboards on a standard desk may be too high or too low for an employee.
- Other problems with the workstation might include poor lighting and noise generated by printers. Sound-dampening covers and internal sound dampening are recommended but still do not reduce the noise adequately. The best solution to date is to put the printers in a separate room or enclose in a noise-reducing cabinet or at least away from the workers' area.
- Backache can be caused by using inappropriate tables or chairs. Adjustable desks and chairs can ease the strain on an employee's neck, back and shoulders.
- Work areas should be designed in a flexible way so that they can be adjusted to meet the employee's particular needs. There should be adequate space for each employee.
- Cables should be kept tidy and positioned is such a way that employees can't trip over them causing themselves to fall or pull computer or peripherals off desks.

Viruses

- Viruses are destructive programs that infect a computer similar to the way biological viruses infect people
- Viruses usually lie dormant for a while and then establish their presence by displaying a message, stopping the computer, or deleting a file
- To protect your system against viruses, you should purchase your software only from reputable dealers
- Run an anti-virus utility and religiously back up the hard drive so that lost data can be quickly and reliably restored
- The greatest carriers of viruses are disks which are illegally copied programs especially games
- A virus is a program code written to replicate by attaching copies of itself to other objects within the system, and normally also having a detrimental effect
- This may range from displaying messages through loss of service to corruption or complete destruction of data
- A program virus will seek out and copy itself into other program files whenever a previously infected program is run
- A boot sector virus copies itself into that sector of a disk and spreads whenever a system is boot loaded from an infected disk
- Viruses are spread when infected programs or disk are transferred to a previously clean system

Multimedia

- 'Multimedia' is a global term for the developing computer technology that can combine text, graphics, hi-fi sound, animation, and full-motion video in a single high-resolution display.
- This has been made possible by the common use of digital recording of text, graphics, sound, and video, coupled with the increased processor speeds required to handle large video files.

The applications of this technology include the following:

- **Training:** As a cheaper alternative to traditional techniques, many large organisations are using multimedia-based systems for staff induction, training in new procedures, and general management training.
- Multimedia foreign-language training systems have also been developed for home, school, and office use.
- **Architectural visualisations:** Using multimedia technology, a building designed on a CAD system can be animated in such a way that a client is able to 'walk through' the building and look at it from a far wider range of views than is possible using CAD.
- **Advertising/promotions Logos, trademarks, and storyboards outlining:** An advertisement can all be created, animated, and given a sound track using multimedia authoring software.
- **Home entertainment:** Variants of multimedia are systems that plug into a domestic television and use a simple remote-control device. Intended primarily as entertainment/educational systems, the applications available include such things as interactive cartoons, games, and an interactive multimedia world atlas.

Systems development

Systems development is the process by which a computerised information system is created.

- A 'system', in this context refers to a collection of computer programs that will act together to handle information so that the needs of the user are satisfied.

The systems-development life-cycle - can be divided into seven stages.

- Each of these stages plays an important part in ensuring that a systems-development project is successful.

Stage 1: Choosing the information system to be computerised
- Which system - Sales, Purchases, Finance or some other -should be computerised? What are the priorities?

Stage 2: The feasibility study
- Once the system has been chosen, which of the solutions proposed will provide the best results? Are the proposed solutions possible and cost-effective?

Stage 3: Full analysis of the system to be computerised
- Exactly what will the chosen system need to do?

Stage 4: Designing how the computerised system will work
- Using the information gained in the analysis stage, designing exactly how the system will do what is required of it.

Stage 5: Writing the programs
- Writing the programs needed to make the system work.

Stage 6: Implementing the new system
- Making sure that the computerised system does what it is supposed to do and, once final testing is complete, implementing it.

Stage 7: Maintaining the system
- Making the slight adjustments and alterations that will be necessary once the system has been in use for some time.

Computer networks

Computer networks are formed by the linking together of computers by means of communications links, using technology originally developed for use with large mainframe computer systems.

- A computer network can vary in size from a couple of microcomputers in the same room sharing printers and storage, to the linking of several mainframe computers located on different continents thousands of miles apart.
- For small-scale local networks involving only short distances, the computers may simply be plugged together without even the need for modems.

Computer Networks:

There are two types of computer network: small local area networks (**LANs**) that link computers in a single building or group of buildings, and large wide area networks (**WANs**) that link computers nationally or internationally.

Local area networks (LAN)

A local area network is used to connect a variety of computers over a limited geographical area, usually a single building or site

- Personal computers are generally not designed to be linked up to form a network, so additional hardware and software are required to make this possible.
- A PC is likely to require a LAN adaptor card, network software, and the appropriate LAN cable.
- A typical PC-based LAN will also have a powerful dedicated PC, called a 'server', that has a large hard disk and a fast memory.
- The server will generally be used to store software or files that need to be available to all users on the LAN, and it may also handle the flow of output to a shared printer.

Advantages and disadvantages of LANs

Summary of Advantages:

- Facilitate the sharing of expensive peripherals like laser printers, modems, and file servers.
- Enable information held on a central server to be shared by a large number of users.
- Applications software may be shared across a network, although some 'network-aware' software will allow only a set number of users at anyone time.
- In an organisation in which several non-compatible computer systems are used, a LAN may be used to integrate them.
- A LAN may be used to offer a wide range of office-automation facilities like electronic mail to users.
- LANs may be used to facilitate 'group working'. An example of this would be allowing a draft document to be accessed over a LAN so that editing suggestions can be attached to it by users other than the author.
- Once the editing process is complete, only the author is able to amend the document if required.
- Many users sharing a single database is another example of group working

Summary of Disadvantages:

- The cost of hardware, software, and cabling.
- Security of data (including the threat posed by viruses) may be a problem if adequate procedures are not adopted.
- When a large number of users are on the system at the same time can cause the response time to become very unsatisfactory.
- Once users are accustomed to working over a LAN, they often become dependent upon it to do their jobs. Any failure in the system can often mean that it becomes impossible for users to work.

Wide area networks (WAN):

A wide area network, will generally use private communications links to connect large numbers of computer terminals over a large geographical area to a mainframe.

- Large organisations like banks, building societies, and government agencies all use WANs that operate over leased telecommunications lines to link together branches and offices throughout the country.
- The automated teller machines (A TMs) provided by banks and building societies to allow access to cash outside banking hours are part of a WAN that is controlled by a computer in another part of the country.
- The laser scanners that are used by many supermarkets at the check-outs may also be part of a WAN that collects information on a minicomputer at the supermarket before passing it on to the mainframe located in the company's main computer centre elsewhere in the country.

Computer Based Training (CBT)

Computers are recognised as a very valuable training tool not only when learning about computers as such but in learning other subjects as well.

- CBT is one of the most popular methods of using computers in education.
- Applications vary from the simplest software teaching a child a basic mathematical skill to the teaching of an elaborate complicated program,
- The special CBT software is generally interactive so the students has to input data as the teaching progresses.

Some advantages of CBT are:

- The student has the flexibility of studying whenever his availability permits
- The student's study times can be as long or as short as his circumstances allow
- The student can work at own pace; not constrained by the obligation to keep pace with another student

Some disadvantages are:

- The student has no regular routine;
- Needs to be strongly motivated or highly disciplined;
- The student cannot consult a tutor if in difficulty
- The student has no interaction with other students;

Backup

- A copy you make of a file in case the original file gets destroyed or corrupted
- Use the Backup command of your computer to back up files on your hard disk
- You can back up files to floppy disks, a tape drive etc
- When you've made a backup file, you can Restore it if your original files are damaged
- Backup copies of files are made as security in the event of the original being destroyed for example through a virus or a damaged hard disk
- The floppy disks holding the Backup copies should be clearly labelled and held in a safe place
- Copy files to an auxiliary storage device in order to have available copies of computer files in case of system fault or failure

    Small office: It will depend on the individual office and the importance of the files
- Once a week might be appropriate for most situations
- Good practice to keep a copy of each printout and file securely - this provides additional security in the event of loss of data
    Banks: Generally banks backup at regular intervals during the day

Advantages of e-Mail

- Quick inexpensive immediate contact can be made to another e-mail account holder anywhere in the world
- Using the cc or bcc facility within the e-mail, numerous communications can be distributed simultaneously
- The attachment facility provides the means of forwarding long files created in a conventional standard software

Disadvantages of e-Mail

- e-Mail exchange can be carriers of Viruses - many records of e-mail attachment containing mass-emailing virus which recipients unwittingly send to their Address Box contacts purely by opening the e-mail
- Unsolicited e-mails: spam

Effects of Computerisation on the Individual:

- Entrance to Leisure centre is controlled by the bar codes on your pass
- Similar card lifts the barrier at your company's car park
- Your local bank will allow you withdraw cash by using an ATM card
- Computer applications make our jobs in offices, hotels etc much easier
- If we are booking into a hotel on the 'phone, the receptionist can quickly tell us by accessing the specialised hotel software the availability of our preferred dates
- Our hotel stay will be be made that bit more smooth by reserving our meals in advance or our requesting that 'wake-up' call - all made possible by the power of computers.

Precautions and Power failure

- See backup above
- Use the special anti-power surge extension leads on all computer sockets
- Also use a UPS (un-interruptible power supply)

Information Superhighway

- This is a 'sound-bite' coined by US Vice-President Al Gore in 1993, comparing the fast growing Internet to the US highway system. It has come to mean the Internet itself.

Y2K Problem

- This turned out to be a damp squib - Large banks, insurance companies, big computerised businesses generally spent millions to put measures in place to prevent a problem which was felt would arise at the turn of the 21st century
- Years within Computer programs were represented by 2 digits only and it was feared that once the year 2000 pealed that all dates in financial transactions would revert to the year 1900 - this did not happen

Consolidation of Theoretical Topics

In order for you to consolidate and retain the theoretical aspects of computers described in this Unit, I have listed below questions in the same order as the topics studied. I recommend that you systematically work through the unit, gradually over a period of time, completing the relevant consolidation question once you feel you understand the subject in hand rather than studying the unit as a whole and then completing all the questions at once.

Exercise 1: Types of Computers:

List *three* points to define the following:

Mainframe:
1._____

2._____

3._____

PC:
1._____

2._____

3._____

Laptop computers:
1._____

2._____

3._____

Dumb Terminal:
1._____

2._____

3._____

Intelligent terminal:
1._____

2._____

3._____

Exercise 2: Hardware v Software:

Distinguish between Hardware and Software:

_____

_____

List three hardware components of a "*typical* personal computer":

_____

Describe three types of Operating System:

_____

Describe three functions of an Operating System:

_____

Exercise 3: Data - 3 Stages:

Describe the 3 stages involved in the processing of Data:

_____

_____

_____

Exercise 4: Electronic Commerce:

Write three sentences describing e-Commerce:

_____

_____

_____

Exercise 5: Internet:

List 5 Pre-requisites before connection to the Internet is possible:

_____

Exercise 6: Application Software:

Describe four types of Application Software:

_____

_____

_____

Exercise 7: Memory Measurement:

Define: **Bit:** _____

Define: **Character:** _____

Define: **Byte:** _____

Define: **Field:** _____

Define: **Record:** _____

Define: **File:** _____

Define: **Kilobytes:** _____

Define: **Megabytes:** _____

Define: **Gigabytes:** _____

Exercise 8: Computer Power

The power of a computer processing data into information is dictated by the following - describe in detail:

- CPU Speed: _____

- RAM: _____

- Cache memory: _____

- Hard disk size: _____

- Clock speed: _____

Exercise 9: ROM

Define ROM:_____

Compare ROM with RAM:_____

_____

Exercise 10: Other Forms of Memory:

Describe any other forms of Memory that you are familiar with:_____

_____

_____

Exercise 11: Input devices:

Describe the following Input methods:

Keyboard:_____

_____

Mouse:_____

_____

Touch screens:_____

_____

Joystick:_____

_____

Tracker ball:_____

_____

Voice input:_____

_____

Document readers:_____

_____

OCR:_____

_____

OMR:_____

_____

MICR:_____

_____

Bar-code readers:_____

_____

Light Pens:_____

_____

Card readers:_____

_____

Graphics pads:_____

_____

Image scanners:_____

_____

Video scanners:_____

_____

Exercise 12: Computer Output:

Describe the following Output methods:

Soft-copy output:_____

_____

Visual output:_____

_____

Audio output:_____

_____

Hard-copy output:_____

_____

Exercise 13: Printers etc:

Define the following range of printers:

Matrix printers:_____

_____

Dot-matrix printers:_____

_____

Ink-jet printers:_____

_____

Thermal printers:_____

_____

Laser printers:_____

_____

Daisy-wheel printers:_____

_____

Line printer:_____

_____

Graph plotters:_____

_____

COM:_____

_____

Exercise 14: Peripherals:

Define the term "Peripherals":_____

_____

Define Secondary storage:_____

_____

Define Computer Speakers:_____

Define **Magnetic disk** and **tape input**:_____

_____

_____

Define **Diskettes**:_____

_____

Define **Optical media**:_____

_____

Define **CD-ROM**:_____

_____

Define **CO-R**:_____

_____

Define **Microform**:_____

_____

Define **Zip Disk/Zip Drive**:_____

_____

Exercise 15: Systems-software utilities:

List 3 points to describe **Utilities**:_____

_____

Exercise 16: Repetitive strain injury (RSI):

Define **RSI**:_____

_____

What can *cause* RSI:_____

_____

What can help **prevent** RSI:_____

_____

Exercise 17: Graphical User Interface: (GUI):

List 3 points describing your understanding of: GUI:_____

_____

Exercise 18: Data Protection Act

List **6** points explaining the origin and purpose of the Data Protection Act:_____

_____

_____

Exercise 19: Data Security:

Describe methods of ensuring Data is secure:_____

_____

Exercise 20: Health and Safety:

Describe 6 steps that should be taken to ensure the health and safety of employees:

_____

_____

Exercise 21: Viruses

Describe what you understand by a computer virus:_____

_____

What steps can be taken to secure your computer system from viruses:

_____

_____

Exercise 22: Multimedia:

What does "Multimedia" mean:_____

_____

Describe 4 uses of "Multimedia": _____

_____

Exercise 23: Systems development

What does "Systems development" mean? _____

_____

List and describe the 7 stages of Systems development:: _____

_____

_____

_____

Exercise 24: Computer networks

Define "Computer networks": _____

_____

What does LAN mean? _____

_____

List some Advantages and Disadvantages of LAN: _____

_____

What does WAN mean? _____

_____

List some Advantages and Disadvantages of WAN: _____

_____

Exercise 25: CBT

What does CBT stand for? _____

Describe at least 3 uses for CBT: _____

_____

List some advantages of CBT: _____

_____

List some disadvantages of CBT: _____

_____

Exercise 26: Backup:

What is "Backup" used for: _____

_____

Does the frequency of Backup depend on the size of the organization? Elaborate:

_____

_____

Exercise 27: e-Mail:

List the **Advantages** and **Disadvantages** of e-Mail:

_____

_____

_____

_____

Management of Files

File Management System

- To have documents stored in an organized and easily accessible way, it is necessary to save files in folders, with meaningful names - such order will facilitate the efficient running of a computer filing system

Files and Folder:

- Whenever a new document is created in a program such as Word for Windows, you save, the document as a file in your computer.
- When you save a file, the file is given a name. Since Windows 95, the file name can have up to 255 characters and can include spaces
- When a file is saved, it is saved in a specific location - a folder.
- When you open a file, the file is found by the disk drive and displayed on the screen

Document Folders:

- Folders are created to help you organize computer files into specific categories
- Folders can hold any number of individual files
- When you save a file that you have created, you can choose the folder in which to store the file
- You can also move files from one folder to another

Program files/folders:

- When you are installing a new Program in your computer, a new folder is created in your hard disk by the Setup process
- All the program files that make the new program run are loaded into the same folder

Viewing the Filing System of your Computer:

- When you turn on your computer using Windows 98, your Desktop should look something like:

Turning on the Computer

- Before you turn on the computer, you must insert the plug(s) into an electrical socket
- The computer can then be started by pressing the on switch on both the monitor and computer base
- The operating system is automatically loaded into main memory as soon as you turn on or boot the computer. The term "booting" refers to the process of loading an operating system into a computer's main memory from diskette or hard disk.
- The operating system consists of the master system of programs that manages the basic operations of the computer including checking malfunction of equipment
- During this booting process, the **config.sys** and **autoexec.bat** files are executed - Windows are **loaded**
- Click on the **Start** button of Windows 98 to display the menu - see the guide to the other applications below on steps to load Word, Excel, PowerPoint, Access and Internet.

config.sys	**Buffer**	**autoexec.bat**
is a configuration file that specifies the keyboard, device drivers and amount of buffers for the computer to use	A buffer is a storage area for temporarily holding data	This file contains instructions that the computer follows before waiting for any commands from user

Switching off the Computer

- Close applications by choosing **File Close** from Menu:
- Select the **Start** button on Desktop, and **Shut Down** from Menu:

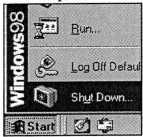

- .. the **Shut Down** dialog box opens - Select **Shut down** option

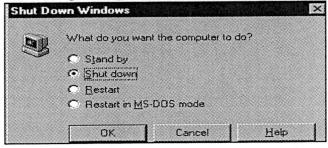

- Click **OK** - Wait as the computer goes through the shutting down process - a quick message will then display - *Shutting down the computer?*
- You can then turn off the switches on monitor and computer base
- Remove plug(s) from electrical socket

Rebooting Computer

- Hold down the three keys: **Control, Alt** and **Delete** simultaneously to reboot.

Browse the Filing system with My Computer

- Double-click the **My Computer** icon on the desktop to open **My Computer** window:

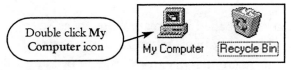

- **My Computer** dialog box opens:

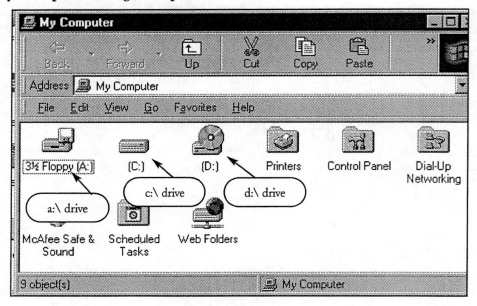

- The disk drives on the computer: (a:) (c:) and (d:) are represented by a **drive icon** and **name**.

- We double-clicked the hard disk (C:) icon - a new window appears, showing the folders (large icons) stored on the *author's* hard disk (You double click the c:\ drive icon on *your* computer and see what folders are displayed)

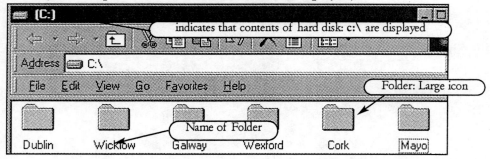

Note to User:

- We will now go through the steps necessary to create the folders listed above.
- We will then add both **Text** and **Word** documents to the **Dublin** folder as well as describing how documents can be created in other applications by the same method
- If you create the folders and documents, as directed, you will be able to practice file management as we move through this unit.

Creating a Folder accessing c:\ drive through My Computer

- Double click c\ drive icon within My Computer - c:\ drive displays like:

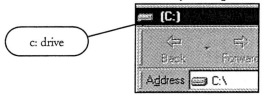

..c:\ must display as above before any folder is created directly into the hard drive

- Select **File New Folder** from Menu:

- "New Folder" icon displays:

- Type in *new* Name for folder, e.g. "Dublin"; hit Return - folder "Dublin" displays

- Continue creating Folders: "Wicklow", "Galway", "Wexford", "Mayo" and "Cork" in the same manner:

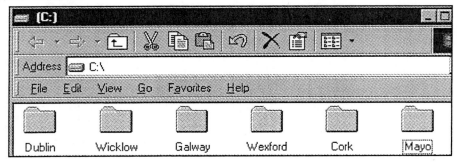

Views

- The View in the diagram above is set to *Large* icons
- To verify: select **View** from **Menu** - Bullet symbol indicates that View is set to Large Icons:

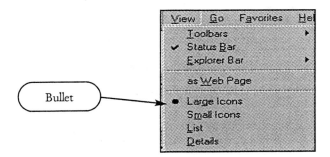

Other Views:

- Other possible Views, available are: Small Icons, List or Details - switch to each View in turn to see how the display varies:

- **Small** Icons View - attainable through **View Small** icons from Menu:

- **List View** - similar to above - folders are listed down one side - also attainable through **View List** from Menu:

- **Details View** - attainable through **View Details** from Menu - Note a Column for Name, Size, Type and Modified:

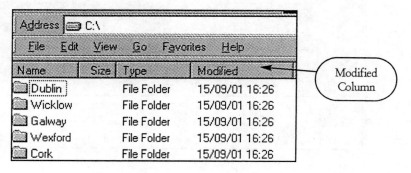

Create a Text File within the Dublin folder

- Double click **c** drive icon - c:\ drive displays
- Select "Dublin" folder, press *Right* Mouse button; select **Open**

- In the Dublin folder, Select **File New Text** Document

Rename a Text File name

- Text document with **.txt** extension is added to the folder. **Rename** by selecting, pressing **Right** button to access drop-down menu, select **Rename**:

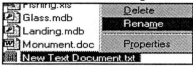

- Type in **name**, for example: **sunshine.txt;** make sure you add the **.txt extension**
- If you display the Dublin folder in **Details View** now, **sunshine.txt** will show as **0KB** in **size**:

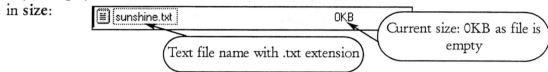

Extensions
All application files have their own unique extension i.e. a full stop followed by 3 letters - **extension** of each file name informs you of the Program the file was created in (i.e. application type):

.doc:	Word	**.xls:**	Excel	**.mdb:**	Access
.ppt	PowerPoint	**.txt:**	Text file		

Add text to the text file:

- The *size* of the text file will change when text is added
- Double click the file name: **sunshine.txt** to open, and type:

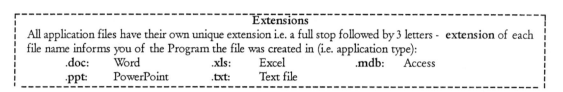

- **Save** with **File Save**. Close with **File Close**
- Through the addition of the text above, the size has *increased* - it now reads: **1KB** in **Details View** - check and see:

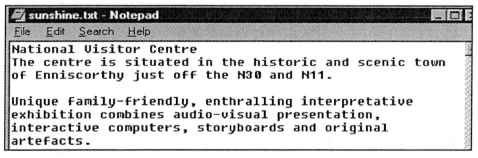

Creating an application document: Word within c:\Dublin folder

- With "Dublin" folder open, select **File, New, Microsoft Word Document**

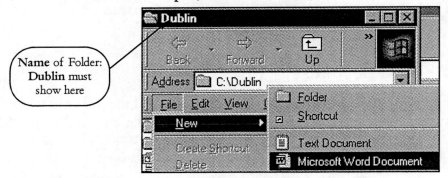

..Microsoft file name displays with the Word **.doc extension:**

New Microsoft Word Document.doc

- Double click and give it a **file name**; our example: name is: **Plantation.doc**
- If you double click this file name, a Word document will open in the same way as a **New** document would open in Word - experiment and see.

Typing text into this Word document:

- **Type** the following text into the **Plantation.doc:**

China has a larger population than any other country in the world. There are over 1000 million people, which means that one in every five people in the world is Chinese. By land size too China is a huge country.
As you would expect in such a large country, there are a great many different landscapes. In the east lie huge cities such as the capital Beijing, Shanghai, Nanjing and Guangzhou. Few Chinese own cars but most have bicycles, and one of the images of a Chinese city is of bicycle jams in the rush hours. In contrast to the crowded cities, in the west are the wide open spaces of the Gobi Desert.

Creating documents in other applications:

- Create **Excel, PowerPoint** and **Access** documents in the same way, i.e. have the **Dublin** folder open and select **File New Excel** etc.
- Use file names displayed below under the contents of "Dublin" folder.

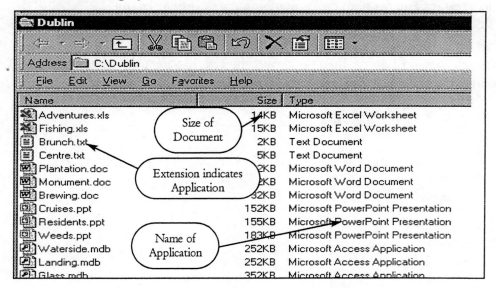

- Key in some data into some files so that the size will not display as 0KB.

Create a Folder within an existing Folder:

- Point at the folder "Dublin" press **Right** mouse button, select **Open**

- The "Dublin" folder opens showing the files this folder contains in **Details** View:

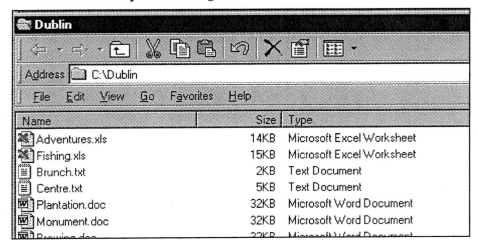

Creating a Folder "Rathfarnham" within the "Dublin" Folder

- With **Dublin Folder** open, select **File New Folder** from **Menu**:

- .. a **new** Folder entitled "New Folder" is created and is listed within the **Dublin folder**

   - we will rename this folder by pointing at the **New Folder** name and pressing **Right** button; select **Rename** from drop-down menu:

- Type in "Rathfarnham" as the **new Folder** name
- Hit **Return** - Folder now displays with new name:

Toolbar

The toolbar provides shortcuts for performing certain tasks and for changing window views:

- Turn on the Toolbar by clicking the **View** menu of the window, and click **Toolbars, Standard Buttons** - *check* mark indicates Toolbar is turned on:

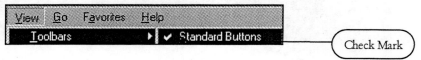

- ..The toolbar appears in the window - our example, the icon for Views is depressed displaying the choices for Views: Large icons etc:

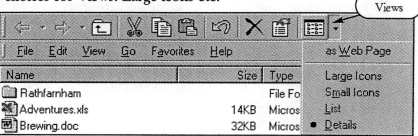

Arrange icons:

By Name:
(Files can also be arranged under Size, Type or Date Modified)
- On the **View** menu, point to **Arrange Icons**, and then click **By Name**:

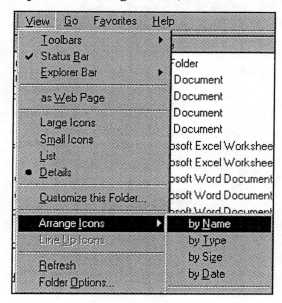

- This **rearranges** all of the icons, so the files and folders appear in alphabetical order at the top of the window under **Name**:

By Size:

- On the **View** menu, point to **Arrange Icons**, and then click **By Size** - Files are arranged according to **Size**:

Name	Size	Type
Rathfarnham		File Folder
sunshine.txt	0KB	Text Document
sunshine2.txt	1KB	Text Document
Brunch.txt	2KB	Text Document

> Files sorted according to Size

Sorting by clicking on relevant bar in Details View:

Name	Size	Type	Modified
Rathfarnham		File Folder	16/09/01 13:23
Adventures.xls	14KB	Microsoft Excel Worksheet	16/09/01 11:12
Brewing.doc	32KB	Microsoft Word Document	16/09/01 11:17
Brunch.txt	2KB	Text Document	16/09/01 11:15
Centre.txt	5KB	Text Document	16/09/01 11:16

> Click on **Name** here to sort in **Ascending** or click again to sort in Descending Order

> Click on **Size** here to sort with the smallest size first or click again to sort with the largest Size first

> Click on **Type** here to sort **grouping** the same type of application files together

> Click on **Modified** here to **sort** files created with the **newest** file first or click again to sort on the **oldest** file first

Auto Arrange:

- If you want to neatly arrange your icons in a window, click **Auto Arrange**

By Type:

- On the **View** menu, point to **Arrange Icons**, and then click **By Type** - Files are *arranged* according to application *type*:

Name	Size	Type
Rathfarnham		File Folder
Glass.mdb	352KB	Microsoft Access Application
Landing.mdb	252KB	Microsoft Access Application
Waterside.mdb	252KB	Microsoft Access Application
Adventures.xls	14KB	Microsoft Excel Worksheet
Fishing.xls	15KB	Microsoft Excel Worksheet
Cruises.ppt	152KB	Microsoft PowerPoint Presentation

> Files can be sorted on **Type** Column by clicking here

By Modified:

- On the **View** menu, point to **Arrange Icons**, and then click by **Date** - Files are arranged according to date *created*:

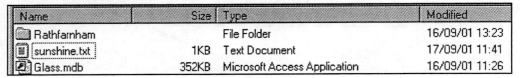

Name	Size	Type	Modified
Rathfarnham		File Folder	16/09/01 13:23
sunshine.txt	1KB	Text Document	17/09/01 11:41
Glass.mdb	352KB	Microsoft Access Application	16/09/01 11:26

Create 2 additional Folders

- With Dublin folder *sorted* on **Name**, Create **two new folders** within the Dublin folder named: **Rathgar** and **Templeogue** - Dublin folder should then look like:

Open Folders simultaneously

- **Open** folder **Rathfarnham** - select folder, point at this folder, press **right** mouse button, select **Open**:

- Folder will open on screen:

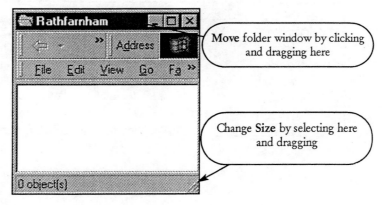

Move folder window by clicking and dragging here

Change **Size** by selecting here and dragging

Note:

- Folders can be moved by selecting folder window, clicking and dragging on Name bar
- Folder window can be enlarged or reduced in size by clicking and dragging on right corner of folder window.

Practice: Moving and Resizing Folder Windows:

- Open **Rathgar** and **Templeogue** folders also - *resize* and *move* folder windows until screen looks like:

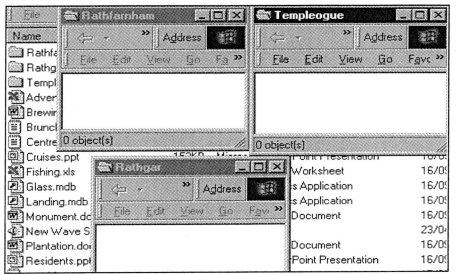

Moving Files from one folder to another:

- Open **Dublin** folder and **Rathfarnham** side by side; adjust size if necessary:

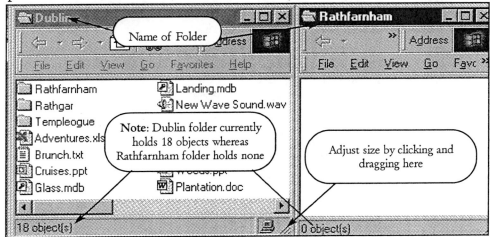

- We are moving *4 files simultaneously - select non-contiguous files by holding down Control key before selecting; Move by clicking on selected files and dragging and dropping in target folder (Rathfarnham) - result will be:

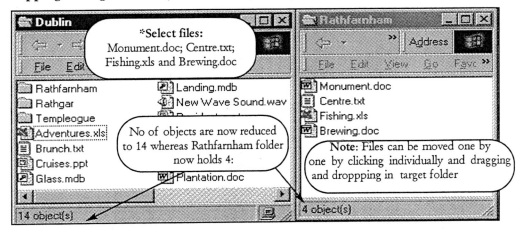

Copying files between Folders

- Procedure is the same as for moving except the **Control** key must be held down when the files are being dragged to the *target* folder - original file is left in source folder (in our case: **Dublin**) and a **copy** is created in the target folder (in our case: **Rathfarnham**)

Copying files from a Folder to the floppy disk: a:

- **Open** Rathfarnham Folder as above
- **Minimise** folders on screen by clicking minimise icon:

- Select **a:** drive icon from **My Computer** window: press **Right Mouse** button, select **Open:**

- ..screen should now look like:

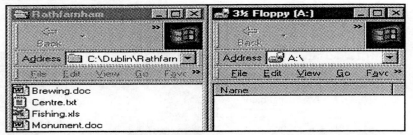

- Select **Monument.doc** in **Rathfarnham** folder, drag to **a:** **drive** - which now looks like:

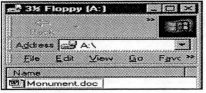

Organizing Files Within Folders

You can structure a computerised filing systems in many ways:
- Have a separate folder for every **aspect** of your work: Letters, Accounts, Budgets etc
- Have a separate folder for each **client**; Each user can have their own set of folders etc
- Files can be **moved** into the folders you create as seen above
- You can also move or create folders **within** other folders

Create folders within folders

- We created the folder *Rathgar* within the *Dublin* folder
- We will now **open** the subfolder *Rathgar* and create folders named *Library* and *Museum* within **Rathgar** folder - the result will be:

With **Rathgar** folder open, select **File New Folder** etc

Copying Misc Files to Library Folder:

- We will now **copy** the files: *Brunch.txt* and *Adventures.xls* to the *Library* folder:

- Select *Library* folder, point at name, press **right mouse** button, select **open** - *Library* folder opens

- Holding down **Control**, Select *Brunch.txt*, *Landing.mdb* and *Adventures.xls* in *Dublin* folder; click and drag to *Library folder* - result will be:

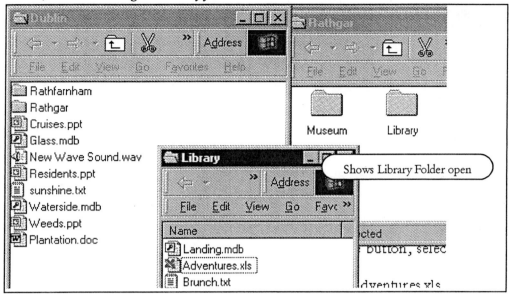

Windows Explorer

- You can use the **Windows Explorer** in the same way as you used **My Computer** for creating folders, moving files etc

Browse through your filing system with Windows Explorer

- You can **browse** through the computer system files with Windows Explorer. You can **display** the same toolbar you used in the **My Computer** windows and change the **view** of folders and files in the same way

- To access Windows Explorer, Click **Start** on the **Start** menu, point to **Programs**, and then click **Windows Explorer**

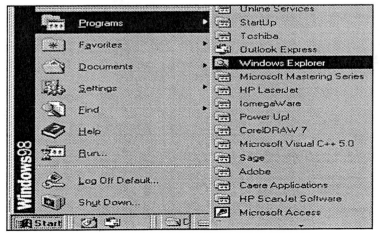

Windows Explorer Window:

- The **Exploring** window appears - As shown in the following illustration, the **left** window displays the computer's entire file structure, including any disk drives, folders

- The **right** window displays the names of the files and folders stored in the item **selected** in the left window - **My Computer** is selected in this example on the **left** side - the **right** side shows the same contents as we were looking earlier at in the **Desktop**:

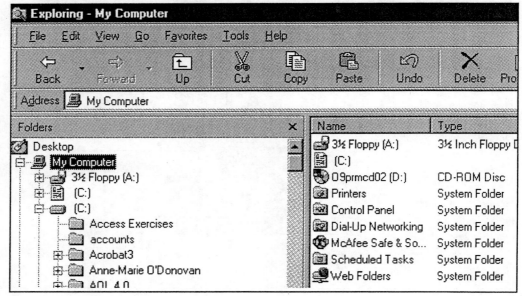

Contents of c:\ Drive

- The contents of the author's c:\ **Drive** is shown by, selecting c:\ on the **left** - the contents - folders in our example (alphabetical order) display on **right**

- Practice on your own computer by clicking on the c:\ drive icon on the left and see what contents are shown on the right.

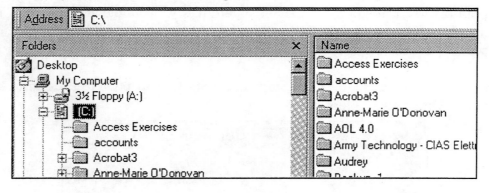

Seeing contents of Folder

- Within **Windows Explorer**, display c:\ drive on **left**:

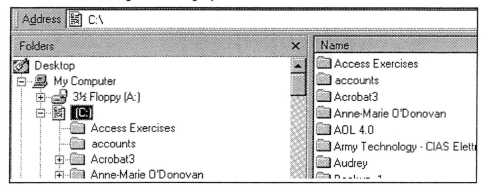

Viewing contents of sub-folder - Rathgar: sub-folder of Dublin

- Move to folder **Dublin** created earlier in the c:\ drive:
- Point at *Rathgar* on right-hand side of screen, press right mouse button, click **Open**

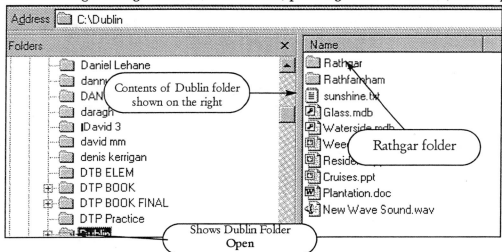

- .. *Rathgar* folder **opens**
- With Rathgar folder open, point at *Library* folder, press **right** mouse button, click **Open** - *Library* folder opens
- Result will be:

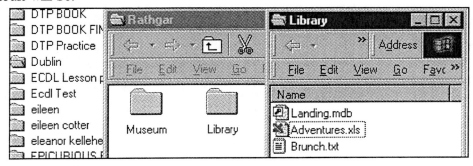

Tip:

- You can *also rename* files with **Windows Explorer**.
- In the **right** window, **select** the file you want to rename, and then from the **File** menu, click **Rename** or, using the right mouse button, select Rename: to rename the selected file

Deleting Files and Folders

- You can **delete** old files to release space for reuse in your hard disk
- Files can be deleted **one** at the time or if you hold down the **Control** key you can select a **range** of non-contiguous files to be deleted
- Deleted files or folders are placed in **Recycle Bin** temporarily in readiness to be deleted permanently when you **empty** the recycle bin
- You can **Restore** the item & reuse it by retrieving it from Recycle Bin instead of emptying the Recycle bin

Recycle Bin

- In **Windows Explorer,** select the **Dublin** folder, hold down **Control** and select the files indicated below:

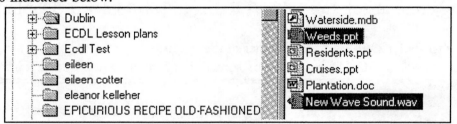

- Press the **Delete** key - a dialog box displays asking you to **confirm** deletion:

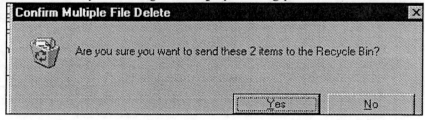

- Click **Yes** - the files are deleted from the folder: Dublin
- The deleted files are now in the Recycle Bin - a holding area on the Desktop for files and folders you no longer need:

Note:

- **Deleted** items stay in Recycle Bin until you explicitly empty it or use the **Recover** command to return them to their folders.

Recover deleted files from Recycle Bin

Suppose you changed your mind about a file or folder you have deleted If you have not yet emptied Recycle Bin, you can retrieve and re-use any item stored there

- We will now recover from Recycle Bin the file: *Weeds.ppt*
- **Double click** the recycle bin - the Recycle Bin window appears, listing the files, folders, and other items deleted since the last time Recycle Bin was emptied - in our case only the two just deleted are showing:

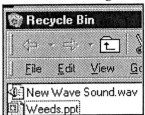

- **Select** file to be restored: *Weeds.ppt*, **File Restore** - selected file is restored to its **original** folder (if you wanted to restore non-contiguous folders, hold down **Control** to select)

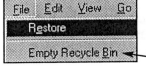

Select to **permanently** delete selected files from Recycle Bin

Empty Recycle Bin

Our example, one file remains in Recycle Bin:

- Select **Empty Recycle Bin** to permanently delete this file

Disk/Floppy Disk Storage

- The hard disk is the most commonly used drive for storing disks
- Floppy disks may be also used to keep a second copy of a file as security against the hard drive malfunctioning
- The hard disk is used to store the software for Windows 98 and all the other applications
- The disk drive is the mechanism that is used to read and write information to and from the disk
- Floppy disk drives are built into the computer base, and the floppy disks are inserted into the disk drive slots
- The hard disk drive is installed internally into the computer base, but it is not accessed from the outside
- Each disk drive has a name that is used to identify each drive:
  The **floppy** disk drive is known as the **a:** Drive
  The **hard disk** is known as the **c:** drive
- The size of the floppy disk is: **3.5"**
- The floppy can be either **high density** or **double density** - most floppy disks are labeled "DD" for double density or "HD" for high density.

Capacity:

- Floppy disk storage capacity measured in **bytes**:
    - 3.5-inch **double density** (DD) - 720 kilobytes
    - 3.5-inch **high density** (HD) - 144 megabytes
    - One **byte** equals about one **character**
    - One **kilobyte** (KB) is approximately **one thousand bytes**
    - One **megabyte** (MB) is approximately **one million bytes**

Formatting a floppy disk

Warning: The formatting process **erases** any information previously stored on the floppy disk

To Format:

- **Place** a floppy disk in the floppy disk drive
- Check to see is it **HD** or **DD** - • **Double-click** the My Computer icon - the My Computer window appears:
- Click the **a:** icon for the drive that contains the floppy disk you want to format
- On the **File** menu, click **Format**:

- - the Format **dialog box** appears:

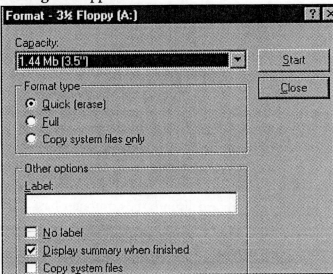

Select the Formatting Options:

Capacity

- In the **Capacity list box,** specify the capacity of the floppy disk
- The capacity depends on whether the floppy disk is a **high-density (HD)** or **double density (DD)** disk

Format Type: Select **Full**

- The **Quick** (Erase) option **erases** all information from a formatted floppy disk
- **Copy System Files Only** copies **system** files to a formatted floppy disk
- Under **Other Options,** be sure that **Display Summary When Finished** is checked Click **Start**
- In the **Formatting** bar at the bottom of the Format dialog box, **tick marks** indicate the status of the formatting process When the bar is filled in, the formatting is **complete,** and the **Format Results** dialog box appears
- In the Format Results dialog box, click **Close**
- The Format dialog box appears again asking you if you want to format another disk -answer **Yes** or **No,** as appropriate In the Format dialog box, click **Close**
- **Remove** the floppy disk from the drive, and **label** it with an appropriate name

Copying from the hard disk to the floppy disk

- In Windows Explorer, select **c:\ drive,** Dublin folder - contents of this folder display on **right:**

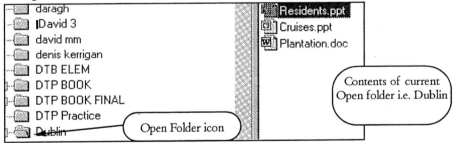

- We will **copy** or (**Send**) a copy of the file: *Residents.ppt* to drive a:\
- Select *Residents.ppt* on the **right;** pointing at the file name, press **right** mouse button
- Select **Send to** - a side menu displays:

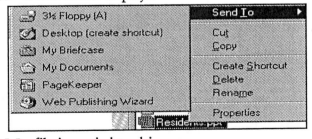

- Select floppy [a] - file is copied to drive a:
- To check, select drive a: in Windows Explorer - contents display copied file:

Note: Files can be copied from the hard disk to the floppy drive in the same way as was discussed earlier copying between folders etc.

Using Find File to Search for Files

- You can use the **Find File** command to search your computer for files By searching, you can locate either program software files, such as, Word, Excel etc or document files - files that you create with any software

Find a document file

- To find a document file, for example, not knowing what folder it was saved in, what application it was created in but you remember the name: "business"
- Click **Start** from **Start Menu**, select **Find**; On Find menu, click **Files Or Folders**:

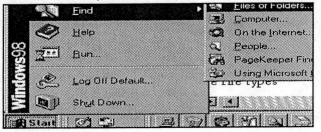

- ..the Find dialog box appears
- Select the Name & Location tab; In the Named box, type Business
- Look in box: Our example: we will look in drive c: and also check the box to search subfolders and then click Find Now:

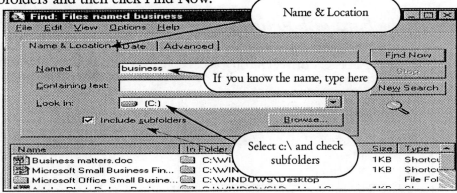

- All files throughout the hard disk that have "business" as **part** of their file **names** are listed at the bottom of the dialog box
- Also listed are the folders in which the files are stored, the file sizes in kilobytes (KB), and the file types - When you see the file you want, double click and the file will open

Find a file containing specific text

- Find a file: we don't know the name but specific text: "house" was used - set up as before but in box: "containing text", type "house", then click Find Now: result will be:

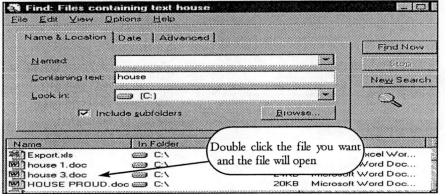

Changing computer's settings

- Click **Start**, and then point to **Settings**.
- Click **Control Panel**:

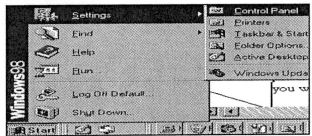

- ..*Control Panel* dialog box opens:

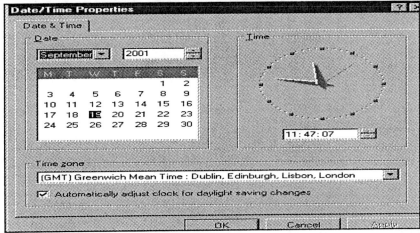

- **Double-click** the icon that represents the settings you want to **change.**

Changing Date and Time within the Computer Settings:

- **Double click** the **Date & Time** icon within the **Control Panel** - dialog box displays:

- Change the **Month** or **Year** by picking as required within the drop-down menu
- Change the **Day** by clicking on the required **Date**
- Change the **Time**: Type required Time; hit **Return** - the **Clock** adjusts immediately

Establish the type of processor your computer has:

- Click **Start Programs, Accessories, Systems Tools, Systems Information** from menu - full detail will display:

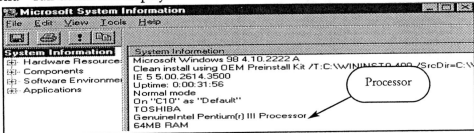

Checking the amount of RAM within the Computer Settings:

- **Double click** the icon for **System** within the **Control Panel:**

- **System Properties** dialog box opens, select **General Tab,** quantity of **RAM** displays:

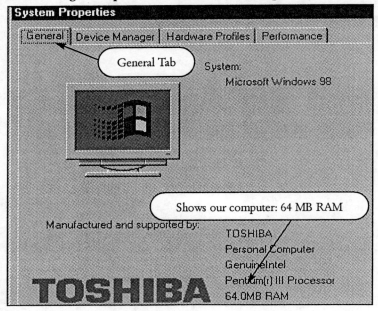

Checking Computer Background Settings within Computer Settings:

- **Double click** the icon for **Display** within the **Control Panel:**

- **Display Properties** - dialog box displays:

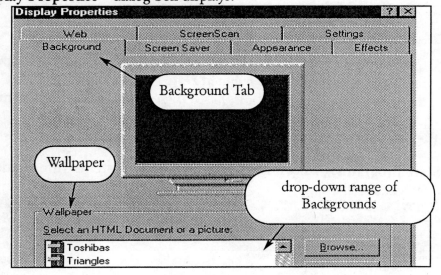

- Select **Background** Tab, change settings by choosing from range under drop-down menu under **Wallpaper**

Printing Progress

- If you are printing a few jobs at the time - the print jobs go into a **print queue**
- The status of the printing jobs can be checked by clicking on the **Printer** icon on the **status bar** (this icon automatically appears once the instruction to print is given)

- Our example - we are currently printing **three** jobs - when we double click the printer icon, the **HP LaserJet 6P** (our default printer) dialog box opens - the jobs are detailed under: **Name, Status, Owner** and **Progress**

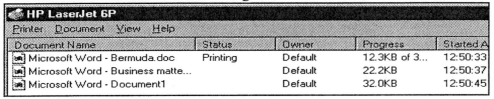

Making a Printer the default Printer

- Click **Start**, point to **Settings**, and then click **Printers**:
- ..Printers dialog box opens - our example, we selected HP LaserJet 6P then selected **Set as Default** from File menu:

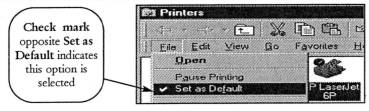

- The **default printer** is thereafter automatically used unless you specify otherwise.

Help Function

Two Help Options:
1. **Application Help:** for aid within Word, for example, click **Help** feature within Word.
2. **PC-related Help:** for guidance relating to the computer itself, use Help facility accessible through Start Menu

1. Getting Help from the Help menu within Word - Help can be sought within other applications in the same way
- Within Word, just click **Microsoft Word Help** on the **Help** menu. - a dialog box opens:
- To scroll through a table of contents for Help, click the **Contents** tab.

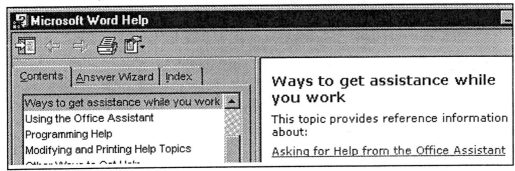

Answer Wizard

- To type a question in the Help window, click the Answer Wizard tab, type question in, our example, we are looking for help on mail merge, click search:

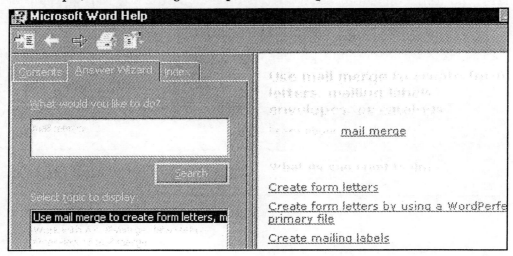

- A range of help topics relating to mail merge display on the right-hand side of the window - we clicked **Create form letters** - the result was:

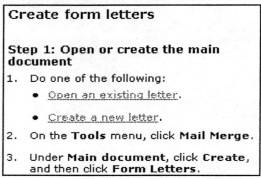

Copying Help text into Word

- If you want to copy this screen into Word, **highlight** text, click **Copy** from Short-cut menu: (right button - mouse):

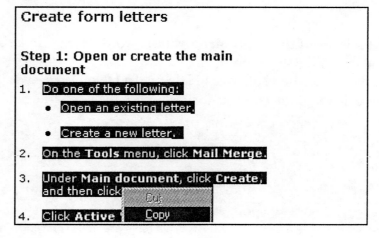

- **Paste** the copied text into a Word page

Index tab within Help

- When you want to search for **specific words** or **phrases**, click the **Index** tab - a range of topics will display in **alphabetical** order
- Our example, we are looking for help on "headers"; we pressed the down arrow until we came to the word "header"; we clicked **Search** - a range of topics displayed:
- Our example, we double clicked **Overview of Headers** - help information displayed on **right**:

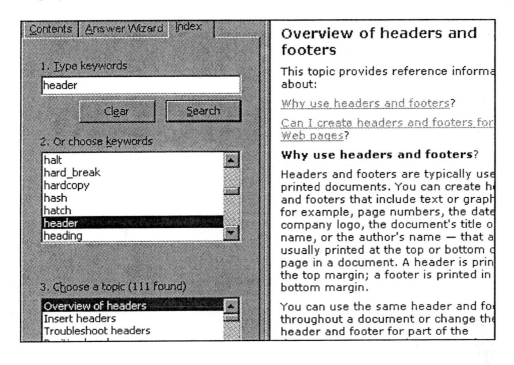

2. Using Help for guidance on the PC in general

- To get help on general usage of the **PC**, use the **Help function** within the **Start** menu:

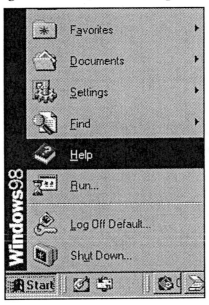

- Use the resulting menus in the same way as the Help menu for Word was outlined above.

Consolidation of File Management

When you have worked satisfactorily through the topics in this Unit, complete the tasks below - they are listed in the same order as they were originally introduced above - where no written answer is required - tick number of task when completed

1. Have a look at the **Desktop** on your own machine and see what folders and icons are displayed.

2. Detail the procedure for turning **on** your computer - number the steps:

   _____

   _____

3. Detail the procedure for turning **off** your computer - number the steps:

   _____

   _____

4. What **combination of keys** are used to reboot a computer?_____

5. Double click the **My Computer** icon on your Desktop - Practice opening and closing the **c:** folder within My Computer on your own computer

6. Create 4 New **Folders** within your hard drive: c:\
   The Folders will be **named**: Antrim; Tyrone; Derry and Armagh

7a. Change the **View** of your c:\ drive to **Large** icons - see can you see your newly created Folders

7b.   Change the **View** of your c:\ drive to **Small** icons
7c.   Change the **View** of your c:\ drive to **List**
7d.   Change the **View** of your c:\ drive to **Details**

8. **Open** the Antrim folder and create a **Text** document within it - **Save** as: Athens.txt - look at the size of this file now in Details View - write down its size:_____

9. **Type** in the content of this text document:

   > The oldest country in the region is Greece. It is made up of the mainland, and many islands in the Mediterranean Sea. One of the world's first great civilisations grew up in ancient Greece. In the ten centuries before the birth of Christ, the people living in ancient Greek cities developed advanced forms of architecture and government, and great skills in mathematics, medicine and other sciences. The most important city was Athens, now the capital of modern Greece.

10. Resave the Athens.txt text file - look in **Details** View at this file again - write its current **size** here:_____

11. In the folder: Armagh, create a Word document; Save it as: Italy.doc - Write down its current size displayed in Details View here:_____

12. **Key** in this text in the Italy.doc file:

> The boot shape of Italy make it one of the most easily recognised countries in he world. Italy lies in southern Europe and is almost completely surrounded by the Mediterranean Sea. The two islands of Sicily and Sardinia are also part of Italy.
>
> Northern Italy has contrasting landscapes of high mountains and flat plains. the northern border is formed by the Alps Today the traditional types of alpine farming have l\largely given way to tourism, both for winter skiing and for summer holidays by the beautiful lakes South of the mountains lies the only large flat region in Italy the plain of Lombardy. This is the most important region for both farming and industry in Italy.

13. **Resave** the Italy.doc file - write its current **size** here:_____

14. In the folder: Armagh, create an **Excel** document; **Save** it as: Balances.xls

15. **Key** in the content of the Balances.xls file:

	Dr	Cr
	£	£
Sales		6500
Purchases	7000	
Lighting	350	
Drawings	500	
Fittings	450	
Debtors	1200	
Creditors		3400
Bank	2100	
Cash	50	
Rent	1235	
Capital		2985

16. Write down the **current size** of Balances.xls file:_____

17. Create 2 subfolders: within the Armagh folder - **Belfast** and **Lagan**

18. **Arrange** icons within Armagh Folder: By **Name**
　　　　　　　　　　　　　　　By **Size** - which is the **largest** file?_____
　　　　　　　　　　　　　　　By **Type**
　　　　　　　　　　　　　　　Date Modified

19. **Open** the three folders: Armagh, Belfast and Lagan - make folder windows the same size and arrange windows side by side

20. **Copy** the files: Athens.txt, Italy.doc and Balances.xls to both the Belfast and Lagan folders

21. **Rename** the files in the Lagan folder as: **Greece2.txt; Rome.doc** and **Creed.xls** - the **extensions** will tell you which file is meant

22. **Copy** the newly named files to the **Armagh** folder - **Arrange** the contents of Armagh folder in **Name** order

23. **Copy** the files: **Greece2.txt** and **Rome.doc** to the **floppy disk**

24. Practice changing **size** of **a:** folder window i.e.
　　　　　　　　　　Minimise window and **Draw** this shape here: _____
　　　　　　　　　　Maximise window and **Draw** this shape here: _____
　　　　　　　　　　Close window and **Draw** this shape here: _____

25. **Open** Windows Explorer on your own computer

26. Display **c:** icon on the **left** and its contents on the **right**

27. Display similarly the contents of the **Lagan** folder

28. **Delete** the files: Greece2.txt; Rome.doc and Creed.xls

29. Restore the file **Greece2.txt** back to its original folder from the **Recycle Bin**

30. **Delete** permanently the files: **Rome.doc** and **Creed.xls**

31. **Format** and **Describe** the process of **Formatting** a floppy disk - number steps:

_____

32. **Find** a file containing the text: "**Microsoft**" in your computer

33. **Describe** how to establish the type of **processor** your computer has:

_____

34. **Describe** how the **Date and Time** of a computer can be changed:

_____

35. **Describe** how you can establish the amount of **RAM** in your computer and describe the steps required:

_____

36. **Check** the amount of **RAM** in your computer and write the **size** here:_____

37. **Describe** how the **Background Settings** of a computer can be changed:

_____

38. **Define** the terms: "**Print Queue**" and "**Printing Status**:

_____

39. **Describe** how you make a **Printer** the "**default**" printer of your computer:

_____

40. **Find** in the **Help** function of your **Word** document procedure for **creating Tables** - **copy** this guide to a **Word document**

40. **Find** in the **Help** function of your PC procedure for **changing Display** - **copy** this guide to a Word document

41. Create a **subFolder named:** Computers into your **drive c:\;**
Create **two subfolders** named: Disk and Drive directly into Computers subfolder
Rename the folder **Disk** as **Floppy.**

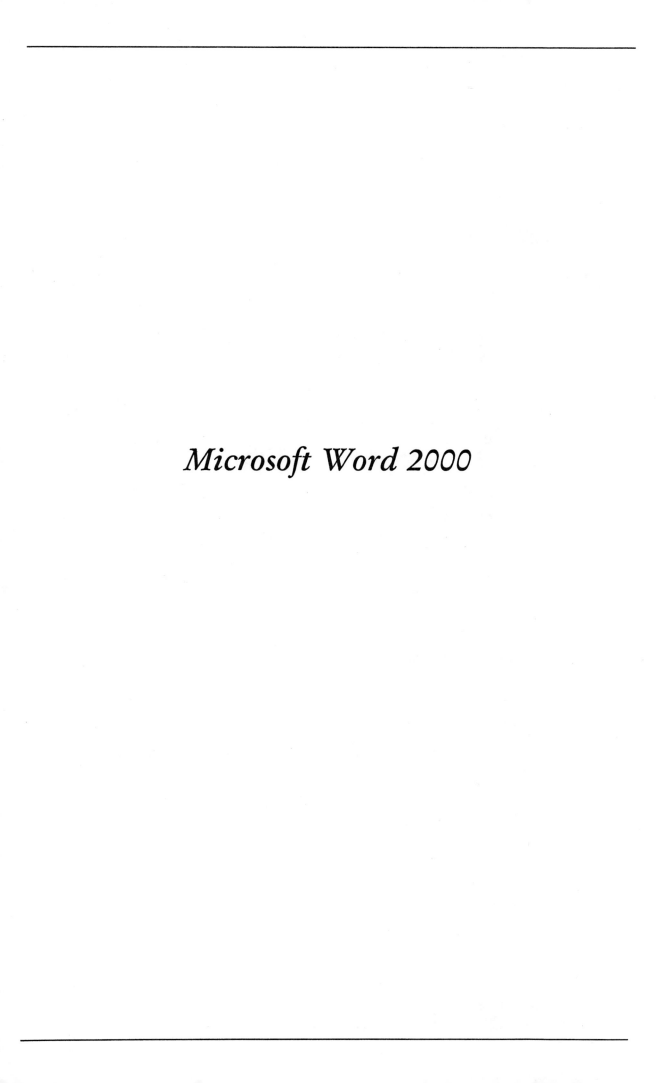

Microsoft Word 2000

Word Processing

Word Processing software is used for the creation of mainly textual material. Such text can be manipulated in many ways such as edited, copied, moved, searched or printed. The most popular word processing software in use today is Microsoft Word. This manual will illustrate the features of Microsoft Word 2000.

Getting Started

- **Turn on** computer - the operating system - in our example: **Windows 98** - is loaded into memory - **Desktop** appears:

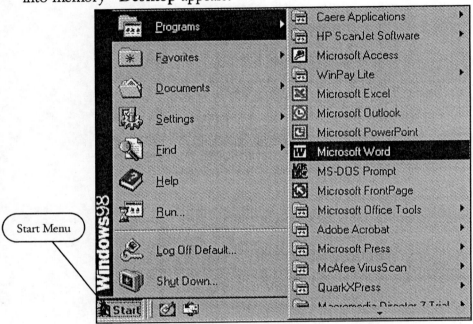

Loading Microsoft Word

- Start **Word** by clicking on the **Start Menu, Programs** and selecting **Microsoft Word.**

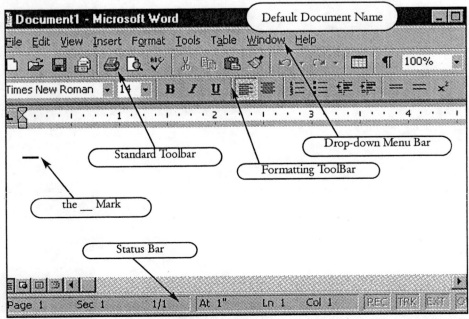

Default Word Document

- A **blank** document (by default entitled **Document1**) opens up - the mark on the screen indicates the position of the cursor (or insertion point) - the point at which text will display automatically as user types.

Menu Bar

- Commands can be selected from the drop-down **Menu Bar** either by clicking on the menu of your choice with the mouse and making your selection or by using the **Alt key** combined with the **underlined letter** of the chosen menu command.

Toolbars

- Toolbars, e.g. **Standard** or **Formatting** are bars made up of icons and displayed **horizontally** at the top of the screen. Clicking on an Icon is a quick way of accessing commands available within your drop-down menu. Add further Toolbars by selecting **View Toolbars** from Menu:

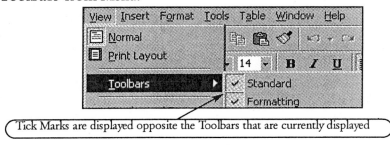

Tick Marks are displayed opposite the Toolbars that are currently displayed

Status Bar

- The Status Bar is the bar at the bottom of the document window that displays information about an operation in progress or the location of the insertion point.

Default

- There are defaults set within all software, e.g. margins, line spacing, font types, are at a preset value, which can be altered with the relevant command.

Methods of Moving around in a Document:

- Hitting the **Return** key moves the cursor to the next line.
- The **cursor arrow keys**:

$$\boxed{\leftarrow \rightarrow \downarrow \uparrow}$$

are used to move cursor in **direction** of the **depressed** arrow key **one** space at the time.
- Use the **Mouse** to move from **one line** to another.
- **Hold** down the **Control** key and press the **left** arrow or **right** arrow keys to move the cursor to the **left** or **right** one word at the time.

- The **Page Up/Down** keys are used to move the cursor up or down a page at the time or use the **Scroll Bars** to move up or across the Document.
- Depress the **Control Key** and **Home key** simultaneously to move the cursor directly to the top of the document.

Margins:

- **Margins** - a pre-defined space - set at the **top, bottom, left** and **right** sides of the document.
- Within Word, the **default Margins** are: **Left & Right**: 1.5"; **Top & Bottom**: 1 ".

Keying in text:

- **Type** in text. As you type, text flows into the open document at the insertion point until it reaches the right margin:

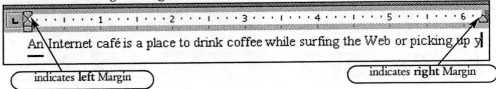

...the text then **wraps** around onto the next line:

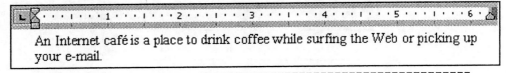

Wrap refers to the way the word processing software determines if the word being typed will fit within the margins; if not, it places that word on the next line

Inserting text within Existing Text:

- **Type** in the text below; Move insertion point to the point indicated:

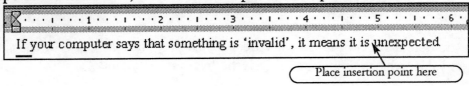

- Type in: "incorrect or" - existing text is pushed forward to accommodate the new text as it is typed:

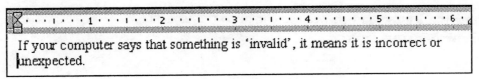

Deleting One Character

- Use **Backspace key** on keyboard to **delete** one character at the time to the **left** or use the **Delete** key on the keyboard to **delete** the character underneath the insertion point

Saving

- Text is only stored temporarily in the memory until it is saved permanently on either the hard or floppy disk using a saving command
- Save permanently by clicking the Save icon on the Toolbar or by selecting File Save from Menu bar. The first time you save a file, a Save as Dialog Box appears:

Save As Dialog Box:

- The default folder is **My Documents**

Folders

- Set up folders for segregating areas of work

To Create A Folder:

- Click the **Up One Level** button to move to the default **c:\ drive**

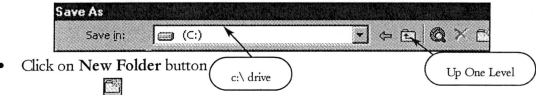

- Click on **New Folder** button

- Type in "Word Processing Tasks" as the **New Folder** name.

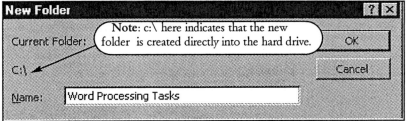

Note: c:\ here indicates that the new folder is created directly into the hard drive.

- Click **OK.**
  ..Word Processing Tasks will now display as the current folder in the **Save As** dialog box:

Naming File in Save As dialog box:

- In the **File name** box, (currently containing the default name: Document1), type in "Task 1" as the file name for the current file. Click **Save**.
- Document is stored *permanently* in the **Word Processing Tasks Folder** under the name: **Task 1:**

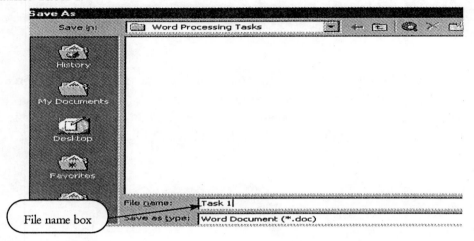

File name box

Closing File

- Select **File Close** from Menu:

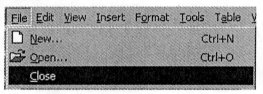

- .. document *closes* on screen

Creating a New Document:

- Click **New** icon on **Standard Toolbar** - *blank* document opens on screen.

Opening File

- Select **Open** icon on **Standard Toolbar** or **File Open** from Menu:

- .. **Open** dialog box opens on screen

- Select folder, e.g.: **Word Processing Tasks**
- Select file name, e.g. **Task 1** - Click **Open** - file Task 1 **opens** on screen:

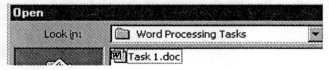

Spelling and Grammar

- By default, Microsoft Word checks *both* spelling and grammar.
  Note:
  If you want to check spelling *only*, click **Options** on the **Tools** menu, click the **Spelling & Grammar** tab, clear the **Check grammar with spelling** check box, and then click **OK.**

To Check - Example of an error in a sentence:

> The quick brown fox jumps over the dog

- Click **Spelling and Grammar** icon on the **Standard** toolbar:

..the Spelling and Grammar dialog box opens up.

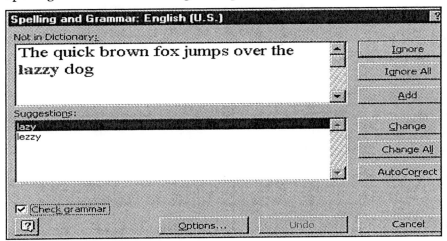

- Errors are highlighted - possible replacement ideas display under **Suggestions**:

- Our example contains one error only: "lazzy" - Click on the appropriate suggestion

- Click on the button entitled: **Change** - appropriate option if change is to be made *once* only - text with error is **replaced** with correct text

- If change is to be made **more than once,** the button entitled: **Change All** is clicked

Show/Hide Icon

- The **Return symbols** and **dots** which represent the **Space Bar** being hit are shown when you click the **Show/Hide** button on the **Standard Toolbar:**

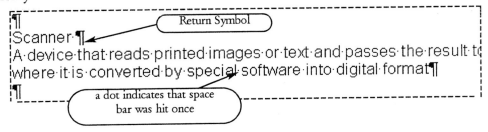

Joining Paragraphs

- To **join** one paragraph to another, it is necessary to **delete** the returns **between** the two paragraphs:

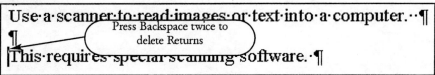

..text is now formed into **one Paragraph** and now looks like this:

¶
Use·a·scanner·to·read·images·or·text·into·a·computer.··Th
scanning·software.·¶

Creating a New Paragraph

- To **create** a **clear line** between Paragraphs, it is necessary to hit the **Return key** twice.

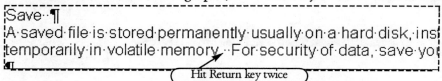

- Place **insertion point** where **new** paragraph is to be created and hit the **Return** key **twice** - Text will now look like:

Save··¶
A·saved·file·is·stored·permanently·usually·on·a·hard·disk,·ins
temporarily·in·volatile·memory.··¶
¶
·For·security·of·data,·save·your·work·frequently.¶

PRACTICE

To consolidate the Word features introduced to date, study the relevant notes, and complete the following exercises:

Exercise 1:

- Identify aspects of a *blank* Word document in the designated text boxes:

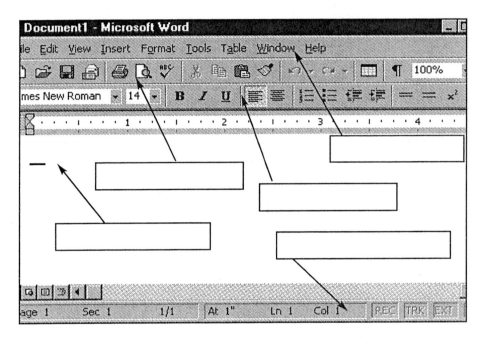

Exercise 2: **Answer the questions below in the space provided:**

- Define in your own words the terms:

Status Bar:_____

Default:_____

Margins:_____

- **Saving:** Where is text held until it is saved?

_____

- **Folders:**
Describe procedure for creating a **new** folder: Number each step:

_____

_____

- **Saving:** Describe steps:

_____

Paragraphs*:*

- *Joining***:** Describe steps required for **Joining Paragraphs** together:

_____

- *New***:** Describe steps required for **Creating a new Paragraph:**

_____

- *Toolbars***:** Name *default* Toolbars & detail the menu command used to turn on Toolbars:

_____

- *Show/Hide Button***:** What is the **Show/Hide** Button - what do you see when you turn on the Show/Hide Button:

_____

- *Opening a File***:** What icon is used to **Open** a File?

_____

- *Closing a File***:** What is the command for **Closing** a File?

_____

- *Deleting One Character:* Describe the *two* methods of **Deleting one Character**

_____

- *Getting Started & Using Word:* Describe the steps involved in **turning on a Computer** and **loading Word for Windows** into the memory

_____

_____

_____

Exercise 3:

- Start **Word** and **Create a new document**
- **Type** in the Exercise below:

> The Fascimile Machine enables visual data to be sent cheaply between firms. The documents are fed into the sender's machine, a copy is made and this is transmitted, to the receiver. The document is then reprinted by the machine. The whole process takes just a minute for each document to be sent to any destination worldwide. Fax machines can receive documents twenty-four hours a day and operate. The system is 100% reliable and prints a message stating how long it took and where it went to. Once the machine has been purchased and installed, the costs are low.

- Create a **folder** and name it "Practice Today"
- **Save** document as **Fascimile**
- **Close File**

Exercise 4:

- **Open** the document **Fascimile**
- **Insert** the following text: - check insertions against the finished document below:

  - "easily and" before "cheaply between.."
  - "fax" between the words: "sender's" and "machine"
  - "via a telephone line," before "to the receiver"
  - after the text "reprinted by the", insert "receiver's fax"
  - "do not need to be attended to" is to be inserted before "operate."
  - After the word: "message stating", type "whether or not the transmission has been successful,"
  - At the end of the document, after the word "costs", insert: "of operation "

- Run **Spell Check** and **Save**
- The *edited* text should now read as follows:

> The Fascimile Machine enables visual data to be sent easily and cheaply between firms. The documents are fed into the sender's fax machine, a copy is made and this is transmitted, via a telephone line, to the receiver. The document is then reprinted by the receiver's fax machine. The whole process takes just a minute for each document to be sent to any destination worldwide. Fax machines can receive documents twenty-four hours a day and do not need to be attended to operate. The system is 100% reliable and prints a message stating whether or not the transmission has been successful, how long it took and where it went to. Once the machine has been purchased and installed, the costs of operation are low.

- **Close** File

Exercise 5

- **Create** a new document
- **Type** in the Exercise below:

> The first AGM of the Club was postponed yesterday after incidents made it impossible to continue. Trouble first started when the secretary declared that the meeting could not proceed because a quorum did not exist. Problems continued though when the treasurer was unable to locate the document. One member then put forward a motion "that meetings be held on Thursdays instead of Fridays", but this failed to be considered as no seconder could be found. A second motion was accepted after a vote by poll. A further three members plus one proxy arrived late and on a point of order declared that the meeting was invalid as they had not received the proper notice. At this the chairman adjourned the meeting.

- In the **Practice Today** folder, **Save** document as "Rathgar"
- **Close File**

Exercise 6

- **Open** the document **Rathgar**
- Make the **insertions** of text as follows:
    - Insert "Rathgar Croquet " before "Club " in the first sentence
    - Insert "a series of " before "incidents"
    - After the word " secretary ", insert "who took charge of the meeting"
    - Insert the sentence: "This however was averted when five latecomers arrived." before the sentence starting with "Problems"
    - After the text: "A second motion", type " relating to new members"
    - "after a vote by poll", insert "but only after a casting poll was used."

- Run **Spell Check** and **Save**
- The edited text should now read as follows:

> The first AGM of the Rathgar Croquet Club was postponed yesterday after a series of incidents made it impossible to continue. Trouble first started when the secretary who took charge of the meeting declared that the meeting could not proceed because a quorum did not exist. This however was averted when five latecomers arrived. Problems continued though when the treasurer who was supposed to read the minutes was unable to locate the document. One member then put forward a motion "that meetings be held on Thursdays instead of Fridays", but this failed to be considered as no seconder could be found. A second motion relating to new members was accepted after a vote by poll, but only after a casting poll was used. A further three members plus one proxy arrived late and on a point of order declared that the meeting was invalid as they had not received the proper notice. At this the chairman adjourned the meeting.

Exercise 7

- **Create** a new document
- **Type** in the Exercise below:

> Ireland joined the EC and has experienced many changes as a result of membership. One of the developments since joining was the signing by Ireland of the Maastrict Treaty which saw Ireland enter with its EC partners into the Single European Market on 1 January 1993. The Single European Market impacted on many aspects, such as Banking. A single market will now exist in financial services. Irish businesses will be able to transact their business with any properly organised financial institution located in the EC. Financial institutions can now set up an office due to the existence of a single banking licence. A European Central Bank was set up in Frankfurt. Existing currencies will be replaced with a currency in the future.

- In the *Practice Today* folder, **Save** document as *Maastrict*; **Close File**

Exercise 8:

- **Open** the document "Maastrict"
- **E**dit as indicated:
    - After the text, "joined the EC", insert "in 1973 "
    - Insert a New Paragraph after the text starting: "membership."
    - After "One of the", and before " developments" insert "most significant"
    - Insert "the Single European Act and" after "of " and before "the Maastrict.."
    - Insert the text: "of the Irish business environment" before ", such as Banking"
    - Insert a New Paragraph after the sentence ending: " ..as Banking"
    - After "Irish businesses", insert "and individuals"
    - After the text "can now set up an office", key in the text: "in any EC country"
    - Type: "There is increased competition for Irish financial institutions." before the sentence starting: "A European Central Bank."
- Run *Spell Check*. *Click Show and Hide* icon to check *Returns* and *spaces*. *Save*
- The **edited** text should now read as follows:

> Ireland joined the EC in 1973 and has experienced many changes as a result of membership.
>
> One of the most significant developments since joining was the signing by Ireland of the Single European Act and the Maastrict Treaty which saw Ireland enter with its EC partners into the Single European Market on 1 January 1993. The Single European Market impacted on many aspects of the Irish business environment, such as Banking.
>
> A single market will now exist in financial services. Irish businesses and individuals will be able to transact their business with any properly organised financial institution located in the EC. Financial institutions can now set up an office in any EC country due to the existence of a single banking licence. There is increased competition for Irish financial institutions. A European Central Bank was set up in Frankfurt. Existing currencies will

- **Close** *File*.

Deleting a Word:

- **Highlight** word to be deleted:

> A special paper tray for a printer

- Press **Delete** key - word is deleted:

> A paper tray for a printer

Deleting a few Words:

- **Highlight** words to be deleted - click the mouse to the left of "- for" and drag the mouse to the right; use **Shift and arrow keys** for more control when highlighting:

> To restart a PC in one of two ways. A cold boot - for a completely fresh start - involves switching it off, waiting some seconds while the hard disk stops spinning, then switching it on again.

- Press **Delete** key - highlighted words are deleted:

> To restart a PC in one of two ways. A cold boot involves switching it off, waiting some seconds while the hard disk stops spinning, then switching it on again.

Deleting a Line:

- Highlight line to be deleted by clicking in the margin to the left:

> More sympathetic to the machine, a warm boot is done with the reset switch. The machine is reset, but the power supply is not interrupted. Macs do all this through keyboard commands.

- Press **Delete** key: text is deleted:

> More sympathetic to the machine, a warm boot is done with the reset switch. through keyboard commands.

Deleting a Paragraph or Block of Text:

- **Highlight** block to be deleted by clicking to the left of the first line and dragging downwards:

> Internet cafe A place to drink coffee while surfing the Web or picking
> e-mail. Good too for getting a first taste of the Internet, as friendly ad
> help will usually be available. Found in towns and cities all over the w
>
> Internet Explorer A leading Web browser from Microsoft. Controversi
> though usefully, it is integrated into Windows 98 and Windows 2000.

- Press **Delete** key and block is erased:

> Internet Explorer A leading Web browser from Microsoft. Controversi
> though usefully, it is integrated into Windows 98 and Windows 2000.

Page Breaks:

- Place cursor at point where **new** page is to be created
- Hit **Control & Return** simultaneously - **new** page is created

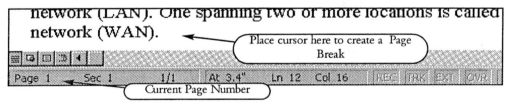

..**New Page** is inserted after the cursor:

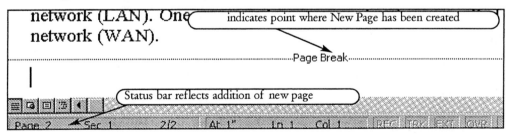

Line Spacing
(By default Line Spacing is set to Single Spacing)

To Change Line Spacing *before* Document is Typed:

- To Set eg **Double Spacing** (one **clear** line in between each line)
- Select **Format Paragraph** command from Menu.
- Select **Line Spacing Double** from drop-down list::

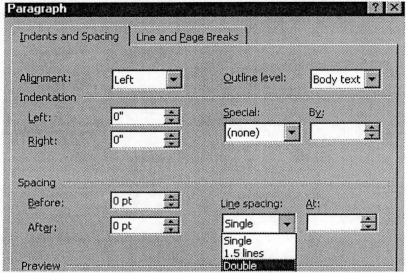

- Click **OK** - Double Line Spacing is set - as the text wraps around from one line to the next, a single clear line will display between the lines of text.

Note: To Apply Double Spacing to **Existing** Text - it is necessary to highlight text *first* before selecting **Format Paragraph Line Spacing** as above

Cut & Paste

Cutting:
- **Highlight** text to be moved:

> A Macintosh program (this is found in the Apple menu) appears as a keyboard on-screen.

- Click the **Cut** icon on the Toolbar

  - text is **removed** from screen and held in the memory - known as the clipboard

Pasting:
- Move cursor to **new** location of text: after the last sentence
- Select **Paste** button from toolbar

  ..text is pasted from the clipboard to the screen

> A Macintosh program appears as a small keyboard on-screen (this is found the Apple menu).

Copy & Pasting

Copying:
- **Highlight** text to be **copied**:

> **The Windows equivalent is Character Map, found in Accessories, Syst Tools.**

- Select **Copy** button from toolbar

..**original** text stays on screen - **copy** of text is placed in memory (clipboard)

Pasting:
- **Move** cursor to location (after "Tools") for copied text and click **Paste** icon
  ..**Copy** of text appears on screen:

> The Windows equivalent is Character Map, found in Accessories, System Tools.
> The Windows equivalent is Character Map, found in Accessories, System Tools.

Setting Margins

- To specify *exact* margin measurements, select **Page Setup** from the **File** menu
- ..the **Page Setup** dialog box opens - click the **Margins Tab**

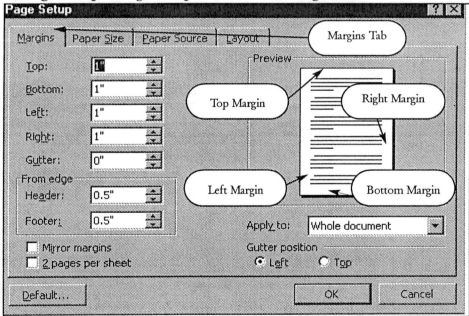

- Enter settings for example: **Top & Bottom = 1"; Left & Right Margins = 1.5"**

- Click **OK**

Choosing a Paper Size

- On the **File** menu, click **Page Setup**, and then click the **Paper Size** tab:
- From the **Paper Sizes** drop-down menu, Select a **paper size** - **A4** is the most commonly used size:

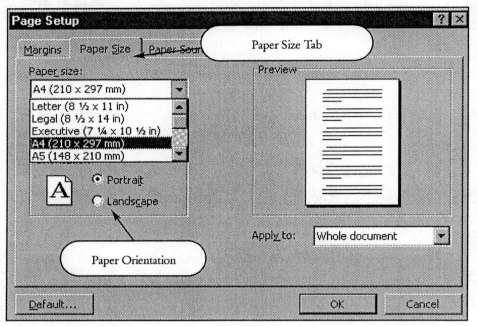

- Select **Orientation**: Choose between: **Portrait** or **Landscape**:

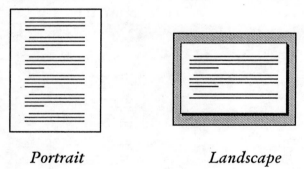

Portrait   *Landscape*

- Click **OK**

Print Preview

- To display each page as it will look when printed, click **Print Overview** icon on Toolbar:

..**Print Preview** dialog box opens

Print Preview dialog box

- **Whole** Page is the default View - Choose from: **Page Width,** 50% etc

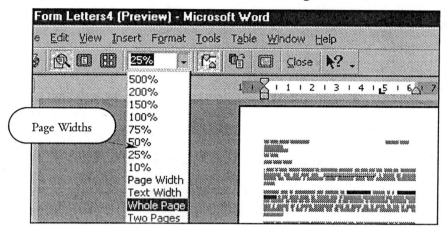

Print Preview Options:

Choose from Icons:

One Page

.. this will give a 25% View of the Current Page

Multiple Pages

..our example: this feature was used to **Preview 8 Pages** of text

- Click and drag on icon to see the effect:

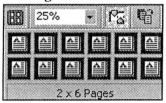

- ..the **8 Pages** in our current document can then be previewed:

Full Screen

- Click to see the **current Page** in 38% View
- Click **Close Full Screen** icon to revert to **default Preview**

Printing

- You can print the **current** whole document **once** by clicking the **Printer** icon on the Toolbar:

Printing Choices:

To print other than the whole document once, select **File Print** from Menu: **Print Dialog box** opens:

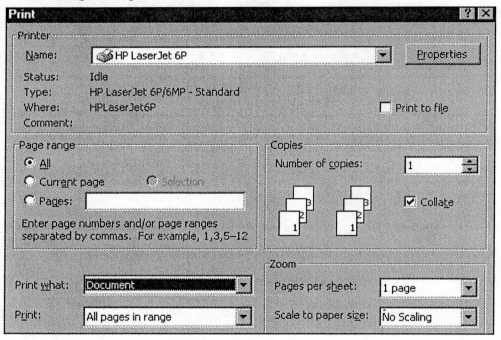

Range for Printing:

Under **Page Range**, choose from:

All:	(This will print the whole document)
Current Page:	(This will print the current page)
Selection:	(This will print current selected text)
Pages:	(Enter in this box the range of pages to be printed, e.g.: 3, 6-8, 11-12, i.e. excluding Pages: 1, 2, 4, 5, 9 and 10)

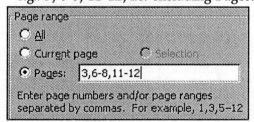

Number of copies:

In the **Number of copies** box, enter the **number** of copies you want to print: e.g. to Print 2 copies: enter 2:

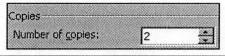

Print to File:

- Use the **Print to File** option when Printing is to be carried out at a **higher resolution** (crisper image - better quality):

..**Print to file** dialog box opens:

- Type in appropriate name, **e.g.: Flyers,** click OK.

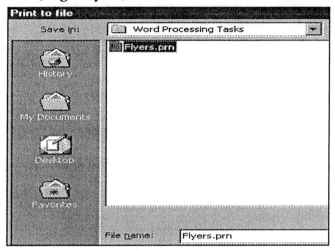

Exercise 9:

- Type in the Exercise below using Margins: **Left** - 1" & **Right** - 1.2"

> Freeze-thaw action occurs in many mountainous areas. Rain enters all the cracks in rock: When this rainwater freezes, its volume expands and expands and the cracks are widened. When temperatures really rise the water thaws. Rain falls again and this process of freeze-thaw action continues until the rock is completely broken down. Freeze-thaw action produces loose rock fragments, which can be seen on all of the mountain sides. These loose rock fragments are called talus or scree rocks.

- Create a **new** folder named "Geographic matters"; **Save** as "Weathering MW"
- **Print to File** using File name: "Weather2" and **Close** file

Exercise 10:

- **Open** file "Weathering MW"
- Using the deletion knowledge acquired above, **Delete** all **words** with a line through

> Freeze-thaw action occurs in ~~many~~ mountainous areas. Rain enters ~~all the~~ cracks in rock: When this rainwater freezes, its volume expands ~~and expands~~ and the cracks are widened. When temperatures ~~really~~ rise the water thaws. Rain falls again and this process of freeze-thaw action continues until the rock is completely broken down. Freeze-thaw action produces loose rock fragments, which can be seen on ~~all of the~~ mountain sides. These loose rock fragments are called talus ~~or scree rocks.~~

- Using **File Save As** feature; Change **Line Spacing** to **1.5**
- **Rename** file as: "Mechanical Weathering MW"

Exercise 11:

- Create a **New** Document; set **Margins** at 1" at both sides; type in the Exercise below.

> Chemical Weathering
>
> The disintegration of rocks as a result of the many chemical changes in the mineral constituents of rock.
>
> Still Mineral Water is an essential requirement for chemical weathering and so is really very active in humid climates. The chief processes are: Solution, Hydration, Carbonation and Oxidation.
>
> Solution is the process by which minerals which are soluble in water are dissolved. With Hydration, some minerals have the power have the power to absorb water. When they absorb this carbonated water, they expand and lose their strength leading to the destruction of the rock.

- In the folder "Geographic matters", **Save** as "Chemical Processes MW"
- **PreView** and **Close** file

Exercise 12:

- **Open** file "Chemical Processes MW"; Change **Margins**: Left & Right: 1.4; Top: 1.1"

> Chemical Weathering
>
> The disintegration of rocks as a result of ~~the many~~ chemical changes in the mineral constituents of rock.
>
> ~~Still Mineral~~ Water is an essential requirement for chemical weathering and so is ~~really very~~ active in humid climates. The chief processes are: Solution, Hydration, Carbonation and Oxidation.
>
> Solution is the process by which minerals which are soluble in water are dissolved. With Hydration, some minerals have the power ~~have the power~~ to absorb water. When they absorb ~~this carbonated~~ water, they expand and lose their strength leading to the destruction of the rock.

- **Delete** all **words** and **lines** with a line through
- **Join the Paragraph** beginning: "Solution is.." to previous Paragraph
- Make a **new** Paragraph at the point: "With Hydration..."
- Turn on **Show/Hide icon** to check the number of Returns between Paragraphs
- Change **Line Spacing** of **First** Paragraph to: **Double**
- Create a **Page Break** at the **end** of the document
- Copy second Paragraph to New Page
- Using **File Save As** feature, **Rename** file as: "Chemical Weathering MW"
- **Print to file** - use **Print File** name: "Chem 32.prn"

Exercise 13:

- Create a **New** Document; set **Line Spacing** to **Double**
- Set **Margins**: *Left*: 1.5" & *Right*: 1.1"
- **Key** in the document below

River Capture

River Capture is the capturing of one river by another extremely small river. Sometimes, a valley with less erosional power is so large compared to the small river flowing through it that it could not have been formed by this river. This misfit river diverting into another river is the remains of a larger river which used to flow through this valley, but which has been diverted from its original course by a second river. These rivers flowing through the soft rocks are parallel to each other and their tributaries. This misfit river has been captured.

River capture is the process, by which water flowing in one river is diverted into another and occurs when one river retreats by headward erosion until it cuts through the divide between it and another stream.

The water of the captured river will flow into the pirate river increasing its volume and its power to erode. The elbow of capture is the point at which river capture occurs. The beheaded river has less erosional power because its water has been diverted. Rivers flow from a central area such as a mountain top resembling spokes on a wheel radiating outwards from the axle. It is a misfit river because it is too small for the valley through which it flows.

- **Save** as "River Capture MW" in the current folder
- **Close** File

Exercise 14:

- **Open** File: "River Capture MW"
- **Delete** Blocks of text listed below:
    - "extremely small river "
    - "with less erosional power"
    - "diverting into another river"
    - "These rivers flowing.. and their tributaries. "
    - "River capture is ..another stream."
    - Rivers flow from a .. from the axle. "
    - "One river must ..capture its water. "

- Change **Margins** to 1" for Top, Bottom, Left and Right
- **Save** under a new name: "Headward Erosion MW"
- **Cut** the first Paragraph and **Paste** to the bottom of document
- Change Line Spacing of second paragraph to 1.5
- Using the **Print** option for "Printing a Selection", Print the last paragraph if facilities permit.
- **ReSave** and **Close** File

Exercise 15:

- **Open** file: "Mechanical Weathering MW"
- Make a **Page Break** at the end of the document
- Using the **Copying and Pasting** feature, make a **copy** of the entire document and **Paste** on to second Page

Edit the copy of the document:

- **Cut** the sentence: "These loose rock fragments are called talus." and **Paste** so that it will then be the first sentence in the Paragraph.
- **Cut** the sentence: "Rain falls again and this process of freeze-thaw action continues until the rock is completely broken down." and **Paste** at the end of the Paragraph.
- Change the **Line Spacing** of the copied paragraph to **Double**.
- **Save** under a new name: "Onion Weathering MW"

Exercise 16:

- **Open** file: "Chemical Weathering MW"
- Make a **Page Break** at the end of the text
- Using the **Copying** and **Pasting** feature, make a **copy** of the entire text and **Paste** on to the next Page

Edit the copy of the text:
- **Cut** the text: "Water is an essential requirement .. Oxidation" and **Paste** so that it will then be the last text in the document.
- **Cut** the sentence: "When they absorb water, .. the rock." and **Paste** at the beginning of the Paragraph.
- Change **Line Spacing** of the second paragraph to **Double** and the **First Paragraph** to **1.5**
- Create **New Page** and make a **copy** of the **first** and **second** paragraphs on this new page
- **Save** under a new name: "Humid Climates MW"

Exercise 17:

- **Open** File "Headward Erosion MW"

Edit as follows:

- Change **Left Margin** to 2" and the **Right Margin** to 1.3"
- **Delete** the first sentence
- Change **Line Spacing** to 1.5
- **Cut** last sentence and **Paste** so that it will become the first sentence in the document
- Create a **Page Break;** make **two** copies of the last paragraph on a **new page**
- **Save** under a new name: "River Diversion MW"
- **Preview;** Change **Paper Orientation** to **Landscape**
- Select **first** Paragraph and **Print** this "selection" once (if facilities permit); alternatively **Print to File; Close** File.

Finding and Replacing:

One or every occurrence of a specific word or phrase can be found and replaced within Word. Below, we will replace every occurrence of the word spring with winter.

- Type in text: "When the ground.." below; Select Edit Replace from the Menu:

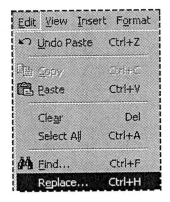

- ..the **Find and Replace** dialog box opens, type in **spring** in the **Find what**: box and type **winter** in the **Replace with**: box:
- When you click **Find Next**, the *first* occurrence of **spring** is highlighted:

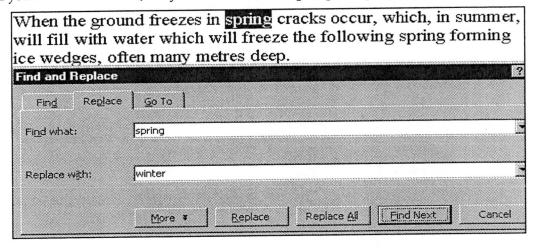

- Click **Replace** key to replace **one** occurrence of the word; click **Replace All** to replace **All** occurrences of the word
- When you Click **Replace All** - this message is then displayed:

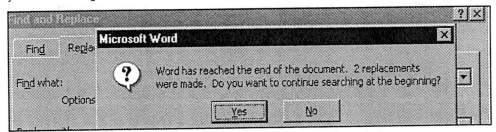

- Click **No**.

Note: Clicking **Find Next** *twice* in succession allows you to **skip** an occurrence *without* replacing.

Find and replace formatting

- Type this text in **Times New Roman:**

> Some Glacial lakes - the Great Lakes of North America - form natural routeways. Where Glacial lakes have drained away, their channels from routeways across difficult terrain.

- We will replace this **Font** with **Arial** for the words: **Glacial lakes** - i.e. the text will remain the same but the **Font** will be changed
- Select **Edit Replace** from menu - **Find and Replace** dialog box opens:
- Type **Glacial lakes** in *both* the **Find** and **Replace** boxes
- With cursor in **Find Box**, Select **More:**

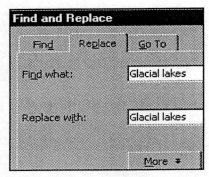

- ..the Find and Replace Box extends downwards to look like:

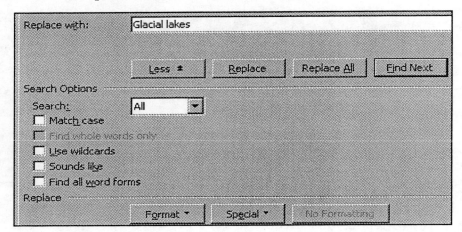

- Click the **Format** button - a drop-up menu displays - select **Font:**

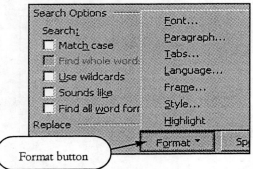

Format button

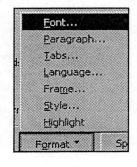

- ..the **Find Font** dialog box opens - select **Times New Roman**, click OK:

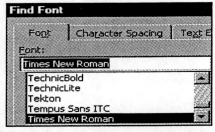

- ..the **Find and Replace** dialog box appears with **Times New Roman** now added below the **Find what** box:

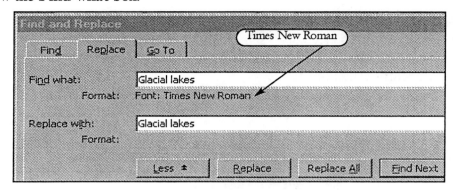

- Click in **Replace with:** box, click **Format, Font** - from **Replace Font** dialog box, select **Arial**, click OK

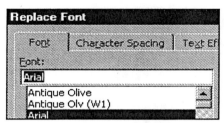

- **Find and Replace** with: dialog box will now look like - click **Replace All:**

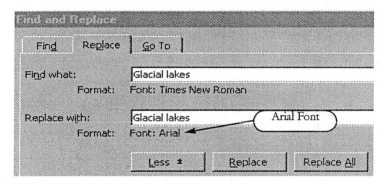

- ..the font of *all* occurrences of **Glacial lakes** changes to **Arial**

Text Alignment

- Text Alignment refers to the text's relationship to the **left** and **right margins**, as in "left-aligned", "right-aligned", "centered" etc For example, the centering alignment feature centers text **between** the left and right margin

- The **default** alignment in Word is **left** - unless the alignment is changed, text automatically displays as it is inputted at the left margin

Aligning Existing text:

- Existing text can be re-aligned by:
- Selecting text and then selecting the relevant Alignment icon on the Toolbar:

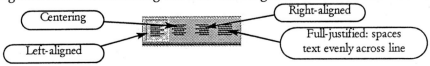

Aligning New text (as it is inputted):

- Relevant **Alignment icon** is selected *before* inputting begins - alignment is applied *automatically* as text is created:

    - **Left-aligned** Example:

    > | Graphics Card |

    - **Full justified** Example: spaces text evenly across line:

    > | Mercedes Benz is |

    - **Right-aligned** Example:

    > | Buffer |

    - **Centering** Example:

    > | Network |

Moving from one open document to another open document

- If memory allows, you can have many documents open **simultaneously** and you can **switch** from one to the other easily - in our example: **three** documents are open at the moment - **Baltimore** is on top.

    To switch to "London" document, select **Window** from menu - all open Word documents are displayed - the "Baltimore" document is the currently opened document as indicated by the **tick mark:**

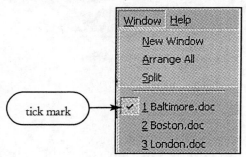

- You **create** 3 documents and **Save** under the names above; let the 3 documents open on the screen. Our "London" document already contains text - **select** the "London" document - "London" document **displays**. **Type** the text below into your "London" document:

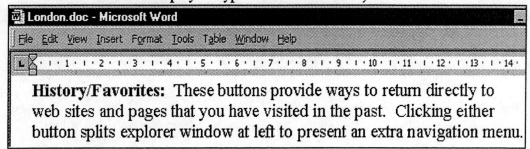

Note: the other two open documents: "Baltimore" and "Boston" will remain available under the **Window** drop-down menu until they are closed.

Copy text from "London" document & Paste to "Boston" document

- **Copy** the **first paragraph** of the "London" document.
- Switch to the "Boston" document by clicking **Window** and select "Boston" document
- Click **Paste** icon - text is **copied** to the screen

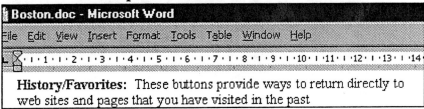

History/Favorites: These buttons provide ways to return directly to web sites and pages that you have visited in the past

Headers & Footers

A header or footer is **text** or **graphics** e.g. a page number, the date, or a company logo. that is printed at the **top** or **bottom** of each page in a document. A header is printed in the top margin; a footer is printed in the bottom margin

To Display Header/Footer Toolbar:

- On the **View** menu, click **Header and Footer** - Toolbar displays Header area:

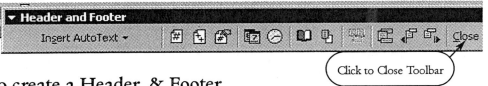

Click to Close Toolbar

To create a Header & Footer

- In the **Header** area, **key in** the Centered Header below:

Header

ROCKET SCIENCE

- Click this icon to switch to the **Footer** area at the bottom of the document:

- In the **Footer** area, key in the Footer below:

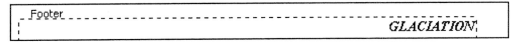

Footer

GLACIATION

Note the purpose of the following icons on the Header & Footer Toolbar - experiment by clicking on individual icons:

- To insert **Page numbers**, select **Page Number** icon: 🔲

(Page Numbers can also be inserted with **Insert Page Numbers** command from Menu)

- To insert **Current date**, select **Date** icon: 🔲

- To insert **Current Time**, select **Time** icon: 🔲

- To **Close** Header/Footer Toolbar, Click **Close button** on Toolbar

Page Numbering

You can **Insert Page Numbers** by using the **Insert Page Numbers** command from Menu - Page Numbers dialog box opens:

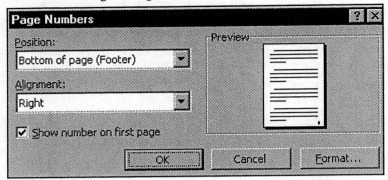

Under **Position Box:**

- The page numbers may be inserted in the **header** or **footer** at the **top** or **bottom** of the page as the drop-down menu indicates:

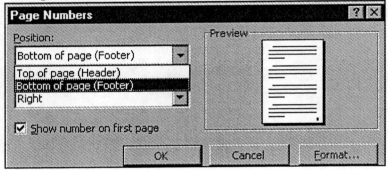

Under **Alignment Box:**

- The page numbers may be aligned e.g. **Left** or **Right** or **Centered:**

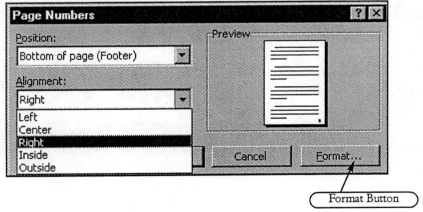

Format Button

Format button - setting options include:

Number Format:

- **Formats of Numbers,** such as: **Roman Numerals, Caps** etc, can be chosen as the drop-down range indicate:

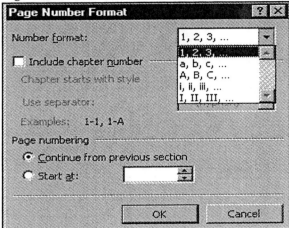

Start Page Numbering

- Click Option for Choices of:

    Default: **Continue from Previous Section:**
    or
    Starting at a **specified Number**

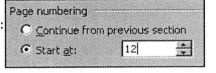

- ..our example, key in **12** as the **Start at** number

Font Type

- Default **Font Types** and **Font Sizes** vary from one software to another - **Times New Roman - Size 10** - may be the *default* **Font Type/Size** for Word for Windows

    whereas Font Type: **Arial - Font Size 12** may be the *default* for **Excel**

To Change Font Type & Size:

- **Highlight** text:

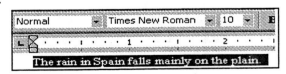

- Click on arrow next to **Font Type Box:** Select **Arial Rounded MT Bold** Font::

Font Size

- Select arrow next to **Font Size** box and select **Size**:

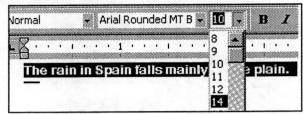

- Text is changed to **Arial Rounded MT Bold, Size 14**

Exercise 18:

- Key in the **text** below. **Save as** "Gresham Hotel MW"

> One of the landmarks of Dublin, dating back to 1817 is the Imperial Motel. At the dead centre of the city, it is within walking distance of Dublin's finest attractions and retains the unique culture, history and atmosphere, yet has all the convenience of any modern convention centre with multi-storey car parking. This year saw a refurbishment programme of the Imperial and the Imperial Metropole's conference and banqueting facilities. Each of these properties offer 38 meeting rooms between them, and can cater for a maximum of 500 representatives. The motel offers a luxury venue with everything today's conference organiser needs: a 24-hour business centre, natural daylight, voice-mail message system, registration lobby, secure multi-storey car park, direct-dial conference phone, full air conditioning, wonderful, cuisine, fitness centre, luxury bedrooms and penthouse suites, travel agency and last but definitely not something many motels can offer, a butler catering to guests' every need.

- Insert a new paragraph at the point: "This year saw"
- Change font for the whole document to Arial Narrow (12)
- Replace any occurrence of the word: "representatives" with "delegates"
- Replace any occurrence of the word: "motel" with "hotel"
- Replace any occurrence of the word: "Imperial" with "Gresham"; at the same time, change the current font for this word to Arial Black, size (14)
- Insert a Header: "The Gresham: a famous Dublin landmark"
- Insert a Footer: "The Gresham has a 24-hour business centre"
- Insert a right-aligned page number in the Footer - the page number is "14"
- Delete the last sentence
- ReSave under the existing file name - let file open on screen

Exercise 19:

- Create a new document and call it "Gresh MW"
- Paste a copy of the first two sentences of the "Gresham Hotel MW" document to "Gresh MW"; close File

Exercise 20:

- Key in the **text** above. **Save as** "Johnstown House Hotel MW"

Meath Further inland, but still close to Dublin is Meath. Johnstown House Hotel and Spa is a unique modern development outside Enfield in Co Meath. It opened this August and is located just 30 minutes from the outskirts of Dublin, on theN4. The hotel is developed around a 1750's Victorian country estate house. Set in 80 acres of stunning parkland landscape with riverside walks, Johnstown House and Spa will offer 125 luxuriously appointed and 17 deluxe suites, a choice of restaurants and a selection of bars and lounge areas. A wide range of conference facilities are available: the conference centre caters for 600 delegates and a selection of nine boardrooms are available for smaller meetings. The conference suites incorporate the latest state-of-the art audiovisual equipment, including back projection and video conferencing and are operated from a single podium point, which controls lighting and sound technologies, including Barco reality 6400 with back projection and zoom lens, video and TV. At the Spa, delegates can relax, unwind and enjoy the ultimate in luxurious treatments, unique heat experiences, and holistic therapies. The modern Spa at Johnstown House is managed by leading international specialists, ESPA, who are associated with some of the best-known Spa developments in Europe. Providing over 3,000 sq m of guest facilities on two stories this state of the art spa facility comprises of 15 private treatment rooms with therapies available from aromatherapy through heat treatments.

- Change font of the first sentence to Times New Roman (10)
- Insert a new paragraph at the point: " The hotel " and at the point: "The conference suites"
- Replace any occurrence of the word: "state of the art " with "modern"
- Replace any occurrence of the word: "Victorian" with "Georgian" - change the font for Georgian to: Arial Rounded MT Bold, size 16.
- Replace any occurrence of the word: "delegates" with " guests "; at the same time, change the current font for this word to Playbill, size (14)
- Insert a Header: "Facilities include a gym and fitness studio"
- Insert a Footer: "18-metre indoor pool"
- Insert a centered page number in the Header - the page number is "21"
- Delete the sentence: starting: "A wide range of conference"
- ReSave under the existing file name - let file open on screen

Exercise 21:

- Create a new document and Save it as: "Enfield MW"
- Using Window drop-down menu, display the file: " Johnstown House Hotel MW"
- Copy the last paragraph and paste into the file: " Enfield MW "
- Change all the font in the " Enfield MW " file to Arial Narrow, size (13)
- Also, create a Header: "Best known spa development in Europe" and a Footer: "Waterfall feature for relaxation"; insert a left-aligned date in the Footer
- Change Line Spacing to 1.5
- Save this file as "Enfield 2"; close all files

Exercise 22:

- Key in the **text** below. **Save as** " Ballymascanlon House Hotel MW"

> Louth Going North along the east coast to Dundalk, an convenient halfway point between Belfast and Dublin (just two and a half hours from Belfast) for activity people is the Kilmichael House Hotel.
>
> A county house set in 130 acres this is a family- run hotel that prides in having a genuine interest in ensuring every guest is made to feel at home, regardless of whether the occasion is activity or pleasure. Having recently completed an - extensive refurbishment project, the Kilmichael is the perfect venue for combining the demands of a activity meeting with some relaxation. The 18-hole golf course designed by the internationally renowned Craddock & Ruddy, will certainly appeal to the golf enthusiast. Set amidst the Cooley landscape the course is as challenging as it is rewarding. Alternatively try a relaxing swim or vigorous workout in the luxurious leisure facilities. Not forgetting the conference facilities, you can choose from one of four meeting rooms, all fully air-conditioned. Video conferencing and a dedicated activity service is also available on request.

- Change font of the first sentence to Times New Roman (10)
- Insert a new paragraph at the point: " Having recently completed " and at the point: "Set amidst the Cooley"
- Join up the paragraph starting: "A county house set in 130" with the previous paragraph
- Insert a Header: "Air-Conditioned Meeting Rooms" in Font Arial Narrow (12)
- Insert a Footer: "Plush Country House"
- Insert a right-aligned page number in the Footer - use the default page number
- Replace any occurrence of the word: " two and a half hours from Belfast " with " one and a half hours from Dublin "
- Replace any occurrence of the word: "Kilmichael" with " Ballymascanlon" - changing the font also to: Algerian, size 16.
- Replace any occurrence of the word: "activity" with " business "; at the same time, change the current font for this word to Playbill, size (14)
- Delete the sentence: starting: "Not forgetting the.."
- ReSave under the existing file name - let file open on screen

Exercise 23:

- Create a new document and Save it as: "Co Louth attraction MW"
- Using Window drop-down menu, display the file: "Ballymascanlon House Hotel MW"
- Copy the last paragraph and paste into the file: "Co Louth attraction MW"
- Change the font of the last sentence in the "Co Louth attraction MW" file to Britannic Bold, size (14)
- Also, create a Header: "18-Hole Golf Course" and a Footer: "Cooley landscape"; insert a right-aligned date in the Header
- Change Line Spacing to Double
- Save this file as "Enfield 2"; close all files.

Emboldening: Bold - Text

- To emphasize text in a dark version of the current font, use Word's **Bold** feature:
- **Select** the text you want to embolden

What you see is what you get

- Click the **Bold** icon on the Toolbar:

- **Highlighted** text is now shown in **bold**:

What you see is what **you get**

Italicising: Italics - Text

- To **italicise** text, use Word's Italic feature: **Select** the text you want to **italicise**:

Splitting a longish document

- Click the **Italic** icon on the Toolbar:

- **Highlighted** text is now shown in **Italics**:

Splitting a *longish* document

Underlining Text

- To **underline** text, use Word's **Underline** feature: **Select** the text you want to underline:

Protected Folders or files

- Click the **Underline** icon on the Toolbar:

- **Highlighted** text is now **underlined**:

Protected Folders or files

Bullets

Bullets can be described as a small graphic used to set off items in a list, examples include: a solid dot, a diamond etc.

Add bullets to existing text:

* **Select** the text to which you want to add bullets:
* Add bullets by clicking **Bullets** icon on Toolbar:

..text displays in Bulleted form:

   * Free Gig Trail all weekend
   * Free Street Entertainment

To remove Bullets

* **Select** the text from which you want to **remove** bullets
* Click **Bullets** icon on Toolbar - bullets are **removed**:

   Free Gig Trail all weekend
   Free Street Entertainment

Paragraph Numbering

Add numbering

* **Select** the text to which you want to **add numbering**
* Add numbering by clicking **Numbers** icon on Toolbar:

..text displays in **Numbered** form:

   1. Access to anything that is password-protected requires a secret password. That can include computers themselves, networks etc.

To remove numbering

* **Select** the text from which you want to **remove numbering**
* Click **Numbering** icon on Toolbar - numbering is **removed**:

> Access to anything that is password-protected requires a secret password That can include computers themselves, networks etc.

To Format Numbered Text with different types of Numbering:

- **Select** Numbered Text:
- Select **Format Bullet Numbering** from Menu:

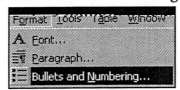

..Bullets & Numbering dialog box opens:
- Select **Numbered** tab: 7 types of Numbering are shown as well as the **None** option - we will now set the Roman Numeral Numbering system to **numbered text**:

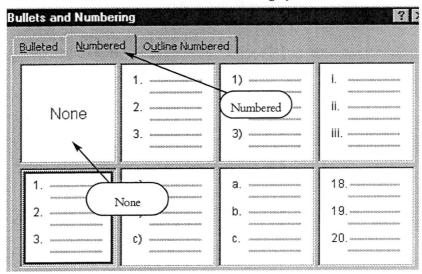

Roman Numeral Numbering:

- Select **Roman Numeral** type if displayed as one of the 7 options, otherwise, click **Customise** button:

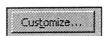

- ..**Customized Numbered List** dialog box opens - From the drop-down menu under **Number style**, select **Roman Numeral** type:

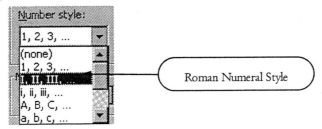

- Settings now displayed include:

Number Style shows: I, II, III
Text Position: Indent at: 5" etc

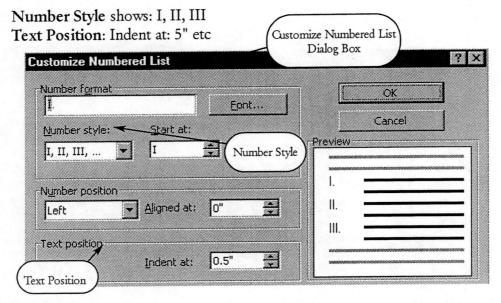

- Click **OK** - numbering on selected text has been changed to **Roman Numerals**:

> I. Emulation allows many different printers to use Hewlett Packard popular software. There is also software that enables a Macintosh emulate a PC.

Another example of Numbering is A B C:

- **Select** text:
- Select **Numbering** icon
- Select **Format Bullet Numbering** from Menu; select **ABC** Format from dialog box:

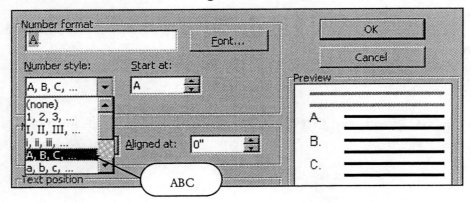

- ..text now looks like:

> A. Emulation allows many different printers to use Hewlett Pack popular software. There is also software that enables a Macint emulate a PC.

Styles

- A **Style** is a **named** set of format settings that can be accessed from the Formatting toolbar.
- A Style can specify a **font type** and **size**. In addition it may also specify **indentation**, **line spacing** and **justification**.
- Applying a Style is a lot faster than manually applying **individual** Formatting adjustments to sections of text and guarantees consistency.
- Word has several **predefined Styles**:

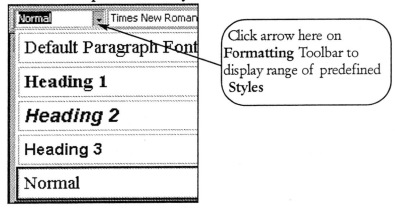

Click arrow here on **Formatting** Toolbar to display range of predefined Styles

Normal Style:

- Example of the **Default** Normal Style: Text is created in the default **font**: Times New Roman (12) without Bold, Italics etc

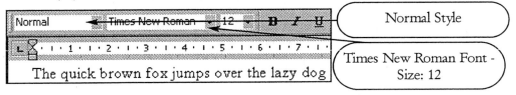

Normal Style

Times New Roman Font - Size: 12

Paragraph & CharactersStyles

- Word predefines Styles can be applied to either selected **paragraphs** or **characters**:

- **Paragraph** Styles are applied to **entire** paragraphs and may include all of the formatting elements listed above. Every paragraph, in a Word document, automatically has the default style, **Normal**, applied to it. As already demonstrated, this Style is based on your default selection of font and size.

- **Character** Styles are applied to any **section** of text and can include formatting such as font type and size, underlining, embolden etc. If you apply a character Style such as boldface to a section of text that is already formatted as italic, the text will then appear as both bold and italic.

Applying a Style

- First **select** the text to be styled
- To **apply a Style** to only **one paragraph**, place the cursor anywhere inside it.
- To assign a **character style, select** the text you want the style to be applied to.
- **Click** on the Style drop-down arrow on the Formatting toolbar
- A list of Styles will appear, with the name in the Style's font.
- Select the **required Style** by clicking on its name. The Style will then be **applied** to the specified text.

Experiment with the predefined Styles:

- Example: Using **Heading 1 Style**
- **Select** text and apply **Heading 1 Style** - see how the **Font** changes: text now displays in Arial Font (16) and **Bold**:

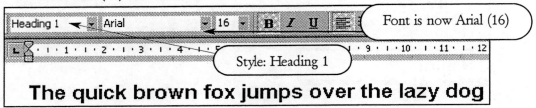

Creating a Style

- **Select** text - apply **formatting** required to selected text, e.g.: Times New Roman 16, Bold Italic:
- In **Style** drop-down list, type in **new Style** name, e.g. Winston

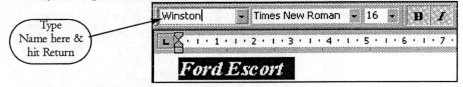

- Hit **Return** - Style named **Winston** is added to the Style drop-down list

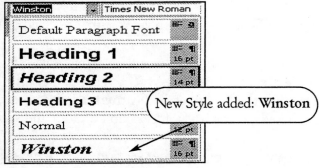

To remove a Style

- **Select** the text and from the drop-down menu, select **Format Style**
- Select **Style** to be **deleted**, e.g. Winston, click **Delete** - style is deleted:

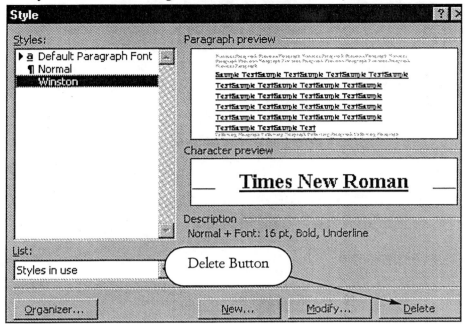

Example of using varying Styles in Practice

- **Key** in the following 4 lines of text:

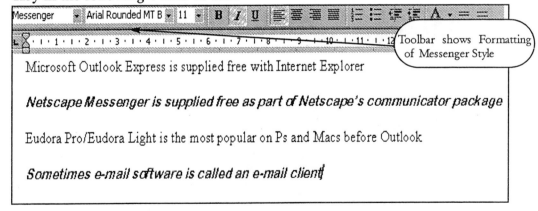

- The **first** and **third** line were created using the **default Normal Style**.
- A **New Style**, named "Messenger" - study Toolbar above and you will see Formatting used - was set up. "Messenger" Style was applied to both the second and fourth line

Procedure for varying Styles when inputting text is:

- Set up any **new Styles** required as above
- When a Style other than default Style is required, click in the drop-down area of the Style box, select **Style** and **type**
- To **revert to default**, click in the drop-down list of Styles and select **Normal**

Change the colour of text and numbers

- **Select** the text you want to **change**:

Do one of the following:
- To apply the colour most recently used for text, click **Font Colour** on the **Formatting** Toolbar
- To apply a **different** colour, click the arrow next to the Font Colour button, and then **select** the colour of your choice, for example, blue:

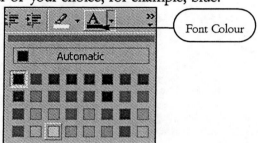

..Colour is applied to **selected** text:

> Aladdin's Cave

Clip Art: Pre-drawn Art

Pre-designed artwork, an integral part of the Windows applications held within a Clip Gallery, can be easily inserted into a Word document:

To Insert a picture from the Clip Gallery:

- Click the area where you want to **insert a picture** or clip art
- Click **Insert Picture Clip Art** from Menu:

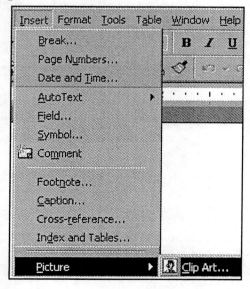

- **Insert ClipArt** dialog box opens:
- Select the **Pictures** tab.. the Clip Art Categories tab:
- Click the category you want - our example, we will double click **Academic**:

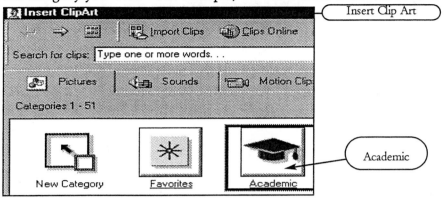

- - range of Academic clips open:

- Select **Clip** required, click on icon: **Insert Clip**..Selected Clip displays on screen:

- Click the **Close** button on the Clip Gallery title bar to close Gallery

Changing Size of Clip

- **Select** Clip - **8 selection handles** appear around the edges of the clip:
- Select applicable selection handle to **stretch** horizontally, vertically or proportionally

Insert a picture from file

- **Click** where you want to **insert the picture.**
- On the **Insert** menu, point to **Picture**, and then click **From File:**

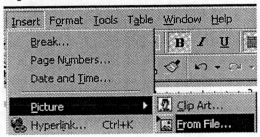

- Locate the **folder** that contains the picture you want to insert.. our example: **Misc** folder containing picture of a soccer ball:

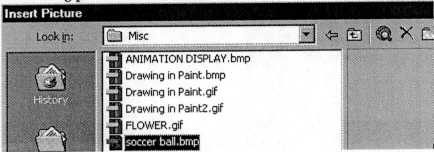

- Double-click this **picture** .. the picture inserts into the screen:

Changing Size of Picture from File

- **Select** Picture - **8 Selection handles** display as before with Clip Art - adjust **size** similarly.

Exercise 24:

- Create a **new** document
- **Type** in the Exercise below:

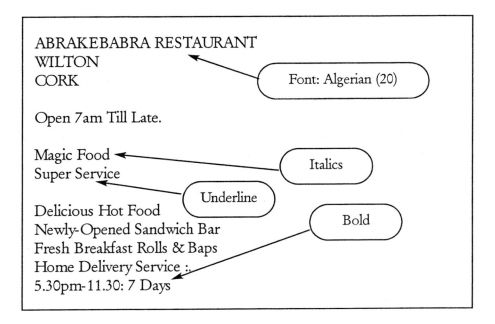

- **Save** as: "ABRAKEBABRA MW"
- Use **Font**: Playbill for body of document - **Size** 14
- Enhance as suggested in illustration
- Resave as: "Newly refurbished MW"

Exercise 25:

- Create a **new** document with 1" **Margins** and **Double Spacing**
- **Type** in the Exercise below:

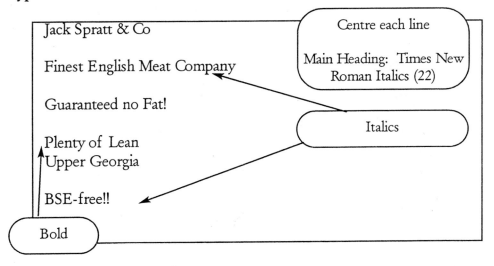

- Make changes as suggested
- **Save** as: "Jack MW".
- **Print to File**

Exercise 26:

- **Create** a new document
- **Type** in the Exercise below - modify as suggested; **Save as** "Park MW"

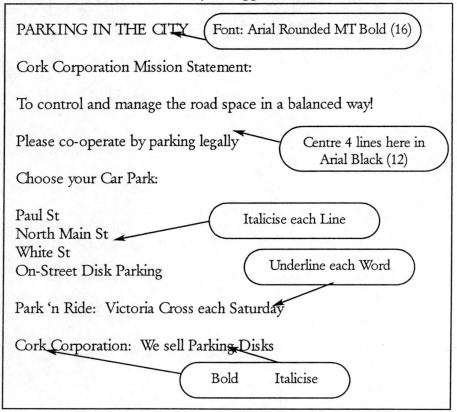

PARKING IN THE CITY — Font: Arial Rounded MT Bold (16)

Cork Corporation Mission Statement:

To control and manage the road space in a balanced way!

Please co-operate by parking legally — Centre 4 lines here in Arial Black (12)

Choose your Car Park:

Paul St
North Main St — Italicise each Line
White St
On-Street Disk Parking — Underline each Word

Park 'n Ride: Victoria Cross each Saturday

Cork Corporation: We sell Parking Disks — Bold   Italicise

Exercise 27:

- Create a **New Document** with **Margin**s: 1.2" at Left & 1.4" at Right
- **Key** in this document applying the suggested enhancements
- Insert a **Clip Art** centered with a **border** below the main heading

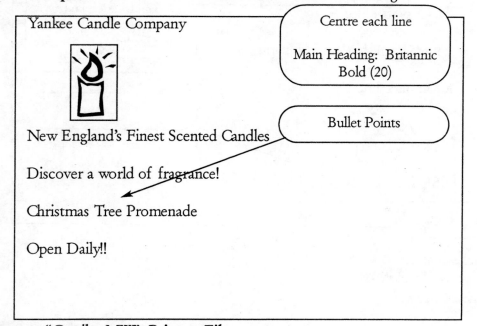

Yankee Candle Company

New England's Finest Scented Candles — Centre each line / Main Heading: Britannic Bold (20)

Discover a world of fragrance! — Bullet Points

Christmas Tree Promenade

Open Daily!!

- **Save as:** "Candles MW"; **Print to File.**

Exercise 28:

- Create a **New** Document with **Margins**: 1.2" at Left & 1.4" at Right
- **Key** in this document applying the displayed enhancements: Bold/Italics/Underline
- Set up a **Style** for sub-headings: Arial (14), Colour: Green - name Style "Skellig"
- Insert suitable **Images** from file similar to our example
- **Change** word "Skellig" to Times New Roman (14) and **colour**: Yellow

One Clear Line between each Heading - use Font of your choice for headings

The Skellig Experience
Valentia Island: *Ring of Kerry*
(beside the main road bridge from the island)

Exhibition Centre Themes

- The life and word of the Early **Christian Monks** on Skellig Michael
- The men of the Skellig **lighthouses** who provided a service to mariners - from 1820-1987
- The **seabirds** of the Skelligs
- The underwater **sea life** of the Skelligs

Audio Visual

- 16-min presentation on the Skellig Michael monastery

Other Facilities

- Refreshment area for light lunches
- Comprehensively stocked retail area

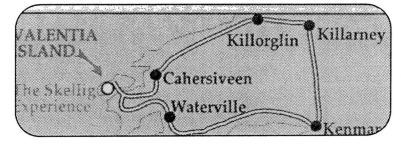

Further Information

- Available from Cork Kerry Tourism at locations: Cork/Killarney

- **Print** once on **A4 Paper** - **Save** to a file named: "Skelligs MW"

Exercise 29:

- In a **New** Document with **Fonts** of your choice, set Margins: 1": Left & 1.3": Right
- **Key** in this document applying the displayed enhancements: Bold/Italics/Underline
- Set up a **Style** for sub-headings, including **Colour**: Blue - name Style "Kenmare"
- Insert and centre **Image** from file surrounded by a thin border
- **Change** word "Kenmare" to Algerian (18) and **colour**: Red

---

KENMARE HERITAGE CENTRE

The Story of Kenmare & Mapped Heritage Trail:

Kenmare was designated a Heritage town by Bord Failte (The Irish Tourist Board) The town was designated under the theme a "Planned Estate Town". The Centre was officially opened in June 1994 by the President of Ireland, Mrs Mary Robinson.

The Centre is located in the Heart of Kenmare town, entrance to the Centre is via Kenmare Tourist Office. There is ample parking space outside the Centre.

A visit to Kenmare is not complete without a visit to Kenmare Heritage Centre.

The Heritage Centre covers themes such as:
- Kenmare Lace Exhibition (Lace Making Displays
- Famous Visitors to Kenmare
- Historical Sites in Kenmare
- The Effects of the Famine on Kenmare
- The Landlords of Kenmare

(Sub-heading)

(Insert the text::
"The Heritage Trail map will
show you at first-hand some of
the delights of Kenmare"
at this point:)

Kenmare Heritage Trail

An integral part of the Experience of the Kenmare Story is to visit the Historical sites after visiting the Centre. All the sites are within walking distance from the Centre and the trail takes about 40 minutes to complete

(- Put list of themes in
1.5 Line Spacing and Italics
- Cut this line and Paste
above "Famous Visitors to Kenmare")

Open Easter to end of September
Admission *Free*

- **Save as** "Kenmare Heritage"; PreView & **Print** on A4 Landscape Paper or **Print to File**
- **Create** a new document, name it "Historical"
- Copy the list of themes from "Kenmare Heritage" to "Historical" file - **Remove** Italics from list - Change **font** to Arial Rounded (MT) Bold (14)
- Insert a **Clip Art** with a border to the left corner below list of themes
- Change **Line Spacing** to Double; **Print** once on A4 Portrait Paper. **Close** File.

Tabs

- Tabs are used to **align** Blocks of data - alignment can be **left, right, centered** or **decimal**.
- Default Tabs are set every **5 spaces.**

Tab setting Procedure:

- To set **precise Tabs.** use the **Format Tabs** command from the Menu bar:

Clearing Tabs:
    Select **Clear All** to clear **All** existing Tabs
    Select **Clear** to clear **one** tab only
- New tab positions are **calculated**: Number of spaces in longest word(s) in each Column must be counted + **spaces** must be allowed between Columns
- Tab Alignment - the relevant **Alignment Type** is selected;
- Tab positions are typed in & **Tab Set** key is clicked to **set** each Tab.

Tab Alignment

- Tabs can have **Alignment**: Left, Right, Centered, Decimal or Bar.
- Tabs can be set to include a **Leader.**

A left-aligned (Straight at Left-hand side) Tab Example:

- Set a **Left-Aligned Tab** for this example:

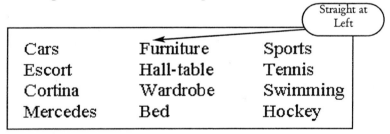

Cars	Furniture	Sports
Escort	Hall-table	Tennis
Cortina	Wardrobe	Swimming
Mercedes	Bed	Hockey

- Select **Format Tabs** from Menu Bar - Tabs dialog box opens - features are as follows:

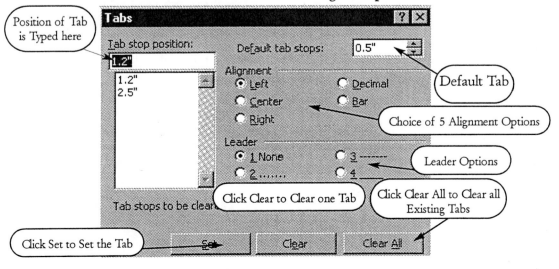

To Set Left-aligned tabs for the exercise on the previous page:

- Click **Clear All** button to clear **all** existing tabs

- In this example, "Cars" Column of Tabs will be typed at the **Left-hand** Margin: **Left-aligned** tabs will be set for **Furniture** and **Sports** Columns.

- To calculate positions of tabs - start counting from the left margin and count the number of letters in the largest word in each column + four spaces in between each column - the results are shown in the Tabs dialog box on the previous page.

Setting Tabs at given Positions:

If you are **given** the Tab settings, of course, no calculation is required

- To set **Left-aligned** Tab at 1.2 - type in **1.2** in Tab Stop **position** box, select **Left Alignment;** click **Set**
- To set Tab at 2.5 - type in **2.5** in Tab Stop **position** box, click **Set** etc

Right-Aligned Tabs example:

- Positions of **right-aligned** tabs are always calculated by counting to the right **edge** of the entry.
- Allow approx **4 spaces** between Columns (Average space between Columns usually 3)

Setting Right Aligned Tabs with given Settings:

- Clear **all existing** tabs in the usual way, select **Right** aligned for this example and set the given Tab settings: **1, 2.5** and **4:**

Settings: 1	2.5	4
Trains	Boats	Planes
Sun	Rain	Mist
Skies	Blue	Mountain
Sea	Shell	Crab
Green	Red	Roses
Hills	Dales	Rivers

- **Ruler Bar** for the given Right-aligned settings will now look like:

Decimal tabs

Decimal tabs are used to **align** numbers on the **decimal point** regardless of **varying sizes** of numbers:

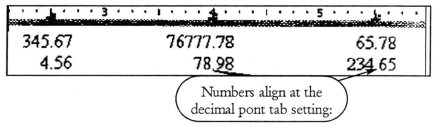

| 345.67 | 76777.78 | 65.78 |
| 4.56 | 78.98 | 234.65 |

Numbers align at the decimal pont tab setting:

Decimal Tab Exercise:

- Calculate and **set** the positions of the decimal tabs in the exercise below.
- Create a **decimal tab** to display the motorist's details:

MOTORING COST

Car Owners	1997	1998
John Walsh	145.67	289.78
Kieran Baker	234.56	1456.65
Diane Creagh	2456.87	98.56
Alice O'Keeffe	432.65	43.45
John Barry	34.56	1234.89
Larry Fox	2344.45	987.65

Centered Tabs

- Centered tabs are used to **align** data in the **centre** of Tab column:
- In the following example, the first Column is entered at left margin, centered tabs are calculated for the other two columns.

To calculate:
- **Count** the number of spaces in Musgrave Park
- **Add four spaces** and **count** to the **centre** point of "Jonathan Cunningham " (biggest word). **Set Tab.**
- **Count** to the centre point of "St Munchin's" for the third Column. **Set Tab.**
- Key in exercise:

Centered Tab Shape

Rugby Pitch	Captains	Opposition
Landsdowne	Michael Whelan	St Munchin's
Musgrave Park	Jonathan Cunningham	Constitution
Landsdowne	Leo Walsh	St Enda's
Musgrave Park	Mike Tanner	St Rita's
Kilkee	Jake Welch	St Munchin's

Change Measurement from Inches to Centimetres:

- Select **Tools Options General** Tab
- From **Measurement** units drop-down menu, select **Centimetres**:

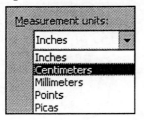

Setting a Centered Tab at a given Setting:

- **Set** a tab at **4 cms, 6 cms** & **8 cms**:
- Change **Measurement** units to **Centimetres**
- Select **Format Tabs Clear All** tabs. As you know the settings you want, there is no calculation involved.
- Select **Centre Alignment** and type in tab settings:
  required: 4, 6 & 8 cms. Click **Set**:

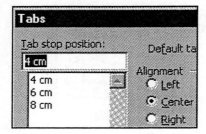

Leader dots

- Leader dots: a **solid, dotted** or **dashed line** that fills the space used by a tab character:
- Leader characters are used to draw the reader's **eye** across the page.
- Choice of Alignment for Tab is made in the usual way, select Leader of choice, e.g.
- Study the example using Leader No 2 in the example below:

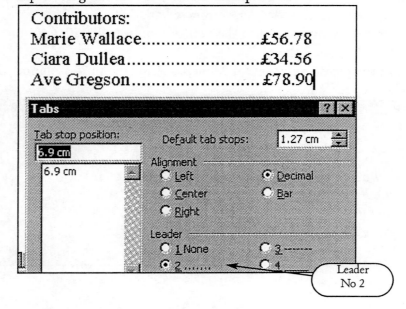

Tables

- A table is made up of **Rows & Columns**.
- You can use tables to hold **aligned numbers** or **text**, which can be **sorted in columns** or **rows**.
- Tables and Tabs are **interchangeable** apart from Decimal and Tabs with Leader Dots.
- Tables are easier to use as the only calculation required is the counting of the overall number of Rows and Columns in an exercise.
- Column **widths** can be adjusted to accommodate varying widths of entries

- **Count** the **Rows & Columns** of this Exercise - **3 Rows** down & **4 Columns** across:

Conferences	Places of Interest	Locations	Restaurants
Packages	Scenery	42	Embassy
Specialist Equipment	Leisure pursuits	54	Seasons

Row   Cell   Column

Creating a Table:

- **Create a table** with **4 Columns** and **3 Rows** - Select **Insert Table** from Menu: ..dialog box opens:

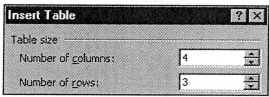

...3x4 Table displays on screen:
- **Input** the data in the newly created Table:

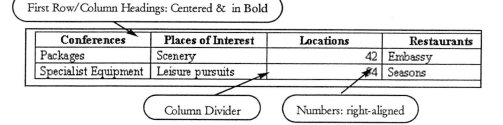

First Row/Column Headings: Centered & in Bold

Conferences	Places of Interest	Locations	Restaurants
Packages	Scenery	42	Embassy
Specialist Equipment	Leisure pursuits	54	Seasons

Column Divider   Numbers: right-aligned

Changing Width of Column:

- Rest mouse **I-beam** on **Column divider** - I-beam changes to a **left/right arrow shape** - Click and hold this shape
- Drag left/right arrow to the left to **reduce** column width & to the right to **widen** column width

Changing Border Thickness in Tables:

- Select **cells**, Select **Format Borders** and **Shading** from menu, select **Width** from dialog box, click **OK**

Emboldening/Alignment of data in Tables:

- **Highlight** data select **Bold** icon/**Alignment** icon

Inserting Rows:

- **Position** cursor in correct location for the insertion of Rows above or Rows below the cursor
- **Highlight 2 Rows downwards** in Table, select **Insert, Rows Below** from Table menu e.g. if you require **2** additional rows to be added below cursor; highlight 2 rows, select **Insert, Rows Above** from Table menu e.g. if you require 2 rows above cursor etc.
- Select **Table Insert Rows** - Required Rows are created **above** first **highlighted** Row

Inserting Columns:

- **Position** cursor in Table in readiness for the insertion of Columns to the **right** Highlight 2 Columns if you require 2 Columns to be created to the right of the cursor; highlight 3 if you require 3 Columns etc.
- Select **Table Insert Columns** - Required Columns are created to the **right** of the **first highlighted** Column

Tables: Deleting Rows/Columns:

- **Highlight** 2 Rows (Columns) in Table if you want to **Delete** 2 Rows(Columns) etc
- **Select** Table **Delete Rows (Columns)** - Selected Rows/Columns are **deleted**

Indentation

You can set **precise** measurements for paragraph indents by using the Paragraph command on the **Format** menu: Example below shows the choices available:

Whole Block: .5" from Left Margin:
- To **Indent** the whole block of selected text by e.g. **.5"**:
- **Select** text, Select **Format Paragraph** from **Menu** - Select **Indents** and **Spacing** Tab
- **Key** in **.5"** in **Left Indentation** Box; click OK: Selected text now starts .5" from Margin - see **Preview** (To Indent from Right also, key in e.g. **.5"** in **Right** box)

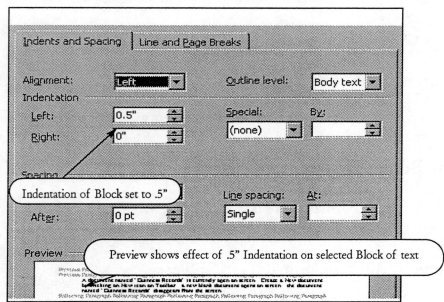

First Line

- To **Indent** the **First line** of **each Paragraph** by e.g. **.5":**
- **Select** text, Select **Format Paragraph** from Menu - Select **Indents** and **Spacing Tab**
- Select **Special** drop-down arrow, choose **First Line:**
- Type **figure** (or accept default): **.5** in **By** box - Click **OK**

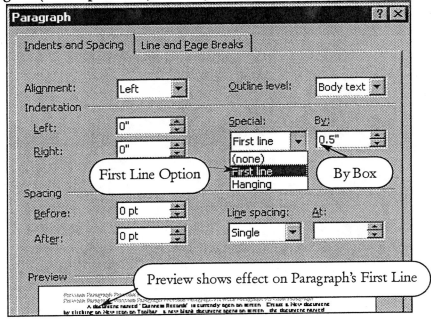

First Line Option

By Box

Preview shows effect on Paragraph's First Line

Hanging Paragraph

- To make each paragraph a **Hanging Paragraph** - the **first line outdented** to left -
- Select **Format Paragraph, Indents** and **Spacing** Tab
- Select **Special** drop-down arrow, choose **Hanging**
- Type **figure** (or accept default): **.5"** in **By** box:

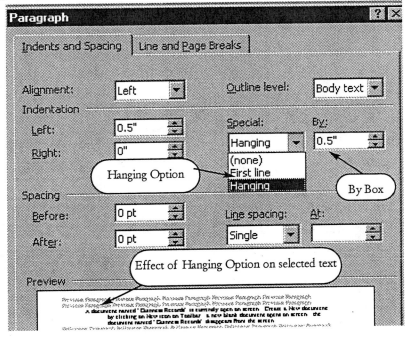

Hanging Option

By Box

Effect of Hanging Option on selected text

Adjusting spacing above and below Paragraph to 10 pts

- **Select** Paragraphs
- Select **Format Paragraph, Indent** and **Spacing** from Menu

  Under **Spacing** options:
- Click in the **Before** box and key in **10 pts**
- Click in the **After** box and key in **10 pts**
  ..adjusted Spacing is shown in the Preview display box

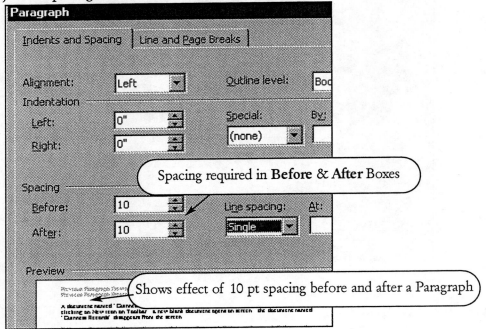

Exercise 30:

- Calculate **left-aligned Tabs** for the exercise below allowing **three** spaces between each Column
- **Enhance** and **Centre** Headings as displayed:

ROCKSAVAGE LEISURE CENTRE			
Evening Clubs			
Monday	Tuesday	Wednesday	Friday
Indoor Soccer	Flower Arranging	Badminton	Drama
Debating	Basket Weaving	Choir Practice	Tennis
Swimming	Aerobics	Weight Lifting	Table Tennis
Painting	Photographic Club	Spanish Circle	Bridge

- Use **Double Spacing** and **Save** as "Activities MW"
- **Print to File**

Exercise 31:

- **Calculate** left-aligned Tabs for the exercise below allowing **three** spaces between each Column

```
+------------------------------------------------------------------+
|                    INTERNET TERMINOLOGY                           |
|                                                                  |
|                      Getting On-Line                             |
|                                                                  |
|   Modem       Connection Software       Indigo      e-mail       |
|   Gateway     ISDN                      ISP         Reply        |
|   Favorites   High Speed Line           WWW         Search Engines|
|   Search      Protocols:                Hypertext   Yahoo        |
|   Browser     Internet Explorer         TCP/IP      Favorites    |
|   Address     Information Superhighway   Home Page   Work-Off-Line|
+------------------------------------------------------------------+
```

- **Enhance** and **centre** as displayed; **Save** as: "TermsMW"
- Change **Font** to **Arial Narrow (14)**; apply **Font Colour:** Blue to **Main** Heading
- **Print once** on A4 Paper or **Print to File**

Exercise 32:

- **Calculate** Tabs for the exercise below allowing **three** spaces between **each** Column
- **Enhance** and **centre** as displayed; Use the space bar to **align numbers** in "Cost" Column under the **decimal** point; alternatively, set a **Decimal Tab** for this Column:

```
+------------------------------------------------------------------+
|            K E S C O   P R I C E   B U S T E R   S A L E         |
|                                                                  |
|                   Lowest price of the Year                       |
|                                                                  |
|  Catalogue No    Item                  Cost       Unit of Sale   |
|  LKI987          Desk Organiser        £19.99     Per Doz        |
|  HG789           Letter Trays          £0.89      Per Set        |
|  LKJ897          Rotamate              £19.99     Each           |
|  GT678           Colourful Waste Bins  £1.99      Each           |
+------------------------------------------------------------------+
```

- **Save** as: "KescoMW"
- Apply **Double Line** spacing; change **colour** of **Headings** for **each** Column to **Yellow**
- Create a **new** Document; **Save** under the name: "Buster MW"; **copy** the last two rows of "KescoMW" to this document
- **Print** both documents to **File**

Exercise 33:

- **Calculate** left-aligned Tabs for the exercise below allowing **three** spaces between each Column

STORES NATIONWIDE

Fresco – Your friendly local Superstore

Jordanstown	Fountain Street	Lapid Shopping Centre
Firgrove	Grand Parade	Oliver Plunkett Street
Winthrop Street	Irish Town Central	Salthouse Lane
Williams Gate Street	High Street	Killarney Outlet Centre
William Street	North Main Street	Frack Shopping Centre

- **Enhance** and **centre** as displayed; **Save** as: "Fresco MW"
- Change **Font** to Arial (14); apply **Font Colour**: Red to Main Heading
- **Print** once on A4 Paper or **Print to File**

Exercise 34:

- Set up the Tabs using the given settings below - **3 Alignment Types**: Left, Centre and Decimal

(1) **Left Tab:** 2.04 cm   (2) **Centre Tab:** 6.4 cm   (3)**Decimal Tab:** 9.8

Leather	Mechanism	£23.45
Sculptured	Assembled	£564.98
Lumbar	Hamper	£456.98
Comfortable	Luxury	£234.56
Adjustable	High Back	£7234.78

- **Save** as: "AdjustableMW"
- **Apply** 1.5 **Line Spacing**; change **colour** of Currency Column to Pink
- **Print** document to **File** - Use **Print File** name: "Adjust44"
- **Close** File

Exercise 35: Tables

- **Calculate** the Rows and Columns required for the Table below - Save as: "Cork Kerry MW"
- Apply a 1 pt **border** to the Table

Major Visitor Attractions in Cork and Kerry		
CORK KERRY TOURISM		
Ballincollig Gunpowder Mills	Blarney Castle Estate	Desmond Castle
Barryscourt Castle	Charles Fort	Mizen Head
Old Midleton Distillery	Ross Castle	Skellig Experience
Doneraile Wildlife Park	Fota Wildlife Park	Killarney Manor
Derrynane House	Millstreet Country Park	Kenmare Heritage

- **Create** a **new** document; name it "Attractions MW"
- **Copy** the document: "Cork Kerry MW" to "Attractions MW"
- **Delete** the last 2 Rows from the Table and the last Column
- Change the Font **Colour** of the Main Titles to: Light Orange
- **Print** both documents to **File**

Exercise 36: Tables

- Set up the **Given** tabs below - tab types are: **Left, Right** and **Decimal.**

Tabs Given: Left: 1.5 cm; Centre: 8.9 cms; Decimal: 11.7 cms		
Accommodation	*Number*	*Cost*
Hotel, B&B	12	£350.99
Apartment, Self-catering	20	£230.70
Half-board, Hotel	30	£120.60
Self-catering Villa	18	£210.70
Half-board: Room only	2	£99.99

- **Key** in exercise and **Save as:** "Accommodation MW"

- **Embolden** and **Italicise** Headings; Apply Font **Colour:** Yellow Number Column
- **Print to File**

Exercise 37a:

- **Key** in the document below in Times New Roman (14) - **Save** as: "Vladimir MW"

A LIFE IN THE DAY OF
WORLD CHESS CHAMPION: VLADIMIR KRAMNIK - Age: 26

Vladimir writes:
It's quite difficult for me to get up in the morning. I like to lie in my bed for 10 minutes and think of nothing - it's my favourite 10 minutes of the day. While I lie there, I gently exercise from top to bottom. Head, neck, fingers - I have exercises for all the body's muscle groups. I don't get out of bed much before noon. Maybe I'll have a sandwich or a yogurt, but lunch is at 3pm, so there's no point having breakfast. Just a cup of coffee. It's two hours before I feel completely fresh.

My apartment is five years old. It's in a good district, just south of Moscow, but it's small. I have one room where I sit at my computer, and one where I sleep. There is a balcony, but it doesn't overlook anything romantic. There are no pictures of me about the place, and the rooms are half empty. There's a bed, a table and two chessboards I keep for training purposes. They aren't expensive gold sets that cost £100,000; they cost £100, and were both birthday presents from my brother.

Believe it or not, I don't care much about money. I've been a millionaire since my world-championship match with Kasparov last year, but I live like a very ordinary Russian citizen. I've never had any wish to live in a castle. And I don't have any special hobbies, like Ferraris. I don't actually have a car: I employ a driver instead. I like having the money, but mainly so I can help my family. My father is an artist and my mother is a music teacher, and they aren't rich. It makes me happy to help them out.

- Apply Double **Line Spacing**; allow 8 pt **spacing before** and **after** each paragraph
- The **First line** of each paragraph is to be **indented** by .3"
- The **Alignment** of the text is to be **Justified**
- Set up **Page numbering** for the document - Right-aligned in the **Footer**; the Format of **Page Numbering** is to be Roman Numerals and the Numbering must start at **25**
- Apply **Paragraph Numbering**: 1., 2. etc to all paragraphs
- Set up a **Style**: Arial Narrow, Bold, Italic, Colour: Orange, **name** it "Chess" and apply this Style to the word "chess" throughout document

- Create a **New Document** - name it "Russian Chess MW"; copy last two paragraphs to new document and key in the the text: below in italics and with a **Bullet**:

I like to lunch out with friends. I wouldn't say I'm on a diet, but I try not to eat unhealthily. I like caviar; who doesn't? But if you eat it every day you don't appreciate its delicate taste. So I eat it every other day. I don't drink at all. Well, sometimes I'll have a glass of red wine or champagne, but it's rare as it affects the brain. Not overnight, but over a long period of time. Suddenly you're not No 1 anymore. You're No 10.

- **Save** and **Print** once on **A4** Landscape Paper

Exercise 37b:

- **Key** in the document below in **Times New Roman (14)**; **Margins**: Top & Bottom: 2.54 cms; **Left & Right**: 3.17 cms - **Save as**: "Amazonian MW"

A m a z o n i a n   C u l t u r e s

What we're looking for is evidence of a vanished civilisation. We know that the mainstream of the Amazon and its tributaries were once home to a population estimated at up to 6m people. The early Portuguese settlers reported bustling, shimmering towns stretching for what seemed like miles along the river. But European diseases, the slave trade and conflict Wiped them out. The towns died. The jungle engulfed them. In equatorial Amazonia, almost nothing organic - cloth, leather, wood, bone - survives longer than a year or so. But ceramics last for ever. And they were good at making those.

These people did not write. The oral tradition of the remaining Amazonian Indians does not operate in a chronological way; For that matter, it makes no distinction between the physical and spirit world. And anyway it is unlikely that today's Indians are directly descended from the people who built the towns and farmed the forest along the Amazon in a period that began maybe 8,000 years ago and lasted until the European incursions of the 16th century.

But who were "they"? We know that they were taller than today's Indian Populations, found in the remote corners of the rainforests. We know that some of them had a sophisticated, shamanic society : where the bones of ancestors were revered and placed in robotic burial urns. We know that at certain points women played a leading role in this society.

- Set up a Centered **Header**: "Amazonian Cultures"
- Insert a suitable **Image from File**, such as the one displayed
- Set up a Left-aligned **Footer**: "Robotic Burial Urns"; include a right-aligned **Page Number**: Small Roman Numerals - **Start** with Number 89
- **Cut** the current last paragraph and **Paste** into position so that it will then be the second paragraph
- Change the **Line Spacing** of last paragraph to 1.5; also **Indent first line** By: 1.27 cms
- Set two **Centered Tabs** at 4 cms and 10 cms - Use these tabs to position the entries: "Portuguese settlers" and "16th century " at 4 and 10 cms respectively
- Apply **Font**: Courier (14), **Colour**: Yellow and *Italics* to all occurences of "Amazon"
- **Copy** image to end of document; **Stretch** image to twice its original size and centre
- Create a **New** document; **Save** it as "Forest MW" - **copy** document: "Amazonian MW" to the new document and make the changes below:
- **Delete** first Paragraph; delete image and **replace** with a Clip Art of your choice
- **Indent** 2nd Paragraph By 2 cms at **both** Left & Right margins
- Allow 8 pt space **Before** and **After** all Paragraphs
- **Delete** existing Tabs; Type in "8,000 years " using newly created Centered Tab: 8 cms.
- **ReSave** - Select first paragraph and **Print** this Selection or **Print to File**

- **Key** in the document below in **Arial Narrow** - vary **size** of font as you see fit
- Set **Margins**: Top & Bottom: 2.34 cms; Left & Right: 3.50 cms
- **Save** as: " Mizen Head MW"

MIZEN HEAD

IRELAND'S MOST

SOUTHWESTERLY POINT!

THE AWARD-WINNING MIZEN HEAD VISITOR
CENTRE -THREE EXPERIENCES IN ONE

Ireland's most Southwesterly Point

- VISITOR CENTRE IN THE IRISH LIGHTS SIGNAL STATION
- THE 99 STEPS
- THE FAMOUS ARCHED BRIDGE
- THE VIEWS UP THE SOUTH & WEST COASTS
- TEA ROOM
- SHOP
- NEW EXHIBITS

OPEN DAILY:
Mid-March, April, May
& October..Daily 10am-5pm

June to September..Daily 10am-6pm

OPEN WEEKENDS:
November-Mid-March..Daily 11 am-4pm

PRICES FOR 2001 :

Adult..	£3.50
OAP/Students..	£2.75
Children Under 12...	£2.00
Children Under 5..	_Free_
Family Ticket: 2 Adults/3 Children...............................	£11 00

Groups _Less 10%_
**IN ANY WEATHER THE MIZEN IS SPELLBINDING!**
MIZEN TOURISM CO-OPERATIVE SOCIETY LTD
Harbour Road, Goleen, West Cork

- Set up a **Style** for Main Headings, name it "Mizen" - it will comprise of: Times New Roman (14), Blue **Colour**
- Add **Bullets** to the Points and other **enhancements**, as displayed
- Insert an appropriate **Image** from file
- Set up a Centered **Header**: "Award Winning Visitor Centre"
- Set up a Left-aligned **Footer**: "Three Experiences in One" in **Bold**. **ReSave**.

Mail Merge

The Mail Merge facility is used to create standard documents: form letters, mailing labels, envelopes etc for more than one recipient - the design ensures that each document appears as an original

There are **3 parts** to the Mail Merge process:

1. Main Document:

Creating a **main** document, which contains the standard information that is to be repeated in each merged document.

2. Data Source:

Open or create a **data source**, which contains the data that **varies** in the merged documents - such as, the name and address of each recipient of a form letter.

3. Merging Process: Merging Main document with Data Source:

- **Merge fields** are **inserted** in the **Main** document - the merge field locations tell Microsoft Word where to **insert data** from the data source.
- **Merge data** from the **data source** into the **main** document. **Each row** (or record) in the **data source** produces an individual **form document.**

Example of 3 Steps involved in Mail Merging a standard document - a letter:

Step 1: Create a form letter

- To create a **form** letter, click the **New** icon on the Toolbar
- **Type** document to be used as **form** letter:

Dear

Thank you for your letter of today.

I am sorry to hear that you were displeased with our hotel standards when you recently stayed with us.

As a small gesture, I enclose a voucher for a mini-break for two in our sister hotel in Galway.

Yours sincerely

Jim Welch
General Manager

- **Save** as "Complaint" - keep file open on screen

- From the **Tools** menu, select **Mail Merge:**

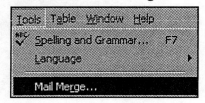

..the Mail Merge Helper dialog box opens:
- Select **Create**, click **Form Letters:**

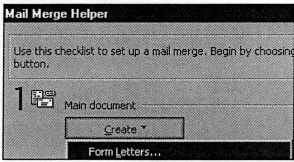

- ..dialog box opens:

-

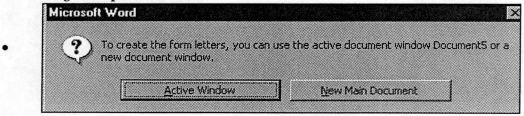

- Click **Active Window**
  ..the active document - the open document where the file named "complaint" is currently displayed becomes the mail-merge **Main** document.

Step 2: Creating the Data Source: (New Names & Addresses)

- Click **Get Data**
- Select Create **Data Source**

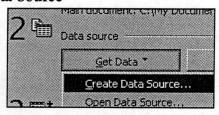

..dialog box opens - showing **Field Names** *preset* in **header** row box.

- Field Names are codes, which will be used to represent the data to be merged - continue with Create Data Source overleaf

Note: *Open Data Source*

- If you have an **existing** file of names and address, you would choose the **Open Data Source** option. If these names and addresses are set up in Table format with Field Names included in the top row of the Table, you set up your Field Names to correspond with these given Field Names.

Create **Data Source** box contains **Field names** in header row box:

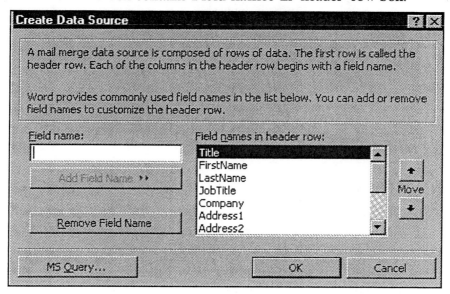

The Data source will comprise of **sets of data** - each set is called a **record** - each item within each record is called a **field** - **Field Name** is the term used to describe the **content** of each field

The letter in our example will be sent to the **3 individuals** in the records below so appropriate Field Names must be set up in the Data Source box to accommodate the fields of each record.

3 Records:

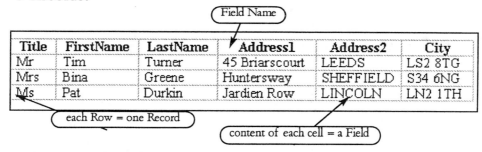

Title	FirstName	LastName	Address1	Address2	City
Mr	Tim	Turner	45 Briarscourt	LEEDS	LS2 8TG
Mrs	Bina	Greene	Huntersway	SHEFFIELD	S34 6NG
Ms	Pat	Durkin	Jardien Row	LINCOLN	LN2 1TH

- We will use **six** of the default **Field Names** to set up these records:

These Field Names are:

Title
First Name
Last Name
Address1
Address2
City - for our purposes here, we will use the "City" field for the Postal Code.

Deletion of Fields:

(The field names that are not required for the data source are deleted)

- To **delete** a field name, select the field name within the header row box, e.g. "Job Title", and then click **Remove Field Name:**

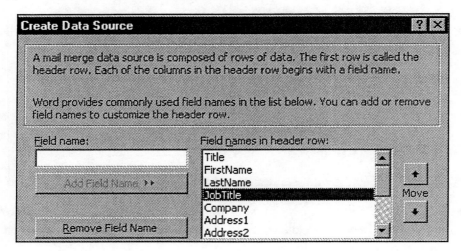

- Continue to **delete** the remaining field names until the 6 field names required are remaining:

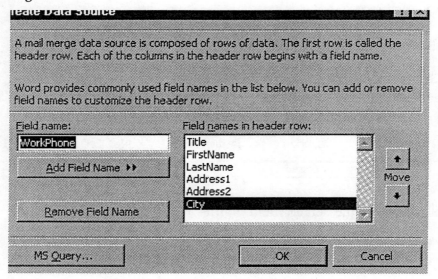

To Create a Field Name, for example: Address3

Instead of accepting the default Field Name: "City", we could have opted to create a **new Field Name** for the third line of the address, i.e. the Postal Code - procedure would be as follows:

- **Remove** Fields not required as before
- Click in **Field name** box, and type "Address3" (**without spaces**):

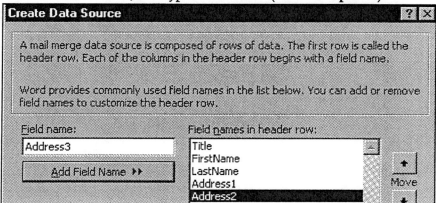

- Click **Add Field Name** - new Field Name **Address3** is added to Header row:

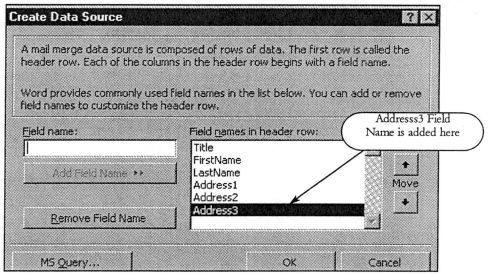

Saving Data Source

- Click **Save** - **File Save As** dialog box opens - Save under meaningful file name: such as: "addresses", Click **Save** - Microsoft Word dialog box opens:

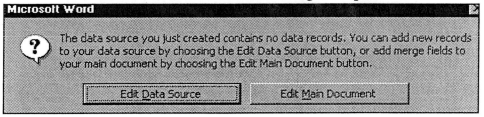

- Select **Edit Data Source** - **Data Form** dialog box opens.

Data Form Dialog Box

Inputting Field Name details of the two records in our example:

- Key in **Record 1** details opposite relevant field names - **Mr** opposite **Title** etc:
- Use **Tab** key to move from one row to the next

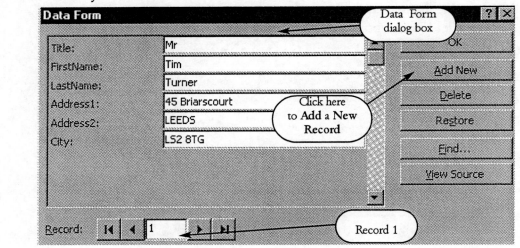

- When all the details of the **first** record have been filled in, click **Add New** each time you want to add details of **another** record - 2, 3 etc
- When all record details have been filled in, Click **OK** to **close** Data Form dialog box and return to **Main document**

Inserting Field Names on Main Document:

- Move cursor to first line of Form letter - a **Mail Merge Toolbar** is displayed (as a result of selecting **Tools Mail Merge** earlier) at the top of the Form Letter:

- Select **Insert Merge Field** button on **Mail Merge** Toolbar - the newly set up **6 Field Names** drop down:

- Insert the **Field Names** at the point where you want the corresponding data to be merged for every letter:
- Select **Title** and field name Title is displayed on screen - Hit **Space Bar** to insert a space **between** Fields
- Select **First Name** Hit **Space Bar**
- Select **Last Name** and hit **Return** key to move to next line etc - **See next Page**

- Insert all remaining fields in like manner until codes representing positions of field names of data source are positioned on the Main Document like:

Mail Merge Helper icon

Step 3: Merging Data Source with Field Names:

- Select **Merge to New Document** icon on **Mail Merge Toolbar:**

- **Data Source** is merged with **Field Names** on Screen - For every record in **Data Source** a separate document is created - **three** letters will be created in our example:

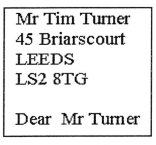

Mr Tim Turner
45 Briarscourt
LEEDS
LS2 8TG

Dear Mr Turner

- Note:

Status Bar now shows: **1/3**, i.e. it is telling us that the cursor is now in the **first** page of a **three-page** document - a page has been generated for each record in the data source:

Another method of adding Field Names to Data Source

To add **additional** Field Names after the **Data Source** file has been saved, another method must be used - our example below has only **3 Field names** for Addresses:

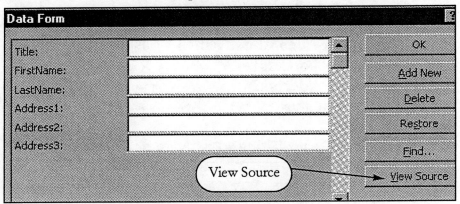

- • - we need to **add** Address4 - procedure is:

- • Click **View Source** on **Data Form dialog box** - a Word document will open displaying the current Field Names in **Table** format:

Title	FirstName	LastName	Address1	Address2	Address3

- • To add **additional** Field Names, a new column must be created for each additional Field name - place cursor at the point where the Columns are to be added, i.e. beyond Address3:
- • Select **Table Insert Columns** to the right from Menu - additional column is added - **type** in Field Name: "Address4":

Title	FirstName	LastName	Address1	Address2	Address3	Address4

- • **Save** and **close** file (**File Close**)
- • The form letter is still open on the screen, click the **Mail Merge Helper** icon on the Mail Merge Toolbar - the Mail Merge Helper dialog box opens, select **Edit** icon:

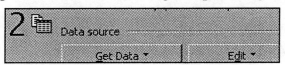

- **Data Source** file name displays, select this file and the **Data Form** opens with the Field Name: Address4 now **included**:

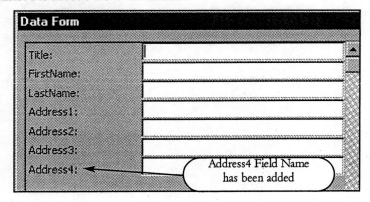

Exercise 38:

- Using the **Mail Merge** facility of Microsoft Word, set up the following letter, which will will be sent to **4 addresses:**

The **letter** for merging is:

> Dear
>
> ### An Ideal Husband by Oscar Wilde
>
> Thank you for your recent query regarding the *Everyman Palace Production* of the above.
>
> I am happy to inform you that this classic play from the very in-vogue <u>Oscar Wilde</u> will run nightly in the Everyman from the 31st October to the 10 November inclusive.
>
> I look forward to seeing you there

Note: Two records contain **4 Lines** of **Address** and Two records contain **3 Lines** of **Address** - you must set up sufficient Field Names to accommodate the **largest** record; Word is programmed **not** to print **blank** lines so the merge will adjust for the smaller records

> Mr Tom Roe 49 Bishop square Midleton Co Cork
> Ms Abby Whitaker The Glade Enniscorthy Co Wexford
> Mr Luke Deane Starry View Briar Road Clonakilty Co Cork
> Ms Nina Curran Avonmore Durrus Bantry Co Cork

Addresses:

Exercise 39:

- Create the **standard** letter for **4 recipients** utilising the **Mail Merge** facility. Merge to the **screen** as before.

- The **letter** is:

> Dear
>
> If you want to Stop Smoking, you can get help.
>
> The Southern Health Board;s Health Promotion Department offers a Smoking Cessation service that can provide individually tailored practical support and assistance to help you in your efforts to stop smoking.

- The **Recipients** are:

> Mr Barry Dunne 56 Friar's Road Callan Co Kilkenny
> Ms Alice Treacy 89 Upper Mount St Tallow Co Waterford
> Mr Nick Taylor 67 John St Milford Charleville Co Cork
> Ms Ber Considine 23 Loretto Road Tralee Co Kerry

Consolidation of all Word features introduced

In the following practice documents, it will be necessary to key in the **basic** document suggested for each Exercise. **Save** under the suggested file name and keep as a **master** file. Use it again and again.

Practice 1:

HOUSE PROUD

When his father former Taoiseach Garret Fitzgerald, got new of his youngest son's Leaving Cert results, he said that his faith in the Irish education had been restored. There were no honours, just passes. But in those days, before the craze of counting points gripped school leavers, Mark Fitzgerald was able to enrol in the college course of his choice.

He may have been an underachiever in an academically brilliant household, but that did not impede Mark Fitzgerald. Today he's at the top of his chosen profession having given it a jolt. As a chairman and chief executive of Sherry Fitzgerald he is credited with creating an estate agency business which is innovate service driven and with a penchant for marketing that has exposed the deficiency of its more traditional rivals.

Sherry Fitzgerald now lays claim to being the largest agent in the Dublin residential market, selling 1,500 second-hand homes last year as well as 8000 new homes. The company is now going countrywide, with an ambitious plan to create a network of 40 franchised agents within three years. Its commercial division. DTZ Sherry Fitzgerald, is among the top five and has set its sights on being number one. To fund all this expansion, Sherry Fitzgerald has been spoken about as a candidate for a stock market listing, although Fitzgerald says that it's speculative and that flotation is just one of a number of options it may pursue.

1. Save the document above using the file name: "Property Market MW"
2. Change font of document to Arial Narrow size
3. Insert blank line after "House Proud"
4. Insert a new paragraph after the sentence beginning "But in those days" and the sentence beginning" Its commercial division
5. Insert the text "Being a good marketer, Fitzgerald is always accessible to the media and agrees, without hesitation to do a personal interview, "before "Today, he's at the top of his chosen profession"
6. Embolden, Colour Yellow and use Italics on all occurrences of the words "Mark Fitzgerald"
7. Delete the word "homes" and replace it with "houses"
8. Cut the words "Garret Fitzgerald" and paste before the word "former Taoiseach"
9. Cut the sentence beginning "He may have been.." and paste before the sentence beginning "Sherry Fitzgerald now lays.."
10. Insert today's date as a header
11. Change the font of "House Proud" to Times New Roman, size 16
12. Type in your name at the bottom of the document in Britannic Bold, size 20
13. Add the page number: 23 to the document in Large Roman Numerals
14. Change the line spacing of the last paragraph to 1.5 and the first paragraph to double
15. Insert a centered footer: "Self-belief is the key to success" in Bold
16. Indent the first line of each paragraph so that the text starts 1 cm to the right of the left margin
17. Create a Table with 4 Rows and 2 Columns - line width of borders to be set to 1 pt

Editor	Number of Issues
Anne Murphy	5
Howard Ellis	6
Kevin Newman	3

18. Merge first row of table
19. Set two centered tabs at 4 cms and 10 cms - Insert the words: "Real Estate" at the first tab and the words "Booming Economy" at the second using the font colour: Green
21. Allow 8 pt Spacing before and after each paragraph in the document
22. Insert an appropriate Clip Art or Picture from file two lines below the heading: "House Proud" - centre in line
23. Save - Print to file; use Print File name: "Sherry.prn"

Data Source:

Create a name and address file: "Addresses" use Tables feature - this will be kept as a master file for the merging exercises.

Name	Address	City
John Murphy	45 Bolton St	Cork
Kay Welch	Upper John St	Limerick
Rita Weir	Friar St	Waterford
Liam Long	Daunt Square	Galway
Frank Furney	Mill Lane	Dundalk
May Wallace	Cork Rd	Dublin

Practice 2:

- **Key** in the document below - **save** as "Railway" - use as a master as before:

> CIE Development
> Extract from Business Post
> The Government's plan to spend £430 million to improve rail safety standards sounds like a bold move to tackle the chronic problems of the service. Analysis of the strategy disclosed by the Minister for Public enterprise, Mary O'Rourke, and the current state of CIE, cast serious doubt on the new initiative. The first striking feature of the minister's strategy is the requirement of CIE to add £70 in new borrowings to the group balance sheet this year as part of the first five-year tranche of investment . Exchequer funds would follow.
>
> O'Rourke's plan should be compared with the scale of the investment recommended in the report by consultants IRMS last year.
>
> In its sometimes damning review of national rail safety they urged spending £590 million over 15 years to bring the network up to acceptable standards. The minister's scheme of investment is based on the period: 1992-2003.

1. Open the document "Railway".
2. Save the document under the new file name: "Irish Rail MW"
3. Change the font in the document to Arial Narrow
4. Create a Header in Blue which will read: "Mary O'Rourke, Minister for Public Enterprise"
5. Insert a blank line after the text "CIE Development".
6. Centre the text: "CIE Development". Put a blank line below "Cork".
7. Justify to the right of the page the text: "Extract from Business Post"
8. Embolden all occurrences of the word "CIE" and change its Font size to 18.
9. Make a new paragraph with the text: "The first striking feature"
10. Delete the text: "in new borrowings"
11. Copy the text: "Analysis of the strategy disclosed by the Minister for Public Enterprise, Mary O'Rourke" to a line on its own below the passage of text leaving a clear line in between.
12. Delete the text: ", casts serious doubt on the new initiative. " and put in a full stop.
13. Apply Bullet Points to each Paragraph.
14. Change the line spacing in the second paragraph to 1.5. Spell check and Save.
15. Insert a picture from a clipart library at the end of the document. Adjust the picture so that the whole document consists of one single page.
16. Insert a page break and type the following text at the top of the new page: "Implementation of a viability plan designed to save £44 million is now about three years overdue". Use the Indent function to make this text start 2 cm to the right of the left margin.
17. Set the Paragraph spacing for below and after each paragraph to 8 pt
18. Set two centered tabs at: 3 cm and 8 cm respectively and type:
    "CIE" at the first tab and "Railway Safety" at the other. Save the document.
19. Use this document as a standard letter in Mail Merge and Merge to the screen using the "Addresses" file above as the Data Source. Save; Print to the file name:Railway.prn".

Practice 3:

- Key in the following text; Save as Bakery; preserve as a master file as before:

> Dear Shareholders, The following, I know will make grim reading but this is the reality for us all as I write. A decision is to be made within the next two weeks on the future of the Mayo bakery company. Keane's. The company went into receivership last January, but the possibility of it being sold as a going concern has not yet been ruled out. Keane's has been trading since 1978. The company's main business was supplying fresh cakes to supermarkets like Superquinn, Tesco and Dunnes Stores, and the decision by Superquinn, its largest customer to terminate its contract last December was a major blow. The decision on whether it would be sold or wound up was likely to be made within the next two weeks. About 55 workers were employed at Keane's at the time the receiver was appointed. It is understood that most of these have been made redundant.
> Keane's made considerable investments in its Charlestown plant. It operated its own distribution network, but costs were high because of its distance from most of its customers. Local TD Michael Ring said he was "not optimistic" that the company could be rescued.

1. Open the document "Bakery" - this is a letter to the Bakery's shareholders
2. Save the document as "Raising Agent MW"
3. Change the font in the document to Courier 12.
4. Insert a blank line after "Dear Shareholders"
5. Insert a new Paragraph before the sentence: "Keane's has been trading" and before "The decision"
6. Insert the text: "It is believed to have substantial debts" before the sentence: "The company's main business"
7. Embolden, change Font colour to Yellow and Italicise, all occurrences of the word "Keane's"
8. Put names of all supermarkets into Times New Roman Font (18).
9. Cut the sentence: "Keane's made considerable.." and paste after the sentence beginning: "Local TD Michael..".
10. Insert today's date as a Header.
11. Change the font of "Dear Shareholders" to Arial Narrow 14.
12. Place the name of Keane's General Manager: Michael Mullins at the end of the letter with four blank lines in between this and the previous line. Place Mr Mullins' title under his name.
13. Change the font size of the General Manager's name of Times New Roman 14.
14. Underline the Manager's name.
15. Embolden all references to months of the year.
16. Add page numbering small Roman Numerals: centered in Footer.
17. Change the line spacing of the last paragraph to double.
18. Insert a Footer that will read: "Crispy pancakes"
19. Spell check and Save.
20. Indent the first line of each paragraph, so that the text starts 1 cm to the right of the left margin.
21. Make this table complete with borders of 1 pt and place it between the last paragraph and the sender in the document.

CAKES	PRODUCTION PER DAY
Queen Cakes	5000
Almond Tarts	3000
Doughnuts	1200

22. Insert the words: "Limited" and "1999" at Centered tabs: 3 cm and 9 cm - Save
23. Open file: ADDRSLIST.XXX. It contains an address list which will be merged with the letter: Insert the three Field Names in the upper left corner of the letter one line after the other: Name; Address; City
24. Merge the letter with the address list. Save your document and close the word processing program.

Microsoft Excel 2000

Spreadsheets

A Spreadsheet is a program that organises **numbers, labels** (text) and **formulas** in **rows** and **columns** for calculating **results**. Spreadsheets have **built-in statistical, mathematical,** or **financial equations** (called **functions**)

In Excel - a popular **spreadsheet program** - a **workbook** is the file in which you work and store your data - each workbook contains many **worksheets** you can organise various kinds of **related information** in a **single file**

A worksheet is always part of a workbook, and is the primary document you use in Excel. You can enter and edit data on several worksheets simultaneously and perform calculations based on data from multiple worksheets When you create a chart, you can place the chart on the worksheet with its related data or on a separate chart sheet.

Getting Started with Microsoft Excel

- Turn on computer: our example - Windows98 is loaded into memory - Desktop appears:

Loading Microsoft Excel 2000

- **Start Excel** by clicking on the **Start Menu, Programs** and selecting **Microsoft Excel:**

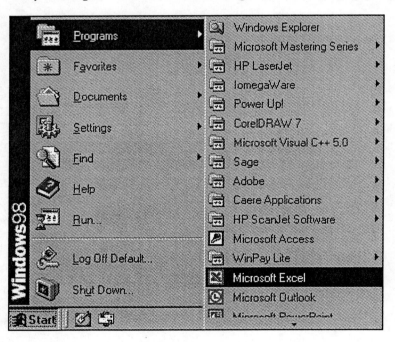

- ..the first (**blank**) Worksheet or Spreadsheet - entitled: **Sheet1** - of a 3-Page Workbook opens:

Worksheets

- The worksheet (named **Sheet1**) is made up of **Columns** (named **A, B, C**) **down** and **Rows** (numbered **1, 2, 3**) **across**
- The **names** of the **3 default worksheets** appear on tabs at the **bottom** of the workbook window
- The **intersection** where a Column meets a Row forms a **cell**
- A cell is **identified** by the **letter** of this Column and Row, e.g. **A5, H6**, etc
- The cell pointer (cell is darkened - indicating **active cell**) is resting in cell **A1** of **Sheet1**
- The **reference** (or **cell address**) of the current cell (**A1**) can be seen in the **top left-hand corner** of the screen in the name box

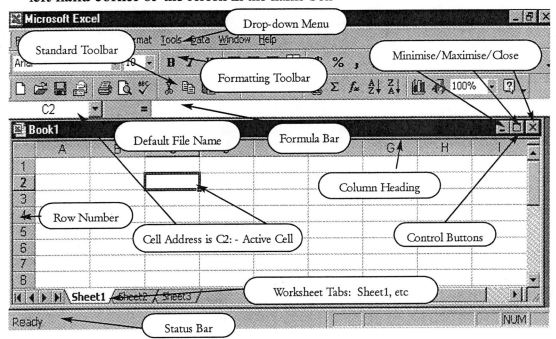

Methods of Moving around in a Worksheet:

- Hitting the **Return key** moves the cell pointer to the **next Row**
- The **cell pointer arrow** keys:

$$\boxed{\leftarrow \rightarrow \downarrow \uparrow}$$

  are used to move the **cell pointer** in the direction of the **depressed arrow key** or use the **Mouse** to move from **one cell** to **another**
- The **Page Up/Down keys** are used to move the cell pointer **up** or **down** a page at the time or use the **Scroll Bars** to move **up** or **across** the **Worksheet**
- Depress **Control Key & Home** key simultaneously to move **cell pointer** directly to cell **A1**
- To **move** from **sheet** to **sheet**, click the **sheet tabs** (**Sheet1, Sheet2** etc) - the **name** of the **active sheet** is **bold**

Default

- A commonly used computer term to describe **predetermined settings** for software features.

Selecting (or Highlighting):

It is necessary to **highlight cells** before many Excel actions, such as, Formatting etc are performed

Selecting a Block (or Range):

- **Select** a block: A1 to A7:
- **Click** in cell A3 with left mouse button depressed
- Hold **button down** and **drag highlighting** to cell A8
- Release button and range: **A3..A8** is selected

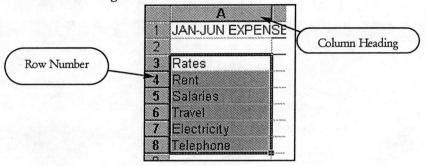

Selecting a Row:	Click on Row Number to Select
Selecting a Column:	Click on Column Heading to Select
Selecting a Whole Worksheet:	Use Control + A to Select

Column Width:

- The **default** width of each Column is **9 Characters:**

F
May
1654
800
29000
900
1276
879

Formula Bar:

- Formula Bar displays the contents of the **active cell**

Deleting Data:

- Press **Esc** key if you want to cancel whole entry **being typed** at any time
- To **Delete** some errors while inputting, press **Backspace** key and **retype**

Example of keying in Numbers & Text in Sheet: A1

- With Cell Pointer in **Cell A1** of **Sheet A1**, type in:

  FINANCIAL YEAR ENDING: 31 DECEMBER 2000

  - the text appears **both** in the **Formula Bar** and **cell** as you type

- Hit **Return** key to store data in **cell** and simultaneously **move** cell pointer to next Row - cell **A2**

- The cell entry is too **large** to fit in A1 so it spills over into cell B2
  (The whole entry will be displayed unless new data is keyed into B2)

- **Experiment** by typing text into B2 - notice that the entry in A1 is truncated at the tenth letter
- **Move** cell pointer back to cell A1 and you will see that the **full** A1 entry is displayed on the Formula Bar

A1	▼	=	FINANCIAL YEAR ENDING: 31 DECEMBER 2000

Book3.xls

Formula bar shows the contents of active cell: A1

	A	B					G
1	FINANCIAL YEAR ENDING: 31 DECEMBER 2000						
2		Jan	Feb	Mar	Apr	May	Jun
3	Rates	1230	1890	1678	1256	1654	178
4	Rent	600	1100	800	800	800	80
5	Salaries	24000	15000	16570	28900	29000	2900

Text is left-aligned in cell by default

Numbers are right-aligned by default

- **Key** in the remaining data (numbers and text) in cells as indicated above:

Default Alignment

- **Text** is **left-aligned** in cell
- **Numbers** are right-aligned

Editing (or Changing) cell contents:

A3	▼	=	Rent

	A	B	C
3	Rent	600	1100

- **Modify** cell A3 to read: Rent **and Rates**

- **Select** cell A3 and **press F2** - known as the **Edit** key - the contents of the active cell are displayed in the **formula bar**

- In the **formula bar,** click to position the **insertion point** after the letter 't',

- Press **F2 key** or double click in **Formula bar** to make **cell A3** active
- Type "and Rates" - **cell A3** should now read:

A3	▼	✕ ✓	=	Rent and Rates

	A	B	C
3	Rent and Rates	600	1100

Saving:

- Data is held in memory (RAM) **temporarily** - Store **permanently** by clicking the **Save** icon on the Toolbar or by selecting **File Save** from Menu bar

- The first time you save a file, a **Save As** Dialog Box appears - the default folder is **My Documents:**

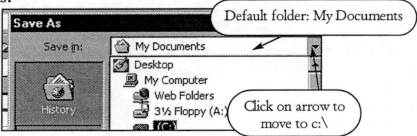

Creating a Folder: (Set up folders to segregate areas of work)

- Move to the default c:\ drive - Click on **New Folder** button

- Type in "Practice" as the New Folder **name**

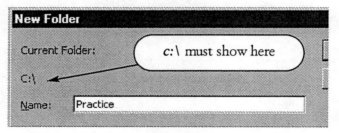

- Click **OK** - thereby creating a folder named "Practice" directly inside **drive c:**

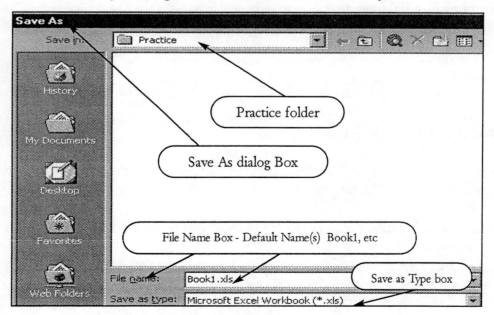

Saving File within Folder "Practice":

- With **File Save As** dialog box open, double click on "Practice" Folder to select - see above:

- **Type** in **Exercise 1** in **File Name Box:**

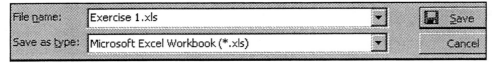

- **Save as** *Type* box - this box, unless changed, always reflects **current** software

- Click **Save** - file saves in Folder "Practice" in drive c:\ - File Save As dialog box closes - **top** of Worksheet now displays the file name:

To Close File

- Click on **File Close** on Menu - file closes

Opening a File

- **Open** files with the **File Open** Command from Menu or by clicking on **Open** icon:

- ..**Open Dialog** box opens - it is necessary to switch to folder in which file was saved

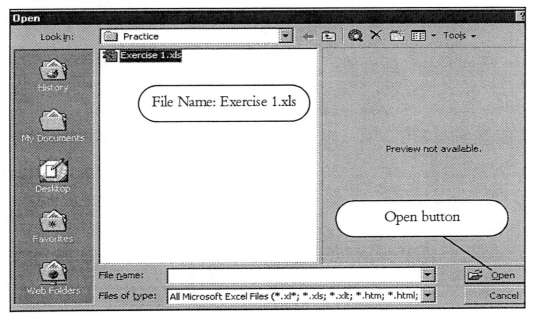

- Move to drive **c:\ icon** - Find folder "Practice" and click **Open** to open folder:
- Click on **File name:** "Exercise 1.xls"; click **Open** button - File opens

---

Formatting: Column Width/Row Height

In a new worksheet:
- The **default** Row **height** is 12.75
- The height automatically adjusts to accommodate the largest font in the row

- The **default** column **width** is 8.43 characters
- Column width does **not** adjust unless you change it

To Increase Column Width:

- **Select** Column or Columns to be widened
- Point to the **right boundary** of the column heading with the mouse
- When the mouse pointer becomes a **double headed arrow**, double click -the column is extended to **accommodate** the **widest** entry

Exercise on Widening Column:

- **Key** in the data below and **widen** Column, as directed:

    i Contents of Column A has flown into Column B:

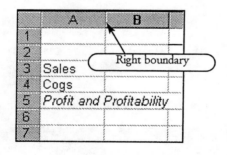

    ii Widened Column A now holds the **full content** of Column:

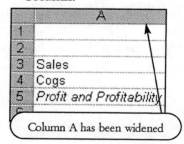

To Decrease Column Width:

- **Select** Column or Columns to be **narrowed**:
- Point to the **right boundary** of the column heading; when the mouse pointer becomes a **double-headed arrow,** and drag to the left until the column has been **reduced** to the required width:

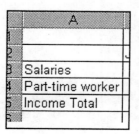

To Adjust Row Height - Row 5:

- Rest the mouse pointer on the boundary of the **row heading;** when the mouse pointer becomes a double-headed arrow, click and **drag** to required height:

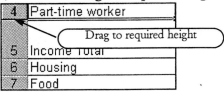

Text Alignment:

- By default, text entries within cells are **Left-Aligned** and numbers are **Right-aligned**
- Using relevant **Alignment** Buttons, Cell contents may be aligned: **Right or Centered:**
- Using **Merge & Centre** Button, headings may be **Centered** over two or more columns:

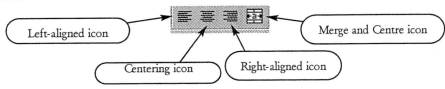

Example of Centering within a Cell:

- Months: Jan-Feb - are **left-aligned** within cells

January	February	March

- To **centre** the months within cells, highlight and click **Centre** icon - result is:

January	February	March

Example of Merge and Centering across Columns:

- **Main Title:** Monthly Income for O'Donoghue's - has been entered in Column A; as there isn't any entry in Column B, text is spreading into Column B - using the **Merge and Centre** feature, we will centre across the Columns: A-E:

Monthly Income for: O'Donoghue's				
	January	February	March	April
Salaries	567.00	900.00	400.00	622.333

- Highlight Title and cells across which the Title is to be centered:

Monthly Income for: O'Donoghue's				

- Click Merge and Centre icon on Toolbar - result is:

Monthly Income for: O'Donoghue's			

Practice

When you are confident that you understand and can apply all the areas introduced in this Unit - complete the exercises below:

Exercise 1:

Study the diagram of a Worksheet introduced in this Unit. **Identify** the features in the diagram below and fill in the detail in ink:

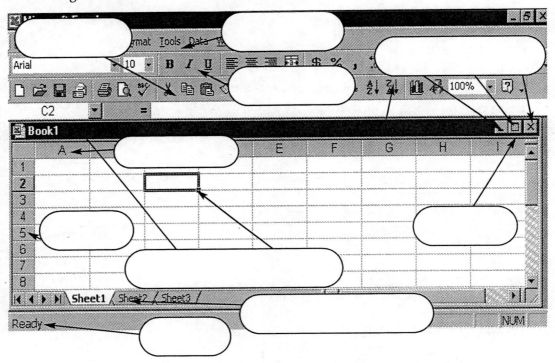

Exercise 2:

- **Complete** the following:

Question	Answer
How many worksheets in a default Workbook?	
What are the default Worksheet names?	
What intersection is a cell formed from?	
What is a cell pointer?	
What is a cell address?	
What does default mean?	
What is the default: (a) Column Width? (b) Row Height?	
What is the Formula Bar?	
Describe two ways of deleting data while inputting	
What is default alignment for: (a) Text (b) Numbers	
What is the Edit key?	

Exercise 3:

- **Move** cell pointer to Cell A5 and **key** in the following Text and Numbers:

	A	B	C
5			
6	Sales		6500
7	Purchases	7000	
8	Lighting	350	
9	Drawings	500	
10	Fittings	450	
11	Debtors	1200	
12	Creditors		3400
13	Bank	2100	
14	Cash	50	
15	Rent	1235	
16	Capital		2985
17			

- Create a **folder**; use your **name** as folder name - make sure you follow the instructions on Folders above - you must go back to the **c:** before you create the folder - use this folder for the remaining exercises

- **Save as:** e.g. "Trial Balance MW" - substitute your initials for "MW" in all the **Saving** suggestions in this Manual.

- **Close** File

Exercise 4:

- **Open** the file: "Trial Balance MW" - **key** in the headings below in the Rows & Columns indicated:

	A	B	C
1	L Griffin		
2	Trial Balance		
3			
4		Dr	Cr
5		£	£

- Using the **Merge & Centre** icon, **merge** the ranges:

    A1..C1 across the Columns: **A, B and C**
    A2..C2 across the Columns: **A, B and C**

- **Highlight** the range: B4..C5 and **centre** within their respective cells

- **Save** and **Close File**

Exercise 5:

- **Key** in the exercise below
- **Widen** Columns, if necessary, to accommodate data
- **Centre** the headings in Row 1 and 3 across 3 Columns
- **Centre** both sets of Headings: "Rooms, 5 Days.." within their respective cells

	A	B	C
1	Corinthian Cruise		
2			
3	BERMUDA		
4			
5	Class	5 Days	10 Days
6			
7	Economy	654	789
8	Standard	678	456
9	Deluxe	435	785
10	Superb	690	677
11	Magestic	349	778
12			
13	JAMAICA		
14			
15	Class	5 Days	10 Days
16			
17	Economy	546	765
18	Standard	567	675
19	Deluxe	554	654
20	Superb	559	543
21	Magestic	447	478
22			

- **Save** as: "Cruise Ship MW" & **Close** file

Exercise 6:

- **Key** in the exercise below
- **Widen** Columns, if necessary, to accommodate data
- **Centre** the headings in Row 2 across Columns: A..G
- **Centre** Headings: Row 4 - within their respective cells
- **Save** as: "Indian Spice MW" - **Close** File

	A	B	C	D	E	F	G
1							
2	SPICE OF INDIA - Monkstown Road Cork						
3							
4		Lamb Korma	Chicken Salad	Pilau Rice	Sirloin Steaks	Onion Nan	Prawn Bhuna
5							
6	Jan	212	289	431	303	190	270
7							
8	Feb	290	329	449	360	266	340
9							
10	Mar	320	354	457	377	321	367

- **Open** file: "Indian Spice MW"
- **Edit** Months so that they will read in full: January, February and March
- **Edit** as follows: "Lamb Korma" should read: "Lamb Bhuna";
                          "Chicken Salad" should read: "Chicken Curry"
                          "Sirloin Steaks" should read: "Fillet Steaks"
- **Save** under a new File Name: "Indian Food MW" - **Close** File.

Formatting: Changing Number Formats

Numbers can be displayed as currency amounts, percentages, decimals, scientific notation, dates, or times with the spreadsheet's built-in formats.

Formatting Cells: Currency Formatting:

- **Highlight** (or Select) Cells: **B6..D1:**

January	February	March
567.00	900.00	400.00
134.00	800.00	700.00
701.00	1,700.00	1,100.00
120.00	134.00	213.00
123.00	156.00	124.00
144.00	178.00	321.00
56.00	43.00	12.00

- Select **Format Cells** from Menu Bar - **Format Cells** Dialog Box opens:
- Select **Currency: IR£ , 2 Decimal** Places:

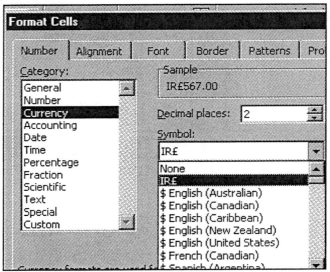

- Click OK.
- Selected **Numbers** are adjusted to display in **Currency Format,** 2 Decimals.

January	February	March
IR£567.00	IR£900.00	IR£400.00
IR£134.00	IR£800.00	IR£700.00
IR£701.00	IR£1,700.00	IR£1,100.00
IR£120.00	IR£134.00	IR£213.00
IR£123.00	IR£156.00	IR£124.00
IR£144.00	IR£178.00	IR£321.00
IR£56.00	IR£43.00	IR£12.00

Borders

Border icon on Toolbar

- Data can be emphasised through the application of **Borders** (of varying thickness), **Shading** or **Colour Borders**
- The Borders **icon** on the **Formatting Toolbar** contains a palette of Borders used for the insertion of borders of varying **thickness** and **positions** - click drop-down **arrow** to display **range** of borders:

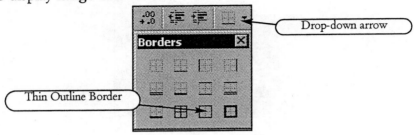

Adding Borders Example - Adding a **thin** border around **selected** data:

- **Highlight** range:

Salaries	24000	15000	16570
Travel	780	9000	756
Electricity	1230	1650	1546
Telephone	870	890	8976

- Click down arrow to the right of the Borders icon, click on the **thin Outline** Border This border will be applied to the **outer** edge of the selected area:

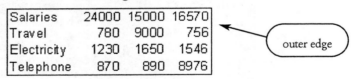

Adding Borders with Format Cells from Menu

Borders may be applied by highlighting text and using the **Format Cells Border** command from the drop-down menu instead of using the Border icon

- **Highlight** text to be enclosed in an **Outline thick** border:

Week Ending : 31 March 2001	
Telephone	15.56
Food	95
Electricity	26
Petrol	15
Milk Bill	9.5
	161.06

- Select **Format Cells** from menu and select **Border tab**:

- A border can be applied to the selected area by choosing from:
  Presets, Preview diagram or specific **buttons**:

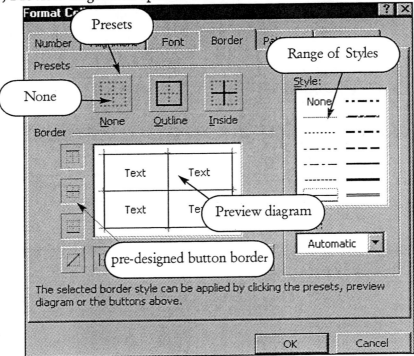

- We need a border **outside** and **inside** each **cell** of the **highlighted** area, so we select **Outline & Inside - Preview** diagram will show the effect of these choices on the **selected** cells:

Week Ending : 31 March 2001		
Telephone	15.56	
Food	95	
Electricity	26	
Petrol	15	
Milk Bill	9.5	
	161.06	

- ..the **chosen borders** are applied to the **highlighted** area

Removing Border

- If you want to **remove** a Border, you must **rehighlight** data and select **None** from Border menu

Inserting Rows/Columns/Multiple Rows/Columns:

- You can insert a **Row(s)** or **Column(s)** within **existing** Rows and Columns

To Insert a Single Row:

- To insert a Row above **Profit and Loss..**: Click in **Row 2**

McKenna's Bakery Dundalk
Profit and Loss for Year ended 31 December 2001

- Select **Insert Row** Command from Menu - Row is inserted as requested:

McKenna's Bakery Dundalk
Profit and Loss for Year ended 31 December 2001

To Insert Multiple Rows:

- To insert e.g. **Two Rows** above the row containing the text: **Alice's Bakery** - select this Row and one Row below.

- Select **Excel's Insert Row** from Menu
- **Two Rows** are inserted above row containing Alice's Bakery

		Alice's Bake

Inserting Columns: To Insert a Single Column:

- Select **Column: B**

	B	C
		Alice's Bakery
	Product	Number sold
	Filo Pastries	300
	Blueberry Pies	56
	Jenny's Specials	77
	Mama Mia's	90

- Use Excel's **Insert Column** Command to insert a **blank** Column to the left:

	B	C
		Alice's Baker
		Product
		Filo Pastries
		Blueberry Pies
		Jenny's Specials

To Insert multiple columns e.g. two -

- Highlight **two columns**, select **Insert Column** - a **new** Column is inserted for each Column highlighted

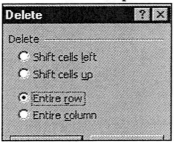

Deleting Rows:

- To **Delete** a **Single Row: Select** the Row, which is to be **deleted**
- Use the **Edit Delete** Command to Delete the highlighted row

Note: If you don't highlight either a row or a column, the **Delete** dialog box opens when you select **Edit Delete** from Menu - an option then has to be selected:

Deleting Columns:

- To **Delete** a **Single Column: Select** Column to be deleted
- Use the **Edit Delete** Command to **Delete** the **highlighted Column**

To Delete Multiple Rows/Columns:

- **Highlight** Rows/Columns to be deleted
- Use the **Edit Delete Entire Row/Column** Command, as appropriate, to Delete the highlighted data

Copying Data: Fill Handle:
(Facilitates copying to **adjacent** cells)

- **Key** in Exercise below;

	Jan
Lodging	2300
Transport	245
Entertainment	267
Meals	122

Highlight the **Jan** Column.

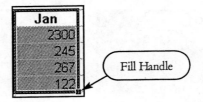

- **Click** in the **last cell** of the column, select **fill handle** - shape **changes** to a black cross - keep **clicking** and drag **two columns** to the right:

	A	B	C	D	E
	Profit and Loss for Year ended 31 December 2001				
		Jan	Feb	Mar	
	Lodging	2300	2300	2300	
	Transport	245	245	245	
	Entertainment	267	267	267	
	Meals	122	122	122	

- Excel fills in **Feb, Mar** - **internal Clock** in computer recognises **Feb** as a month and automatically uses the **Excel fill** feature to create the **next consecutive** month ie **March**

Copying Data (or Replicating): Copying to non-adjacent cells
(Original data is **copied** - **not removed** - to be **pasted** elsewhere)

- **Highlight** Data to be copied
- Click **Copy** icon on Toolbar

(or **Edit Copy** from Menu)
- Position cell pointer in **second location** of data and click **Paste** icon:

- (or **Edit Paste** from Menu) - the copied data **displays** at this point

Cutting Data: Removes data from cell for relocation elsewhere

- **Highlight** Data to be moved
- Click **Cut** icon on Toolbar

(or select **Edit Cut** from Menu) - data is cut from cell into memory:

- Position cell pointer in new location of data and click **Paste** icon:
  - the cut data **displays** at this point

Exercise 7:

- Key in the Exercise below:

SOCCER CLUBS OF THE 21 CENTURY				
January 1 2001				
CLOTHES' REQUIREMENTS FOR YEAR				
Club	Shirts	Pants	Hats	Gloves
Blackburn	234	134	334	434
Aston villa	123	333	323	423
Manchester	112	132	334	312
Leicester	225	325	625	325
Juventus	361	331	461	361
Blackburn	345	445	345	545
Chelsea	221	446	421	521
Newcastle	111	236	511	311
Liverpool	226	326	326	266

- Save as: "Soccer MW"
- Use Merge and Centre & Centering Alignment, as required for headings
- Format Numeric Columns to £ Currency, 0 decimal places
- Add one new row above top title - key in the text: Records' Copyright - Centre across Columns
- Add a Column to the left of the "Club" Column. Enter the heading: "Secretary" for this Column in the same Row as: "Club", "Shirts" etc
- Larry Somers is the Secretary for Blackburn; enter the 8 other Secretaries names in the remaining rows: Jim Barnes, Dick Willis, Con Sheehan, Mike Tanner, Rick Long, Milo Welch, Leo Dowling and Harry Kidney
- Add a Thin Outline Border to the exercise
- Save under a new name: "Clubs MW".
- Copy the last two rows to Rows 20 & 21
- Resave and Close File.

Exercise 8:

- Key in the Exercise below:

Stock 1 April, 1995	
Sales	4,786
Purchases	
Carriage inwards	
Return outwards	789
Wages	
Rent & Rates	
Communication Expenses	
Commission	
Sundry expenses	
Buildings	
Debtors	
Creditors	12,347
Fixtures	
Loans from K Kenny	22,000
Drawings	
Capital	65,000
J Clarke audited all figures	

- Save as: "K Kenny Trial Balance MW" - Close File

Exercise 9:

- Open the file: "K Kenny Trial Balance MW" - this file will be amended by adding further Rows and one extra Column as well as making other changes so that it will look like the document below
- Compare both files carefully and then made adjustments as required: use F2 key for modifying the text entries:

Example of where original text is to be modified - use **F2** to edit and key in additional text

Trial Balance as at 31 December 2002		
	Dr	Cr
	£	£
Stock 1 April, 1995	17890	
Sales		
Purchases	45675	4,786
Carriage inwards	4321	
Carriage outwards		7654
Return outwards		567
Wages and Salaries	18456	
Rent & Rates	4355	
Communication Expenses	333	
Commissions payable	456	
Insurance	765	
Sundry expenses	324	
Buildings	543	
Debtors	3450	
Creditors		23,000
Cash at Bank	12345	
Cash at Cash	25456	
Fixtures	7554	
Loans from K Kenny		23,682
Drawings	3456	
Capital	454	
	856	87,000
J Clarke audited all figures		

- Format to $ Currency with 2 Decimal places; delete the £ symbols
- Delete single rows: "Fixtures & Capital" use Control key to select non-consecutive rows
- Insert two Rows above Cash at Bank; cut the Rows: "Loan from.." & "Drawings" and paste into the newly created Rows
- Delete the rows left blank by the cutting
- Delete the remark: "J Clarke..." (with Delete Key)
- Copy column B and paste to a clear part of the Worksheet - Format this block to £ Currency with 1 Decimal place
- Delete Column C
- Save under a new name: "Rodgers Trial Balance"

Exercise 10:

- Key in the data below in Columns A & B - Save as "Mitchell MW"

	Jan
Salaries	10000
Building operations	1300
Travel	850
Suppliers	500
Depreciation	1200
Equipment Maintenance	750
Shipping Expense	400
Data Processing Costs	2100
Printing & Duplicating	640
Other	534

- Insert a Row at Row 1 for the insertion of the Title: "Running Expenses for Mitchell & Company for 2001"
- Use the AutoFill feature to fill the data in Column B to Columns: C-M inclusive - Note the months fill in automatically in sequence, i.e. Feb, Mar etc
- Expenses for each month were the same as above apart from some changes which should be entered as follows - Use the Autofill where applicable:

	Jan	Feb	Mar	Apr	May	Jun	Jul	Aug	Sep	Oct	Nov	Dec
Salaries	10000	7800	6900	6900	7600	8080	4000	8900	7000	8600	8700	8900
Building operations	1300	9000	7700	7500	6789	4567	8765	5678	5433	3333	6700	6655

- Apply a border between each Column and a thin border Outline
- Save as: "Mitchell Enterprises MW" - Close file

Exercise 11:

- Key in the following exercise - Save as "Antonio MW"

Antonio's Wholesale	
Item	Number of Items
Dessert Spoons	60
Napkins	90
Sugar Bowls	30
Tablecloths	45
Dinner Plates	50
Side Plates	45
Saucers	60
Cups	30

- Merge and Centre main heading across Columns; enclose whole exercise in Borders - around the outside and between each cell
- Insert a Column to the left of the "Number of Items" Column - Name this Column: "Cost per Item"; Insert Rows, as required in the modified document below - fill in detail of new Rows and Columns
- Edit "Number of Items" to read "No.."; place a thick border below main Title
- Finished exercise should look like:

Antonio's Wholesale		
Item	Cost per Item	No of Items
Dessert Spoons	IR£2.50	60
Tea Spoons	IR£2.00	70
Napkins	IR£4.00	90
Sugar Bowls	IR£3.45	30
Knives	IR£5.00	90
Tablecloths	IR£25.00	45
Dinner Plates	IR£4.00	50
Soup Spoons	IR£3.00	65
Side Plates	IR£2.50	45
Saucers	IR£3.00	60
Cups	IR£2.00	30

- Save under a new file name: "Antonio's Platters". Close File.

Formulas:

- A **formula** is a sequence of values, cell references, names, functions or operators that produces a **new value** from **existing values**

Adding Formula:

- Several methods can be used to **add** figures within Excel - the most commonly used method is the **AutoSum** - this method will add the **highlighted** range using the = **Sum** formula - see Example below: =sum(B5..B10) - this means the spreadsheet is instructed to **add** all the **consecutive** numbers in the range between **B5 and B10**.

Method:

- **Select** Range to be added:

	B
4	Number Purchased
5	5500
6	4500
7	650
8	990
9	897
10	458
11	
12	

- Select **AutoSum** icon from Toolbar:

- **Total** of calculation appears in **bottom** cell; Formula displays in Formula Bar:

		B	C
B11		=	=SUM(B5:B10)
4		Number Purchased	NO BOUGHT
5		5500	*Adding Formula*
6		4500	
7		650	
8		990	
9		897	
10		458	*Total of Calculation*
11		12995	

Adding: non-Contiguous cells

- To **add** contents of cells: C6, D9 and E10 (i.e. non-contiguous cells) together type the =**Sum** directly into cell where the answer is to go, open a **bracket**, select each relevant **cell** in turn, type a **comma** between Cell addresses, **close brackets** - the result will be: =SUM(D6,D9,E10) - See **Formula Bar:**

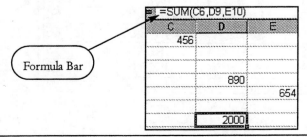

Formula Bar

AutoFilling Formulas: (Relative Cell Addresses)

- The AutoFill feature can be used to **copy** the 'action' of the formula to other similar length range(s) This is known as copying the **relative** cell addresses.

Example:

The **AutoSum** feature is used to add **range: B2..B5** - formula shown in **Formula Bar:**

B6 ▼	=	=SUM(B2:B5)		
A	B	C	D	E
	Q1	Q2	Q3	Q4
LODGING	2300	2450	3300	2560
TRANSPORT	245	545	565	245
ENTERTAINMENT	267	475	278	546
MEALS	122	222	232	172
	2934			

- Select the **AutoFill** feature on the corner of the cell pointer in cell **B6** and **drag** to the range: **C2..C5** - the action of the adding formula - the adding of **4 consecutive figures** - is **copied** across and **applied** to the relative cells of columns: **C, D** and **E.**

C6 ▼	=	=SUM(C2:C5)		
A	B	C	D	E
	Q1	Q2	Q3	Q4
LODGING	2300	2450	3300	2560
TRANSPORT	245	545	565	245
ENTERTAINMENT	267	475	278	546
MEALS	122	222	232	172
	2934	3692	4375	3523

Subtraction:

- The subtraction formula requires two parts:
  - (1) an operator to begin the formula: =
  - (2) two cell addresses separated by the subtraction sign: such as: =B6-B7

To find the Taxable Income of John Gibbons below, see the following example:

Steps in Subtraction:
- Click in **B5**(cell where result is required) Type =
- **Select** cell **B3** Type - Click cell **B4** - **=B3-B4** displays in **B5**
- Press **Return** - Result is shown in **B5** - Formula is displayed in **Formula Bar**

	A	B
1	Employee	John Gibbons
2		
3	Salary	50000
4	TFA	12000
5	Taxable Income:	=B3-B4

B5 ▼		=	=B3-B4
	A		B
1	Employee		John Gibbons
2			
3	Salary		50000
4	TFA		12000
5	Taxable Income:		38000

Multiplication

- The symbol for Multiplication is *

- To multiply **C1 by C2:**

VLOOKUP	▼	X	✓	=	=C1*C2

	C	D	E
1	67		
2	87		
3	=C1*C2		

C3	▼		=	=C1*C2

	C	D	E
1	67		
2	87		
3	5829		

- Place cell pointer in C3 (the cell where the result is required)
- Type in =C1*C2 & hit Return
- Result shows in C3 - Formula can be seen in formula bar

Division:

- The **Division** symbol is /

Example of how Division is used:

- Place cell pointer in **D2** (the cell where the result is required)
- Type in **=C2/B2**
  (the "/" is a key on the numeric keyboard)

VLOOKUP	▼	X	✓	=	=C2/B2

	A	B	C	D
1	Food	Quantity	Total Cost	Cost per Item
2	Bread	12	11.76	=C2/B2
3	Butter	4	3.48	
4	Tea	5	7.35	
5	Sugar	6	4.56	
6	Milk	2	1.35	

- Hit **Return** - Formula can be seen in formula bar
- Result in **D2** is filled to the relevant cells with AutoFill
- Our example: **Result** is formatted in **Irish punts** with **2 decimal** places:

D5	▼		=	=C5/B5

	A	B	C	D
1	Food	Quantity	Total Cost	Cost per Item
2	Bread	12	11.76	IR£0.98
3	Butter	4	3.48	IR£0.87
4	Tea	5	7.35	IR£1.47
5	Sugar	6	4.56	IR£0.76
6	Milk	2	1.35	IR£0.68

Font Colour

- Click the down arrow of the drop-down menu of the **Font Colour** icon on the **Formatting Toolbar** to display a palette of colours used for the shading of text:

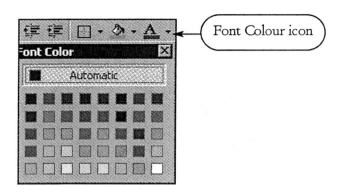

To Apply Font Colour

- Select text

| Classification of Export Produce |

- Select a **Font Colour** from Palette, e.g. Red -
  ..selected text now displays in Red:

| Classification of Export Produce |

Fill Colour

- The **Fill Colour** icon on the Formatting Toolbar contains a palette of colours used for the *shading* of cells:

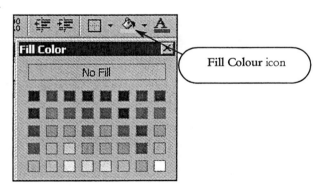

Using Fill Colour

- Highlight cells, as displayed - hold down Control to select ranges:
- Select Colour e.g. Green from Menu - highlighted cells now display in the shade green:

Week Ending 31 March 2001		
Telephone	15.56	
Food	95	
Electricity	26	
Petrol	15	
Milk Bill	9.5	
	161.06	

Week Ending 31 March 2001		
Telephone	15.56	
Food	95	
Electricity	26	
Petrol	15	
Milk Bill	9.5	
	161.06	

Insert a new Worksheet

- The default Worksheets are:

- ..Sheet3 is the active Sheet, Insert an additional Worksheet into your Workbook by selecting **Insert Worksheet** from Menu:

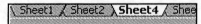

.. new Worksheet is added to the left of the Sheet3 Tab

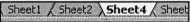

Move Worksheet

- To move worksheet, select tab and hold down mouse button - icon for a Page appears;

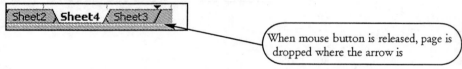

- Keep the mouse button depressed and drag the Sheet tab to the new location:

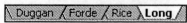

When mouse button is released, page is dropped where the arrow is

Rename Worksheet Tabs:

- Double click each Worksheet Tab Name in turn and key in new name:

Sorting Data

- Sort rows in **ascending** or **descending** order based on the contents of one column
- Click a **cell** in the column you would like to **sort by**:

```
Rent
Rates
Machinery
Salaries
Advertising
```

- Click *Sort Ascending* by clicking on this icon:

  ..the Column will be *sorted* like:
```
Advertising
Electricity
Freight
```

- Click *Sort Descending* by clicking on this icon:
  ..the Column will be *sorted* like:
```
Rent
Rates
Machinery
```

Font Style: Bold/Italic/Underline

Formatting Toolbar

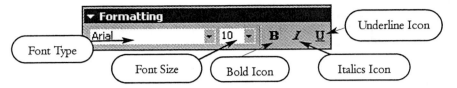

To embolden/italicize/underline data you have two options:

- Before you start typing, turn **on** Bold/Italic/Underline, as required by selecting relevant icon on Formatting Toolbar and type - text is emboldened/italicized/underlined as it is created

or

- To embolden/italicise/underline **existing** text: highlight text and select relevant icon - emboldening/italicizing/underlining is applied to existing text

Example of "Rainfall" in Bold, Italics & Underline:

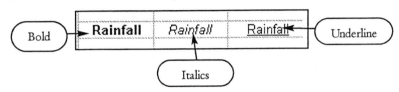

To select non-contiguous data:

- Hold down Control key as you select by dragging mouse button
- Release mouse button as you move to highlight next range but keep Control down until all required text is highlighted

Example:

- To embolden (make darker) the Column Headings and Dates in the following example, you must: Hold down Ctrl and Highlight range as indicated before clicking the Bold icon on the Formatting Toolbar:

Date	Particulars	Discount	Details	Purc
Jan-07				
Feb-07				
Mar-07				
Apr-07				
May-07				
Jun-07				
Jul-07				

Formatting: Font Type/Font Size/Font Style

Font Type & Size:

The default Font Type generally within the Excel software is set to Arial with the Font Size set to 10

Example of changing the default **Font Type** and **Font Size** to Arial Rounded MT Bold

- Click in cell A1 - in Formatting Toolbar, current Font Type and Size displays:

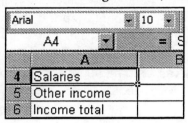

To Change Font Type

- Select data:

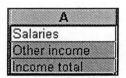

- Click on arrow to display the **Font** drop-down list on the Formatting Toolbar, click on **Arial Rounded MT Bold**:

- Click on arrow to display the **Font Size** drop-down list on the Formatting Toolbar, click on **12**:

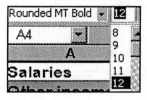

- Selected range: now displays in Arial Rounded MT Bold, Font Size: 12:

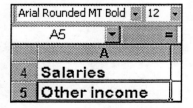

Exercise 12: Adding

Study and practice the **Adding, Subtracting, Multiplying** and **Division** examples given above before completing these tasks:

SUNSHINE CATERERS						
	Scones	Fruit cake	Doughnuts	Queen Cakes	Apple Tart	Total
January	400	670	356	534	446	
February	400	370	456	534	456	
March	400	330	776	534	457	
April	400	270	556	534	345	
May	400	470	456	534	345	
June	400	370	556	534	348	
Total						
Total sales of confectionery for Jan - Jun 2003						

- Key in this Adding Exercise in Sheet 1 of a new Workbook
- Use the AutoSum to add the number of Scones sold
- Use the AutoFill feature to Copy the adding formula to the other Columns.
- Use the AutoSum feature also to total the individual monthly sales in the appropriate cell - copy to remaining cells.
- Merge and Centre main headings & embolden
- Centre Column Headings within Cells and Italicise
- Name Sheet 1 Tab: "Sunshine" - Enclose whole exercise in a thin outline border
- Save as "Caterers MW"

Exercise 13: Adding

- Key in the Adding Exercise in Sheet 1 of a new Workbook - use the AutoFill feature to copy "Q1" to Column C, D etc - the system will recognise "Q1" represents a Quarter and will give the next Quarter references in sequence

Brookside Leisure Activities for Year Ending: December 31 2002					
	Q1	Q2	Q3	Q4	Total
Athletics	120.00	330.00	335.00	654.00	
Basketball	567.00	430.00	442.00	432.00	
Hockey	540.00	887.00	552.00	224.00	
Soccer	334.00	553.00	456.00	336.00	
Total					

- Use the AutoSum to Total the income from Q1
- Use the AutoFill feature to Copy the adding formula to the other Columns.
- Use the AutoSum feature also to calculate the Total income from each Sport - copy to remaining Columns
- Merge and centre main heading;   Centre Column Headings within Cells
- Change Font to Arial Narrow (12); Underline "Total"
- Save as: "Leisure Pursuits MW"
- Name Sheet1 Worksheet tab as: "Brookside"
- Copy the whole exercise and Paste to Sheet 2 - this tab is to be named: "Complex"
- In the "Complex" Worksheet, Edit "Hockey" income to read:

Hockey	340.00	600.00	452.00	300.00

- Delete the row relating to "Basketball" - note the Adding formula adjusts to take account of the change in numeric entries - ReSave & Close File

Exercise 14: Subtraction

- Key in the Subtraction Exercise in Sheet 1 of a new Workbook in Arial (12)

	2001	2002	2003	2004	2005
Sales	60000	65000	87600	68900	76000
Cogs	23400	25600	66700	2435	26789
Profit					

- Save as "Cogs"
- Calculate Profit by subtracting cost of "Cogs" from "Sales" for the year "2001"
- Copy Formula to remaining years using AutoFill
- Rename Worksheet Tab as "Profit"

Exercise 14: Addition & Subtraction

- On **Sheet 2,** set up the Exercise below - Save as "Garner MW"

James Garner's Maintenance Records					
	Q1	Q2	Q3	Q4	Total
Lodging	2300	2450	3300	2560	
Transport	2450	545	565	245	
Entertainment	267	457	278	546	
Meals	122	222	232	172	
Sub Total					
Less Allowance	670	780	369	467	
Deficit:					

- Calculate the Total expenses for Q1 - Copy to remaining Quarters
- Total the "Lodging" Row; Copy to remaining Rows
- Deduct Allowance for Q1 - Copy to other Quarters: Change Font Colour to Red
- Rename Worksheet Tab: "James G"
- Embolden and Centre all Headings. ReSave and Close

Exercise 15: Subtraction

- On Sheet 3, set up the Exercise below - Save as "Zicco MW"
- Calculate the "Outstanding" figures, by subtracting "Payment" from "Balance"
- Rename Worksheet Tab: "Ziccos4"

ZICCO's NIGHTCLUB				
First Quarter				
Supervisor	Account No	Balance	Payment	Outstanding
Butler, Tom	23-45-98	IR£346.00	IR£123.00	
Collins, John	23-56-78	IR£234.00	IR£223.00	
Rodgers, Dick	34-66-33	IR£567.00	IR£125.00	
Lee, Mike	34-66-88	IR£123.00	IR£215.00	
Cutbert, Lara	34-455-66	IR£342.00	IR£225.00	
Sorenson, Lisa	43-55-66	IR£632.00	IR£125.00	
Burke, Tim	12-34-56	IR£123.00	IR£222.00	

- Insert a new Worksheet after "Ziccos4"; Name this new Worksheet: "Roget66"
- Paste whole worksheet: "Ziccos4" to "Roget66" - pasting should start at C12 - this means: click on C12, click the Paste icon - the copy will drop downwards from C12
- Fill Column A with Green. ReSave

Exercise 16: Addition & Subtraction

- Insert a new worksheet in the current Workbook - Name it "Savings77"
- Set up the Exercise below in Courier (10)- Save as "Conor MW"

BUDGET FOR JONES' FAMILY												
Conor O'Dowd: Monthly Income & Expenditure for Year Ended: 31 Decembere 2002												
	Jan	Feb	Mar	Apr	May	Jun	Jul	Aug	Sep	Oct	Nov	Dec
Pay Cheque	1500	1500	1500	1500	1500	1500	1500	1500	1500	1500	1500	1500
Expenses:												
Mortgage	600	600	600	600	600	600	600	600	600	600	600	600
Car Loan	350	350	350	350	350	350	350	350	350	350	350	350
Petrol	80	90	70	65	45	78	56	45	76	90	67	56
Telephone	90	85	45	55	67	87	66	44	44	56	66	66
ESB	55	67	65	45	55	76	33	77	77	77	65	65
Credit Card	120	130	140	120	120	200	130	140	120	130	130	130
Insurance	65	65	65	65	65	65	65	65	65	65	65	65
Total Expenses:												
Monthly Savings:												
Annual Savings:												

- Total Expenses: Jan; AutoFill to remaining months - Change Font Colour to Blue
- Calculate "Monthly Savings" for Jan by subtracting Expenses from Cheque amount - AutoFill to remaining months
- Calculate the "Annual Savings" by adding the Savings accumulated each month
- Edit the months to read in full, such as: "January" for "Jan" etc
- Underline and Centre all Headings. ReSave; Close Workbook

Exercise 17: Multiplication

- In a new Workbook, key in the exercise below; Format and Centre, as required:
- Fill the two Main Heading cells with Yellow. and Fill Column A with Green

Daily's Fresh Fruit			
Week Ending 31 May 1999			
Product	Units Sold	Cost per Unit	Total Cost
Plums	13	$2.00	
Apples	12	$1.50	
Pears	26	$3.00	
Damsons	19	$4.00	
Oranges	12	$1.75	
Kiwi	16	$2.50	
Peaches	18	$3.00	

- Save as: "Daily's Fruit MW"
- Set up the Multiplication formula in the cell below "Total Cost" for calculating the expenditure on Plums; Copy to remaining cells using AutoFill
- Name current Worksheet: "Fresh Fruit".   ReSave file

Formatting: Dates

The next exercise will involve **dates**. The computer's **internal clock** referred to earlier recognises dates as well as Months, Days of the Week, etc

Example:

- When you type in a date, for example: **12 March, '97** below - the internal clock recognises the entry as a **date format.**
- To verify this, select **Format Cells Number** from Menu (date entry is currently selected) - notice that Date is selected under **Category,** and a particular **Date Format** is selected under **Type:**

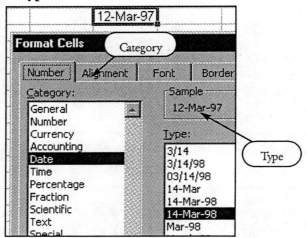

- To select another **Date Format,** make a selection under **Type**

Exercise 18: Multiplication

- Set up the Exercise on Wages:

WAGES RETURNS					
Week Ending: 27 April 2001					
Name	PRSI No	Date Hired	Total Hours	Hourly Rate	Gross Pay
Joe Staunton	123-456-789	23-Jun-98	40	IR£12	
Kit Donovan	324-567-876	12-Jul-97	30	IR£14	
Brid Lynch	435-678-767	25-Jul-98	25	IR£10	
Aine Curtin	765-678-987	4 Aug 199	40	IR£10	
Ber Barry	546-678-789	12-Feb-97	35	IR£10	
Dora Twomey	546-789-098	27-Oct-98	30	IR£12	
Luke Dale	876-567-890	25-Jul-97	35	IR£14	

- Align Headings; Format Dates in "Date Hired" Column
- Under "Gross Pay", set up Multiplication formula; AutoFill to other cells
- Name Sheet tab: "Wages"
- Save as: "Wages MW"
- Close File

Exercise 19: Multiplication

- Refer back to Exercise 10 - open file named "Antonio's Platters" or retype Ex 10

Item	Cost per Item	No of Items
Dessert Spoons	IR£2.50	60
Tea Spoons	IR£2.00	70
Napkins	IR£4.00	90
Sugar Bowls	IR£3.45	30
Knives	IR£5.00	90
Tablecloths	IR£25.00	45
Dinner Plates	IR£4.00	50
Soup Spoons	IR£3.00	65
Side Plates	IR£2.50	45
Saucers	IR£3.00	60
Cups	IR£2.00	30

- Insert a Column to the right of "No of Items"; Title Column: "Total Cost"
- Set up a multiplication formula for calculating the total cost of the items under the new Column.
- Save as: "Antonio's Expenditure". Close File

Exercise 20a: Multiplication

- In a new Workbook, set up the Exercise on Photographers' fees:

Day	Date	Customer	Description	Photographer	Hours	Fee per Hour	Total Cost
Crosbie's Photographic Studios							
Macroom Co. Cork							
Week beginning: 7 July 2001							
Sun	July 7, 2001	Rena Corcoran	Wedding	Kim Rice	7	£25.00	
		Harry Curtis	Graduation	Leo Brown	5	£35.00	
		Frank Pilmore	Confirmation	Ana Ball	8	£40.00	
		Alice Butler	Reunion	Fred Rice	4	£20.00	
		Dorry Cooke	Graduation	May West	3	£30.00	
		Billy Grant	Child's Birthday	Dan Mills	6	£35.00	
		Al Morris	Holy Communion	Eric Tobin	4	£40.00	
						Total Cost:	

- The Days and Dates can be filled using AutoFill - Fill these Columns with Blue
- The photographers' fees vary, so calculate individual fees under "Total Cost"
- Name the current Worksheet "Crosbie"; name Sheet 2 "Wilson"
- Copy whole worksheet: "Crosbie" to "Wilson" starting with cell E10
- Edit "Wilson" worksheet - he also has photographic studios but the address is: "Lee Valley Ovens Co Cork"
- Wilson employed the same phographers for the week commencing 14 July - Edit the dates accordingly; delete Columns on: "Customer" and "Description"
- Enter the hours worked for the same sequence of Photographers: 10, 12, 5, 6, 8, 10 and 12 - Enter these figures in Green Font
- Add an additional Photographer: Marie Welch - she was also employed by Wilson for 5 Hours on 16 July - her Hourly Fee was £40 - calculate the cost of her work
- Save Workbook as "Photos" and Close

Exercise 20b: Division

- Grandon Appliances re-stocked - input details of the overall cost of each appliance
- Calculate (using Division formula) in the Column entitled "cost per item" how much each item costs:

Grandon Appliances Entertainment Centre			
Appliance	Total Cost	No bought	Cost per Item
32" TV's	275	20	
Programmable VCR's	225	20	
Speakers	234	15	
CD Players	198	5	
Tape Decks	345	10	
Amplifiers	234	6	

- Format the "Total Cost" and "Cost per Item" Columns in £ currency with 2 decimal places
- Fill Column A & B with shading; change Font Colour of all numbers to green
- Name Worksheet "TVs"; Insert an additional Worksheet; name it "Speakers"
- Copy the first three Rows of "TVs" Worksheet to "Speakers" WorkSheet starting with cell A10. Save

Exercise 21: Division

- Calculate the cost of each individual item of Furniture in the Exercise below - create it in Arial Font (12)
- Key in all the figures in Font Colour Yellow and the Text in Font Colour: Green
- Format the "Total Cost" and "Cost per Piece" in Dollars, 2 Decimal places

Woodfield Furniture Company			
	Number	Total Cost	Cost per Piece
Chairs	400	IR£9,000	
Tables	340	IR£4,567	
Stools	550	IR£5,468	
Wardrobes	234	IR£2,345	
Dressing Tables	345	IR£6,890	

- Enclose each cell in a medium-sized Border
- Centre the Main Heading across the Worksheet
- Name the Worksheet Tab: "Furniture55"
- Insert a New Worksheet and Name it "Furniture99"
- Copy contents of "Furniture55" to "Furniture99" - start pasting from cell B12
- Save as "Furniture56"

Freezing Titles:

- To keep the contents of a **Row** or **Column** in view as you scroll, you must **freeze both horizontal** and **vertical titles**
- **Select** a Row below any rows you want to freeze or select a **Column to the right** of any columns you want to freeze
- Choose **Window Freeze Panes**: a **Horizontal Line** is created which indicates that all the rows **above** the line are frozen; a **Vertical** line indicates that all the columns to the **left** are frozen - see Example below

Note: To **remove** freezing, select **Window Unfreeze Panes** from Menu

Example: shows the freezing of Column A & Row 1:

	A	B	C	D	E	F
1	Street Levies	Jan	Feb	Mar	Apr	May
3	Patrick	1.95	1.95	1.95	1.95	1.95
4	Castle	1.3	To Freeze at this point: Click in B2			34

Select **Windows Freeze Panes** - Column A and Row 1 are frozen - indicated by Vertical/Horizontal lines

Page Breaks

- If you want to print a worksheet that is larger than one page, Microsoft Excel divides it into pages by inserting **automatic** page breaks based on the **paper size, margin** settings, and **scaling** options you have set

Horizontal/Vertical Page Breaks:

You can change which **rows** are printed on the page by inserting **horizontal** page breaks; you can insert **vertical** page breaks to change which **columns** are printed on the page

Manually Insert a Horizontal/Vertical Page Break in a Row:

Horizontal:
- Select Row, Select Insert Page Break:

Vertical:
To Manually Insert a Vertical Page Break in a Column:
- Select **Column**
- Select **Insert Page Break**: - a **Vertical line** is created to the **left** of the **selected Column**

Removing Page Breaks

- To **Remove one** Page Break: **Drag** on page break line until it is **outside** the **Print** area
- To Remove **all** Page Breaks: Choose **Reset All Page Breaks**

Print Preview

To access **Print Preview,** click the **Print Preview** icon:

..Preview screen opens:

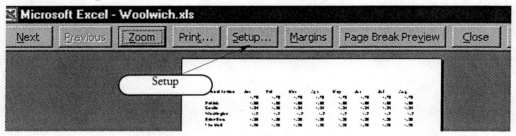

To change the way your worksheet prints - click the Setup button

..Page Setup Dialog box opens:

The Page Set Up Dialog Box has 4 Tabs:

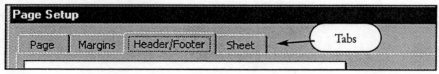

Choose from Tabs:

Page
Margins
Headers/Footers
Sheet Tabs

Page Tab:

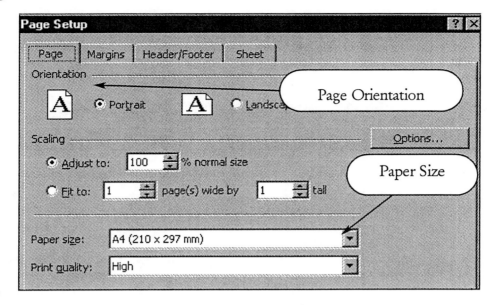

Orientation:

You can set the orientation of the worksheet to **Portrait** or **Landscape**:

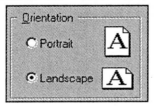

- The **default** Orientation is **Portrait**: data is printed **vertically** on page
- Choosing **Landscape** option will print worksheet **horizontally** on page

Paper Size:

- Worksheets can be printed on different **sizes**:

  To set **Paper Size** to **A4**:

- Click drop-down arrow and select **A4 Size**;   Click OK

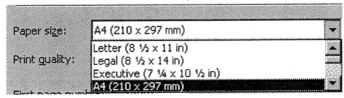

Changing Margins:

* Select the **Margins** tab to change:
  - **margins** settings
  - **centering** on page
  - **header/footer** positions

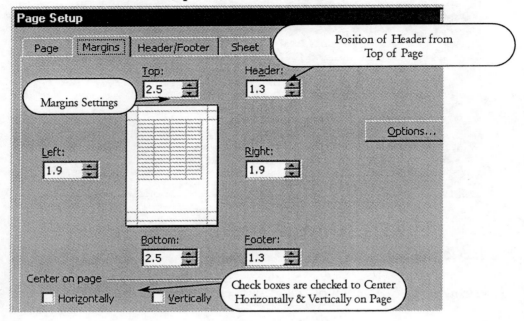

Change Margin Settings:

* Change **Top/Bottom/Left/Right** Margins to **1"**.
* Type in **1** in each of the settings boxes. Click **OK**
  (This setting will allow an **inch** of space between **data** and **edge** of paper in **4 place**s)

Centering document on Page

* To **centre** a document on the **length** of the page, select the option **Vertically**
* To **centre** a document on the **width** of the page, select the option **Horizontally**

Headers & Footers Tab

* To automatically **repeat text** -such as a **page number, worksheet title**, or **date**, you can add **headers** or **footers** to your **printed worksheet**
* **Headers** appear on the **top** of the page
* **Footers** appear on the **bottom** of the page
* You can use the **built-in** headers and footers in Excel or **create** your own

To Use a Built-in Header(Footer)

- Select **File Page Setup Headers/Footers** Tab
- Click the **drop-down arrow** under **Header(Footer)** to Choose a **built-in** Header:

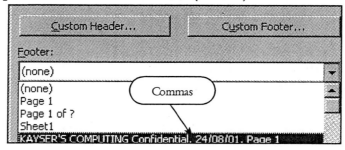

Note: commas indicate the part of the Header that will be displayed on the **left, centre** and **right**, respectively

- Delete "**Confidential**" and the **built-in Header** will then display like:

To create a new Header:

- Click **Custom Header** under **Header Footer Tab:**

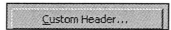

.. **Header Footer** dialog box opens:

Set up Header as follows:

- Click in the **Left** section and click **Date** icon to display **current date**
- Click in the **Centre** section, and type **Irish Society in the 21st Century**
- Click in the **Right** section and select the **Page** icon

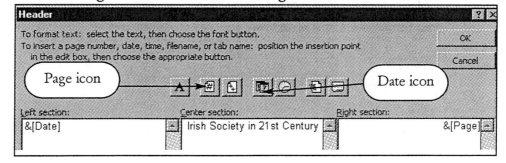

- This will result in the Header:

Sheet Tabs

- Select **Sheet** tab
- Select the relevant option button to:
    - turn **gridlines** on or off
    - print the **row** and **column headings**
    - **Black and white**
    - print a **draft** copy of your worksheet

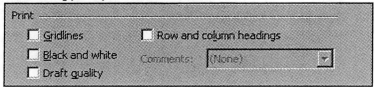

Printing:

Spreadsheets can be printed in **whole**, in **part**, with **values**, with **formulas**, with/without **borders**

- To **Print All Sheets** in Workbook, click **Print** icon on Toolbar

Print Defaults:

- To change the **print defaults** before printing, select **File Print** from Menu ..**Print Dialog** box opens:

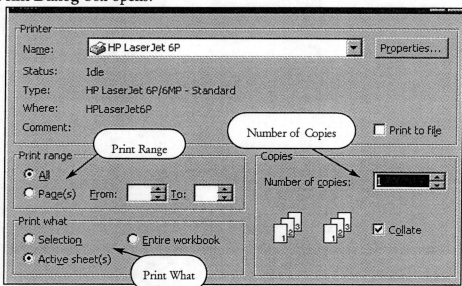

Make choices from:

- **Print Range:** *All* is default
- Select **Pages:**

    Key in **5** opposite **From** and **10** opposite **To** to Print the **Pages 5-10**

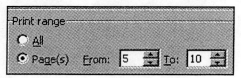

Print What

- Choose from:
    - **Selection** - this option will print any highlighted text only
    - **Active Sheet** - this option will print the worksheet currently displayed or open
    - **Entire workbook** - this option will print every sheet within the whole workbook

Copies

Number of Copies: Type in Number required - 1 is default

Print to File

- Use the **Print to File** option when Printing is to be carried out at a higher resolution (crisper image - better quality)
- Select **Print to File** option from dialog box: ☑ Print to file
- **Print to File** dialog box opens- type in file name, e.g. "Expenses"; click OK

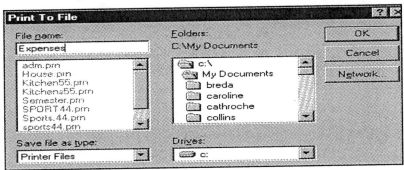

Wrap Text within a Cell:

- Displays multiple lines of text within a cell
- If Text is too big to be accommodated across the cell, you can **Wrap** the text around to the next line within the cell

Example:
- Select the cells you want to format

      Cost per Item
- On the **Format** menu, click **Cells**, and then click the **Alignment** tab.
- Under **Text control**, select the **Wrap text** check box.
- Under **Text Alignment**, we chose **Center** for both **Horizontal** and **Vertical** Alignment - see **Options** under drop-down arrow:

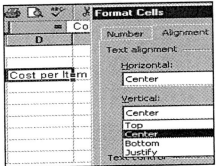

- Click OK - text **Wraps** around within cell:

Exercise 23:

- Set up the exercise below - a Projection for years: 2001-2004
- Main Heading is centered across Columns in Algerian Font (18)
- Sub Heading is centered across Columns in Algerian Font (12)
- Fill the Headings Row with Green and the %s in Yellow

PROJECTION OF BUSINESS CAPITAL							
TOWER CARD COMPANY							
Expenses	2001	% Inc for 2002	2002	% Inc for 2003	2003	% Inc for 2004	2004
Rent	30000	10%		10%		10%	
Rates	3000	12%		12%		12%	
Machinery	40000	13%		14%		14%	
Salaries	200000	16%		16%		16%	
Advertising	1200	12%		18%		18%	
Electricity	3400	13%		13%		13%	
Freight	3000	12%		10%		10%	

- The expenses for 2001 are given; calculate the projected expenses for future years using the predicted increases (multiplication formula required)
- Save as: "Tower Card"

- Set up a Header:

04/10/01	Tower Card Company

- Set up a Footer:

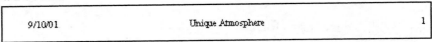

9/10/01	Unique Atmosphere	1

- Insert a Horizontal Page Break
- Paste a copy of the Projected Expenses to the next page; Save
- Centre both Horizontally & Vertically on the Page
- Preview Page and switch Orientation of Page to Landscape
- Print once on A4 paper
- Print to Print File also

Exercise 24:

Mr & Mrs Mitchell are planning 50th Wedding Anniversary celebrations. As facilities vary between venues, the number of guests they can invite will be determined by their choice of Hotel.

- Set up the analysis below to help them make their decision
- Enhance as suggested and use your own choice of Fonts

50th Wedding Anniversary for Monica and Dominic Mitchell				
25-Feb-01				
Costings for 4 Hotels — Varying Number of Guests				
	Hotels			
Menu	Maryboro	Wiltern	Bohemo	Licerne
Mussel Terrine	IR£6	IR£6	IR£8	IR£7
Homemade Soup	IR£4	IR£5	IR£4	IR£5
Roast Sirloin Beef	IR£20	IR£22	IR£25	IR£26
Grilled Salmon	IR£22	IR£23	IR£20	IR£22
Chocolate Marquis	IR£10	IR£12	IR£14	IR£13
Tea/Coffee	IR£3	IR£3	IR£3	IR£3
Cost per Person:				
	Maryboro	Wiltern	Bohemo	Licerne
Number of Guests:	50	100	150	200
Total Cost per Hotel:				

- Set up a Right-aligned Header:
    Congratulations are in order!
- Type in the Date of the Anniversary also at the left of the Header line

- Set up a Centered Footer:
    Golden Celebrations just for you!

- Name Worksheet: "Hotels"

- Insert a Vertical Page Break
- Paste a copy of the analysis to the next page

Modify:
- Add an additional Hotel: Montrose
- The number of Guests possible here is: 250 - the prices are the same as for the Maryboro except Salmon costs £25 - Calculate; Save
- Centre both Horizontally & Vertically on the Page
- Preview Page and switch Orientation of Page to Landscape
- Print once on A4 paper
- Print to Print File also

Statistics

Statistical Functions include:

- **COUNT**: This function determines the **number** of number entries in a list.
- **AVERAGE**: This function finds the **Average** of a list of Values. i.e. sum of the values divided by the number of values summed.
- **MAX**: This function searches a list of values and displays **largest** value in list.
- **MIN**: This function searches a list of values and displays **smallest** value in list.

An **example** of the four Statistical functions above based on the **Range: A1..E1** is shown below:

	A	B	C	D	E
1	456	654	678	456	655
2					
3	*Examples of Formulas:*		*Formula entered as:*		Range: A1..E1
4	Count Formula:		=COUNT(A1:E1)		
5	Average Formula:		=Average(A1:E1)		
6	Max Formula:		=Max(A1:E1)		
7	Min Formula:		=Min(A1:E1)		

Graphs

- To make Data instantly understandable, spreadsheets allow data to be displayed Graphically
- The more common types of graphs include: Bar, Line, Stacked Bar: and Pie.

Bar:
A bar graph represents the data points in series by bars of different heights.

Line:
A line graph shows the points of your data range or ranges plotted against the Y axis.

Stacked Bar:
A stacked bar graph places the values in each series on top of each other for any other point on the X axis. The total height of a bar this represents the total values in all the series plotted for any given point.

Pie:
A pie chart shows one range of values. It represents the percent each value is of the total by the size of the pie wedge assigned to that value.

XY:
An XY graph plots the values in one series against those in another.

Creating a Graph:

Creating a Graph from **consecutive** Rows

- Highlight data to be used - it is essential that 2 sets of Labels are included in Highlighting:

Items	Qty	Total Cost
Doors	89	623
Tables	76	532
Chairs	66	462
Wardrobes	84	588
Sofas	92	644

Labels

Note:
If Graph is to be based on data on **non-consecutive** rows, Holding down **Ctrl** key and releasing mouse button allows you to *skip* rows in selection

Items	Qty	Total Cost
Doors	89	623
Tables	76	532
Chairs	66	462
Wardrobes	84	588
Sofas	92	644

- Click on the **Graph icon** on the Toolbar:

..the Chart Wizard dialog box opens - select **Column**:

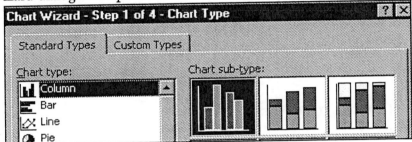

- Click **Next** to go to next Step: **Chart Source Data:**

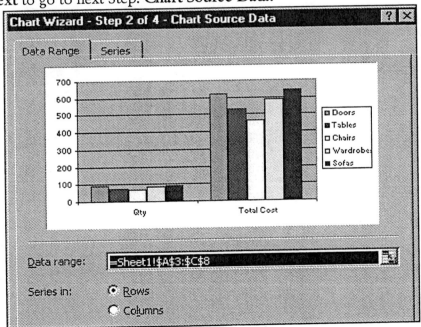

- Select Series in **Rows:**
- Click **Next** to go to next Step - **Chart Options:**

Chart Options:

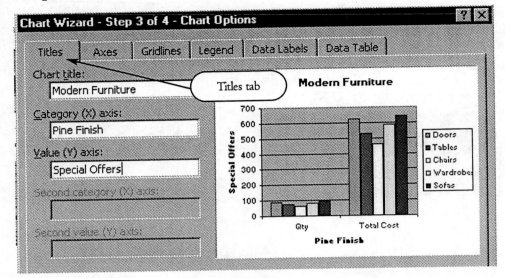

- Click **Titles** tab; key in:
- Chart **title:** "Modern Furniture" •
- Category **X Axis:** "Pine Finish" .
- Value **Y Axis:** "Special Offers"

- Click **Next** to go to last Step: **Chart Location** - accept suggestion - current worksheet - **Sheet 1**:

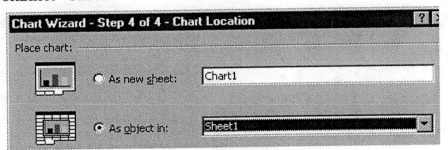

- Click **Finish:** Completed Column Chart displays:

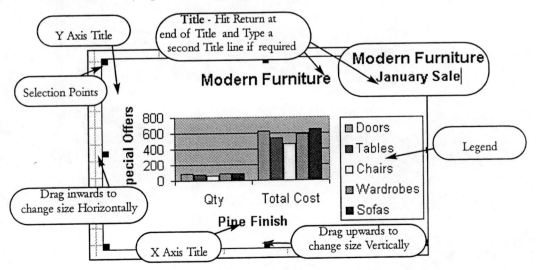

Moving Chart

- Select Chart by pointing and clicking - **8 Selection Points** display around edges
- Click anywhere on Chart - hold mouse button down and **Move** Chart as desired.

Resizing Chart

- Click on **Selection points** and adjust size as required

Add data labels to the chart

The chart **type** associated with the selected data series determines the type of **label** you can add.

To add data labels to a **data series**, click the data series, i.e. a group of related points plotted in a chart that originates from rows or columns on a single worksheet. Each data series in a chart has a unique **colour** or pattern.

To add a Data label to the data Series in the Chart above:

- Select the **related points** of the data series:

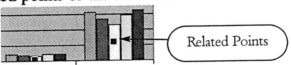

- On the **Format** menu, click **Selected Data Series**:

- Select **Data Labels** tab, select the **Show Label** option:

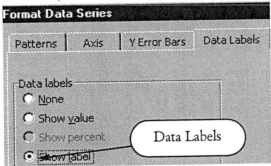

- Click **OK** - **Data Series** is shown with Labels:

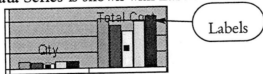

Change Graph type to Pie & show Percentages:

- Select **Chart**
- Select Chart from Menu, select **Chart Type:**

- Select **Pie:**

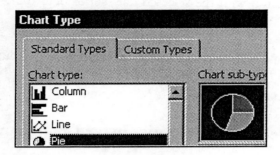

- Click **OK** - Chart has now changed to **Pie Type** on screen:

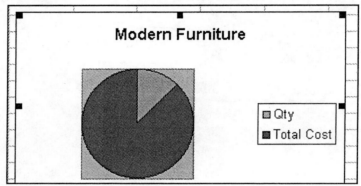

- Select **Chart** - Select **Chart Options** from Menu:

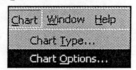

- Select **Data Labels, Show Percent** - Click **OK** - Pie displays applicable **Percentages:**

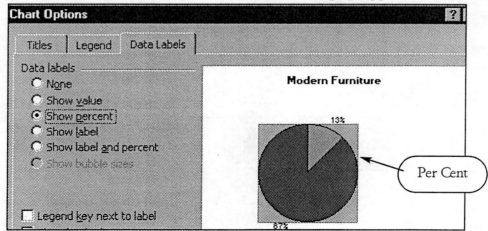

Change Colour in Bar of Chart

- Open **Column Chart** created above:

- Select **Bar** to be changed:

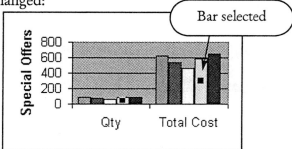

- Select **Format Data Series:**

- Select **Patterns**, select required **Colour**, for example: **Green:**

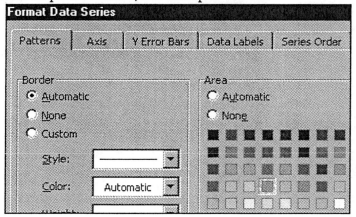

- Click **OK**
  ..selected Bar changes to selected Colour:

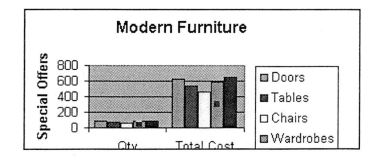

Exercise 25:

- In a new Workbook, set up the Analysis of Tests
- Calculate the Average, Max, Min and Count results in respective Columns

June Brophy's Result for 1st Year								
Dorcrest Comprehensive School								
Course	Test 1	Test 2	Test 3	Test 4	Average	Max	Min	Count
Irish	56	58	60	62				
English	67	65	63	61				
Maths	75	66	57	48				
Biology	55	59	63	67				
Economics	47	59	71	83				
Geography	65	60	55	50				
Business	58	62	66	70				

- Name Worksheet: "Results1"; Save as "Dorcrest MW"
- Name Sheet2, "Results2"; Copy contents of "Results1" to "Results2" Worksheet - start the Pasting from cell E12
- Edit "Results2" details - "Test 1" to "2001a" etc - see below:

2001a	2002a	2001b	2002b	2001c	2002c	2001d	2002d
56	60	58	56	60	64	62	60
67	55	65	75	63	51	61	71
75	75	66	57	57	57	48	39
55	60	59	58	63	68	67	66
47	63	59	55	71	87	83	79
65	58	60	62	55	48	50	52
58	59	62	65	66	67	70	73

- Recalculate formulas for Average, Max etc. Save

Exercise 26:

- Create a Bar Graph based on "Results1" details - exclude Statistics Columns
- Use "Dorcrest Comprehensive School" as Main Title and "June Brophy" as SubTitle
- Use "First Year" as X-Axis Title and "Co Limerick" as Y-Axis Title
- Make a copy of this Graph in "Results1" Worksheet; Change Bar Type to Pie
- Show Percentage Label on this Pie Chart
- Change colour of two slices of Pie to Green and Yellow

- Create Column Graph based on data from "Results2" Worksheet - Use Results up to 2002b inclusive; Subjects: Irish, English and Business only
  Note: Remember to include Labels at the top and side when selecting; hold down Control key as you select so that you can exclude rows of data
- Use "Graph for End of Year Report" as Main Title
- Use "2002 Inclusive" as X-Axis and use "Extra Tuition" as Y-Axis
- Add Data Labels to Graph
- Colour 2 Bars: Blue and Red
- Print Graph only - you must select Graph first before Print command in order to print the graph only - Save

Exercise 27:

- In a new Workbook, set up Forester's Return below
- Calculate Total Cost, Selling Price Total - from these two figures, calculate Profit:

Forester's Greengrocer							
Week Ending 31 March 2002							
Product	Unit	Number Sold	Cost per Item	Total Cost	Selling Price per Item	Selling Price Total	Profit
Apples	Each	48	IR£0.50		IR£0.60		
Pears	Each	56	IR£0.45		IR£0.55		
Bananas	Per Kilo	66	IR£1.34		IR£1.44		
Plums	Per Kilo	30	IR£2.34		IR£2.44		
Oranges	Each	50	IR£0.30		IR£0.40		
Nectarines	Each	34	IR£0.45		IR£0.55		
Avocados	Each	30	IR£0.35		IR£0.45		

- Set up 4 Columns beyond the Profit Column - entitle Columns: Average Profit, Max Profit, Min Profit, and No of Fruit Types (Count Formula)
- Set up Statistical Formulas in the new Columns - the range for calculations will include all the figures in the Profit Column
- Name current Worksheet: "Fruit"; name Sheet2 "Greens"
- Copy contents of "Fruit" Worksheet and Paste to "Greens" Worksheet starting Pasting at cell A20
- Sort Product Column into Ascending Order
- Make a Pie Chart using 1st 4 Columns - Colour a slice of the Pie Pink and another slice Light Orange; Include %s in Graph
- Print one copy of both Worksheets and close Workbook

Consolidation of all Excel features

The following **4 practice documents** are intended to revise all the Excel for Windows features introduced to date.

Practice 1:

John Murphy owns a small computer company - at the end of Q1 in 2002, he calculates his profit for the previous 3 months

1. Set up his income from computer related products and his outgoings from general expenses
2. Save under file name: "Enterprises MW"

John Murphy Computer Enterprises	Jan	Feb	Mar	Income from each source	Average Monthly Income
INCOME					
Hardware					
Computers	3220	4450	3450		
Monitors	2000	3000	2000		
Printers	500	600	500		
Disk Drives	750	800	750		
Total income from Hardware:					
Software					
Spreadsheets	350	450	300		
Word Processing	450	550	500		
Database	450	650	590		
Graphics	600	700	450		
Total Income from Software:					
Overall Income:					
EXPENDITURE					
Rent	2300	2300	2300		
Rates	1200	1200	1200		
Advertising	600	600	600		
Wages	700	700	700		
Electricity	260	260	260		
Total Expenditure:					
Net Income					
Total Expenditure:					

3. In the row flagged: Total Income from Hardware, set up a Formula to calculate funds generated by sales from Hardware for each month
4. In the row flagged: Total Income from Software, set up a Formula to calculate funds generated by sales from Software
5. In the row flagged: Overall Income, add the Total income from Hardware and Software for each month
6. In the row flagged: Total Expenditure, add the cost of the monthly expenses
7. In the row flagged: Net Income set up a formula to determine the profit when expenses have been allowed for
8. In the column: Income from each source, Total the individual income each quarter from the different categories of sales
9. Under the Column flagged, Average Monthly Income, calculate the average income for the quarter for each category
10. Insert a Row above Graphics, and input the income from CAD:
    CAD   200   400   650

11. Adjust Formula range, if necessary, so that CAD income is included in all relevant calculations above
12. Format whole Spreadsheet to £ Currency, 2 Decimal places Name this Worksheet tab: Murphy
13. Insert a new Worksheet before Murphy's Worksheet, and name this Worksheet: "Computers"

14. Copy the contents of the Murphy's worksheet to the Computers Worksheet
15. Switch to Murphy's worksheet; make a Bar Graph from the Rows: Computers, Printers and Disk Drives for the months: Jan - Mar (Remember to hold down Control when excluding rows from graph)
16. Colour the bars of the Graph to: Green, Yellow and Red
17. Create a Pie Graph on the Computers Worksheet - base this graph on data from Rent, Advertising and Electricity (Remember to include the months: Jan-Mar when selecting data for Graph); Show Data Labels in Graph
18. Colour slices of Pie to: Orange, Pink and Turquoise; show percentages in Graph
19. Sort on Expenditure Column
20. Print to file named: Computer Enterprises.prn; Save and close Workbook

Practice 2:

Barry Long owns a furniture company. He wants you to set up a spreadsheet which will detail buying price and selling price of furniture. He wants to calculate the Total cost of Buying, Selling and Profit per Item. He will also require the Average Selling Price.

1. Create the following spreadsheet::

Code	Furniture Item	Qty Bought	Cost Price per Item	Total Cost Price per Item	Selling Price per Item	Total Selling Price per Item	Profit on each Item
GH6789	Tables	56	£80		£90		
KL9087	Chairs	60	£45		£60		
LO987	Cabinets	80	£56		£74		
MI0987	Dressers	79	£120		£145		
HY789	Hall Tables	56	£78		£90		
HY789	Telephone Tables	80	£60		£85		

2. Calculate the "Total Cost Price per Item" starting with the "Tables" and copying to remaining items
3. Calculate the "Total Selling Price per Item" starting with the "Tables" and copying to remaining items
4. Calculate the "Profit on each Item" starting with the "Tables" and copying to remaining items
5. Insert a Column on the right; entitle this Column: "Average Selling Price of Items"
6. Create an Average formula opposite "Tables" based on "Total Selling Price per Item"
7. Copy to remaining cells
8. Create a Bar Graph based on "Tables" and "Telephone Tables" and "Qty Bought"; the title for the Graph is to be: "Wilson's Furniture Range"
9. Include Data Labels in Graph
10. Change Bar Colours to: Green and Yellow
11. Name this Worksheet: "Furniture"; Create a new Worksheet and name it: "Furniture 56"
12. Copy all the data as well as the Graph to the "Furniture 56" Worksheet; change Graph Type to Pie
13. Change colours of Pie to: Red and Orange; include Percentages
14. Save; Print to File using Print file name: "Furniture.prn"
15. Close Worksheet.

Practice 3:

The Treasurer of Dromgina Sports Club wants to analyse the income from the various sporting activities for the first 4 quarters of 2001. The Committee are also interested in finding the average income for each sport during the year and to display graphically.

Sports Revenue					
2001	Q1	Q2	Q3	Q4	Average
Athletics	120	330	420	235	
Hurling	230	430	530	453	
Football	540	640	440	345	
Soccer	654	854	638	456	
Total					

1. Create the following spreadsheet:
2. Total the Q1 Column and copy to other Columns
3. Find the Average income from each sport entering the formula in the relevant cells
4. Add a Border around the whole table and between each cell excluding heading
5. Format all figures to 2 decimal places except Total line which is to be formatted to £ currency
6. Add a header in the left corner: "Sporting Returns"
7. Add a footer in the right corner: "Christy Ring"
8. Name Worksheet tab "Activity"
9. Open a second worksheet and name it "Sport"
10. Copy all data from the "Activity" worksheet to the "Sport" Worksheet
11. Add a new Row: fill in the detail as follows:

Basketball	130	430	390	330

12. Copy the Average formula to the Basketball Row
13. Print one copy of the "Activity" Worksheet to a Print file under file name "Sports44.prn"
14. Edit the income shown for "Soccer" in the "Sport" Worksheet - this should read:

Soccer	660	890	654	466

15. Create a Bar Chart in the "Activity" worksheet based on the Quarterly Income from : "Athletics", "Football" and "Soccer"
16. Add "Fitness for Tomorrow" as the title
17. Modify colours of bar chart to yellow, green, blue
18. Copy bar chart from the first worksheet to the second
19. Change Chart type in the "Sport" Worksheet to Pie - change one segment colour to Pink
20. Change Font Colour for all Sports to Yellow in "Activity" Worksheet
21. Save and Close Worksheet
22. Open spreadsheet again and Centre Main Heading across the four Columns - change font to: Times New Roman (20)
23. ReSave and close

Practice 4:

The Managing Director of Maher's Electrical Company wants the company's records updated to include the detail in the following worksheet:

Electrical Goods Sales	Jan	Feb	Mar	Average
Microwave	5345	6433	6422	
Hob	6544	4432	3563	
Iron	4356	4643	5453	
Dishwasher	2345	4732	5455	
Total	18590	20240	20893	

1. Key in the data above
2. Total the Jan Column - copy to other months
3. Format cells: B4..D7 to thousand marker with one decimal place
4. Find Average of columns - enter formula and copy to relevant cells
5. Add a Border around the outer edge of the table
6. Format Total Column to $ Currency with 2 decimal places
7. Add a centered header: "Kitchen affairs"
8. Add a footer in the left corner: "Domestic issues"
9. Name Worksheet tab "Electrical"
10. Open a second worksheet and name it "Utensils"
11. Key in "Kitchen matters" in Row 1 in the "Utensils" Worksheet thereby replacing the original heading
12. Copy all data from the "Electrical" worksheet to the "Utensils" Worksheet
13. Print one copy to a Print file under file name "Kitchens55.prn"
14. Create a Pie Chart in the "Electrical" worksheet from the data detail relating to: "Microwave", "Hob" and "Dishwasher" - exclude Average result from Graph
15. Add percentage labels to chart
16. Add "Labour-saving devices" as the title
17. Modify segment colours of pie chart to yellow, green and blue
18. Copy pie chart from the first worksheet to the second
19. Save and close Worksheet
20. Open Worksheet again and italicise as well as change the Font (Arial - 16) of the main heading in the "Utensils" Worksheet; fill this Row with Green also:
21. Save Spreadsheet "Province" in a template file format to a disk and close.

Microsoft Access 2000

Databases

A database is a collection of integrated data that share common characteristics Data is anything you want stored for future frequent referral. Data within Access - the database application within the Microsoft Office suite - can be text, numbers, memos, OLE objects etc

Getting Started with Microsoft Access

- **Turn on** computer: Our example: Windows98 is loaded into memory; Desktop appears:

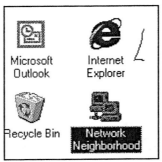

Loading Microsoft Access

- **Start** Access by clicking on the **Start Menu, Programs** and selecting **Microsoft Access:**

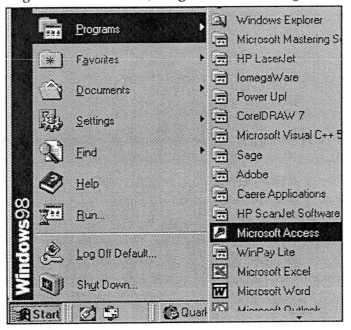

- ..the Microsoft Access Dialog Box opens (this dialog box displays once only - immediately after you turned Access on) giving you a choice of ways of creating a New Database using a Blank Database or a Database Wizard or Opening an Existing Database:

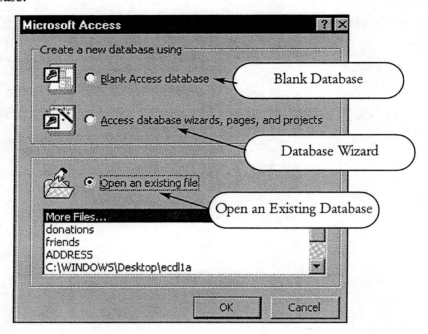

Creating a New Database:

- Cancel the Opening Screen by clicking on **Cancel** button
- Click **New** icon on Toolbar:

- ..**New** dialog box opens; click on **Database** icon; click **OK**:

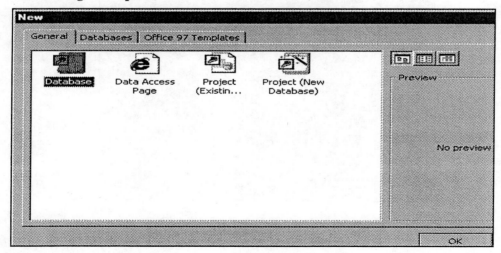

..**File New Database** dialog box opens:

- Create a **folder**, for example: **Access Exercises**
- Key in an appropriate file name, for example: **Practice1:**

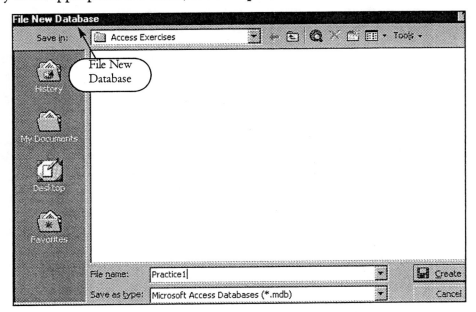

- Click **Create** - a new dialog box entitled with your chosen database name: **Practice1:** Database opens:
- Tabs for: **Tables, Queries, Forms, Reports**, etc are displayed:

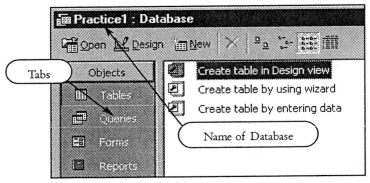

- In practice (in the workplace), one database is opened for related Tables, Forms etc

Example: Roche's Superstore has many departments: One **Database** is created called "Roche's Superstore'
- One **Table** has been created for each Department within Roche's database:

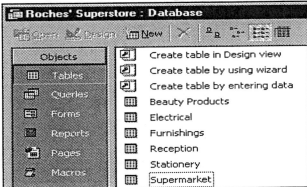

- You can compare a database to the **drawer** of a Filing Cabinet - the **tables** represent the **files** in the drawer - each **separate** but **enclosed** in the same drawer

Tables

- A Table is a **collection** of **related data** (about the same subject), made up of **Rows** and **Columns.**
- This is a typical example of a Table - a "Customers" table - consisting of Columns & Rows made up of related data:

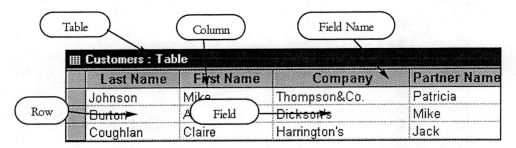

- The term "**Table**" describes the collection as a whole, made up of **Rows** across and **Columns** down
- "**Field names**" describe the contents of each **column**
- Each **row** contains a "**Record**" - A record is a set of information about the same item Each record is made up of individual "**Fields**"
- A "Field" is an **element** of a table that contains a specific piece of information

Creating Tables in Design view

We need a **Table** to hold our **Employees details**. The Design of the Table must be set up before **employee data** is inputted

- Have the "**Practice1**" database open on the screen:

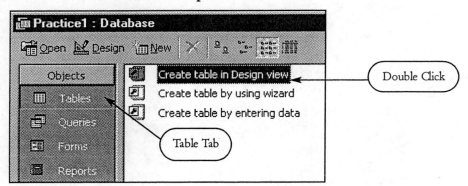

- Select **Tables tab**, and then double click **Create table in Design View** - a **blank** Table Design box entitled **Table1** - a Table, consisting of **3 Columns** entitled: **Field Name, Data Type** and **Description** opens:

Field Name	Data Type	Description

Designing the Fields in Tables

The Design of the Table in Design View involves:
- The keying in of appropriate **Field Names** for each field in the Table
- The selection of **Data Types**, and
- The keying in of **Descriptions** (optional)

Setting up Field Names:

- Click in the cell below the Column entitled Field Name and type the **Field Name**

Data Types:

- The **characteristics** of a field that controls what **kind** of data a field will hold
- Fields set to Text or Memo data type will allow the field to store **either** text or numbers
- A Field set to Number data type will accept **only** numbers
- The numerical data of a number field can be used in **calculations**
- The **Currency** data type will accept numeric values only - the currency symbol, as such, is not typed directly into cell - the **default** currency of the **computer system** is automatically applied to each **number** provided the data type is set to **currency**

Choosing a Data Type:

- Select an appropriate **Data Type** from the drop-down menu in the **Data Type** Column:

Table2 : Table		
Field Name	Data Type	Description
	Text	
	Memo	Properties
	Number	
	Date/Time	
General Lookup	Currency	
	AutoNumber	
	Yes/No	
	OLE Object	
	Hyperlink	The data typ
	Lookup Wizard...	the kind of

Description

- Text giving further **information** about the field can be keyed in the Description Column (this is optional)

Example of Description keyed in **Design View:**

Field Name	Data Type	Description
Employee No	Number	Numbers used must be in the 900's

- Description content displays in Datasheet View when relevant field name is current:

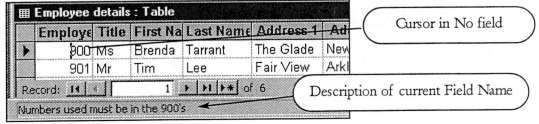

Designing "Employee Details" Table:

- Key in the **Field names** and choose the applicable **Data Type** for each of the 9 required **Field Names** - let the **Description** Column blank

Field Name	Data Type	Description
Employee No	Number	
Title	Text	
First Name	Text	
Last Name	Text	
Address 1	Text	
Address 2	Text	
Address 3	Text	
Department	Text	
Date of Birth	Date/Time	

> **Primary** key is one or more fields whose value or values uniquely identify each record in a table

> An **Index** key speeds up searching and sorting in a table based on key values and can force uniqueness on the rows in a table. The primary key of a table is automatically indexed

Primary key

The field **Employee No** is an ideal primary key field - each employee has a **unique** Employee No, i.e. no two employees will have the same No

- Select Employee No field name for the Primary key by selecting the **Row selector** for the desired field:

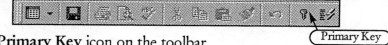

- Click the **Primary Key** icon on the toolbar
- ..the **Employee No** Field Name will be flagged with a **Key** symbol:

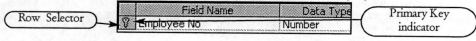

Selecting an Index Field:

- Select the field that you want to create an **index** for, e.g. "Date of Birth"
- In the **lower portion** of window on the **General** tab, click in **Indexed** property box, and click **Yes (Duplicates OK)** or as in our example: **Yes (No Duplicates)**: ensures that no two records have same data in this field.

Saving the Table Design

- **Save** the table design by clicking the **Save** icon on the toolbar:

- **Type** "Employee Details" as the **name** for the table in the Save As dialog box:

- Click **OK**.

Views

- The structure for each Table is set up in **Design View** - data is inputted into the Table in **Datasheet View**
- The **View icons** for **Design** and **Datasheet** look like:

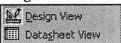

- Practice switching from **one View** to the other by clicking on **either** Design or Datasheet icons

Datasheet View:

The records will be keyed in **Datasheet View**:

- Click the **Datasheet View icon** on Toolbar and the Table opens in Datasheet View
- Datasheet View displays a screen similar to a spreadsheet in a **Row/Column format** with the **Field Names** displayed horizontally - **each Row** of data will represent a **record** of the table:

Employe	Title	First Na	Last Name	Address 1	Address 2	Address 3	Depa

Employee details : Table

Add data to Table

- **Key in** the following data under relevant field names
- Press **TAB key** to move from **field to field** and to move from the end of **one record** to the start of **another**

Employe	Title	First Na	Last Name	Address 1	Address 2	Address 3	Departme	Date of Birth
900	Ms	Brenda	Tarrant	The Glade	Newmarket	Co Cork	Accounts	12/03/74
901	Mr	Tim	Lee	Fair View	Arklow	Co Wicklow	Personnel	28/07/70
902	Ms	Sandra	Higgins	Sea Crest	Ennis	Co Clare	PR	19/03/78
903	Mr	Fred	Hawe	The View	Cashel	Co Tipp	Marketing	30/04/80
904	Ms	Sue	Rice	Ivy Leaf	Shannon	Co Clare	Accounts	12/04/80
905	Mr	Jack	Lane	My Way	Gort	Co Galway	Sales	23/07/81

- When you move from the end of one record to the beginning of another - the Table **automatically saves**

Editing Records

If the details of a field need to be changed, **Edit** as you would in a word processing package:

- **Move** the cursor to the relevant field:
- **Delete** with Backspace key, if necessary
- Type in **New Data**, if required

- **Run** by clicking on the **Run** icon - any record relating to the specified criteria: "Accounts" will display:

Employe	Title	First Na	Last Name	Address 1	Address 2	Address 3	Departme
900	Ms	Breeda	Tarrant	The Glade	Newmarket	Co Cork	Accounts
904	Ms	Sue	Rice	Ivy Leaf	Shannon	Co Clare	Accounts
907	Mr	Jim	Stewart	The Mill	Tralee	Co Kerry	Accounts

- **Save** as "Employees in Accounts":

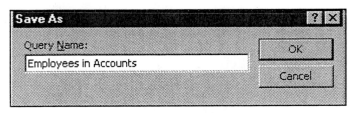

Finding Fields meeting one Criteria OR the other:

- Our example, we will find the fields: Department = "Accounts" entered in the **Criteria** Row OR "PR" entered in the **or** Row - this will produce a result if **either** criteria is met

Field:	Address 2	Address 3	Department
Table:	Employee details	Employee details	Employee details
Sort:			
Show:	☑	☑	☑
Criteria:			"Accounts"
or:			"PR"

- Click **Run** and the Record meeting both criteria display:

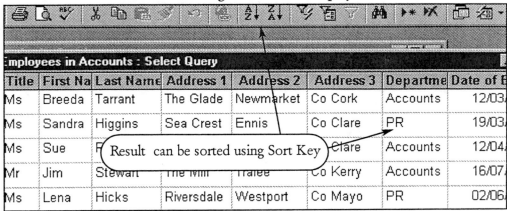

Title	First Na	Last Name	Address 1	Address 2	Address 3	Departme	Date of E
Ms	Breeda	Tarrant	The Glade	Newmarket	Co Cork	Accounts	12/03,
Ms	Sandra	Higgins	Sea Crest	Ennis	Co Clare	PR	19/03,
Ms	Sue				Clare	Accounts	12/04,
Mr	Jim	Stewart	The Mill	Tralee	Co Kerry	Accounts	16/07,
Ms	Lena	Hicks	Riversdale	Westport	Co Mayo	PR	02/06,

Result can be sorted using Sort Key

Sorting Records - Datasheet View

- With **cursor** in Column to be sorted, click on **Sort** icon
- **Sorted** records look like:

Address 3	Departme
Co Mayo	PR
Co Clare	PR
Co Kerry	Accounts
Co Clare	Accounts
Co Cork	Accounts

Sorting in Query Design View

- Records in Queries can also be sorted in **Query Design** View - click in **Sort Row** under the relevant **Field Name;** choose from **Ascending** or **Descending** - Records will display as requested when the query is **Run:**

Field:	Address 2	Address 3	Department
Table:	Employee details	Employee details	Employee details
Sort:			
Show:	☑	☑	Ascending
Criteria:			Descending
or:			(not sorted)

- **Save** as "Accounts or PR employees"

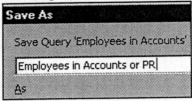

Finding Records that meet BOTH criteria:

- Our example, we will find the records that meet both criteria:

  Sex = "M" and **Employed from Year:** >1996

- both criteria entered in the Criteria Row - this will produce a result **only** if **both** criteria are met::

Field:	Present	Sex	Employed from Year
Table:	Employee details	Employee details	Employee details
Sort:			
Show:	☑	☑	☑
Criteria:		"M"	>1996

- Only **one** record meets both criteria:

Employe	Title	First Na	Last Name	Departme	Date of Birt	Present	Sex	Employ
903	Mr	Fred	Hawe	Marketing	30/04/80	☑	M	1997

- **Save** as below:

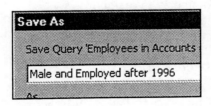

Finding records that meet the Yes/No (also known as Logical) field "Yes"

- **Logical** fields when set up initially in a Table can be entered as either "Y" or "N" - however when using a Logical field in a **Query criteria,** "Y" must be entered as "**Yes**" and "N" as "**No**"
- **Inverted commas** are automatically added to **Text** criteria e.g. "**Accounts**" but Logical criteria displays **without** inverted commas - **Yes**

To find records of employees "Present", enter the Logical data as:

Field:	Date of Birth	Present
Table:	Employee details	Employee details
Sort:		
Show:	☑	☑
Criteria:		Yes

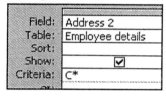

Yes entered here

- **Run** the query - the result is:

Date of Birt	Present
12/03/74	☑
19/03/78	☑
30/04/80	☑
12/04/81	☑
16/07/78	☑

Wildcards

Using Wildcards - an **asterisk** "*" can be used to represent any data in different positions

- To find Employees with "Address 2" starting with C with different endings: use C* - asterisk can be substituted for anything:
- Under the appropriate Field name, enter: C*:

Field:	Address 2
Table:	Employee details
Sort:	
Show:	☑
Criteria:	C*

- **Run** to get the result::

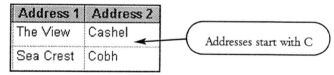

Address 1	Address 2
The View	Cashel
Sea Crest	Cobh

Addresses start with C

..**both** addresses start with "C".

Another example of a Wildcard:

Find **Last Names** starting with "H" with Misc endings:

- Set up **Criteria** as:

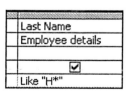

Last Name
Employee details
☑
Like "H*"

- **Run** to get the result: - all **Last Names** start with "H":

Employe	Title	First Na	Last Name
902	Ms	Sandra	Higgins
903	Mr	Fred	Hawe
908	Ms	Lena	Hicks

Other Wildcard Examples:

To find Records where "Address2" contains "l": use *l* - asterisk can be substituted for letters before and after the "l":

Address 1
Employee details
☑
Like "*l*"

- **Run** to get the result:

Last Name	Address 1
Tarrant	The Glade
Rice	Ivy Leaf
Stewart	The Mill
Hicks	Riversdale

- .. all the Address1 records above contain the letter **"l"**

Show Row:

Change the Query to **exclude** certain Field Names by **deselecting** the **Check Box** in the **Show** Row

- **Deselect** (by clicking) **check boxes** for: **Department** and **Date of Birth** fields:
- Switch to **Design View**
- In the **Show** Row, under the relevant **Field Name**, deselect check Box to **remove** Check Mark for the Fields that you **don't** want to display:

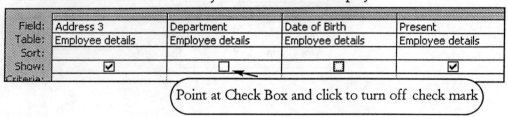

Field:	Address 3	Department	Date of Birth	Present
Table:	Employee details	Employee details	Employee details	Employee details
Sort:				
Show:	☑	☐	☐	☑
Criteria:				

Point at Check Box and click to turn off check mark

- Click **Run** - display excludes deselected Field Names

Exercise 5a
- Create a Query based on the Table: "Books", created above - use all Field Names and Save as "Book List"

Exercise 5b
- Create a Query on the Table: "Books" again, but base Query on the Fields: Publisher, Author and Title of Book only
- Save as "Book Deals"

Exercise 5c
- Using Books Table, create a Query
- Set up the Criteria: Year of Publication = 1998
- Save as: "1998 Books"

Exercise 5d
- Using Books Table, create a Query
- Set up the Criteria: Cost: >13 under "Cost"
- Save as: "Books over $14"

Exercise 5e   OR
- Using Books Table, create a Query
- Use both the Criteria: "Publisher" = Beacon Press OR "Number of Pages": >400
- Sort on Number
- Save as: "Great Buys!"

Exercise 5f   AND
- Using Books Table, create a Query
- Use both the Criteria: "Year of Publication" = 1997 AND Cost = $12.99
- Sort on Cost
- Save as: "Reads of the Day"

Exercise 5g   Wildcard
- Using Books Table, create a Query
- Use all Fields - Base the Query on the Wildcard: T* set up under "Title of Book"
- Sort on Title of Book
- Save as: "Publisher's Delight"

Exercise 5h   Wildcard
- Using Books Table, create a Query
- Use all Fields - Base the Query on the Wildcards: *B* set up under "Author"
- Sort on Title of Book: Ascending Order
- Save as: "First Editions"

Exercise 6a
- Create a Query based on the Table: "Customers", created above - use all Field Names and Save as "Customers 2000"

Exercise 6b
- Create a Query on the Table: "Customers" again, but base Query on the Fields: Last Name, Company Name and Member of Association only
- Save as "Exclusive"

Exercise 6c
- Using Customers Table, create a Query
- Set up the Criteria: Year of Birth >1970
- Save as: "Young Entrepreneurs"

Exercise 6d
- Using Customers Table, create a Query
- Set up the Criteria: Member of Association = Yes
- Save as: "Members Only"

Exercise 6e   OR
- Using Customers Table, create a Query
- Use both the Criteria: "Date of Affiliation" > 1st June 1998 OR Member of Association = No
- Sort on Last Name
- Save as: "Golden Customers"

Exercise 6f   AND
- Using Customers Table, create a Query
- Use both the Criteria: "Partner's Name" = John AND Year of Birth = 1973
- Sort on Company in Descending Order
- Save as: "Star Customer"

Exercise 6g   Wildcard
- Using Customers Table, create a Query
- Use all Fields - Base the Query on the Wildcard: L* set up under "Company Name"
- Sort on Last Name: Ascending Order
- Save as: "Loyal Customers"

Exercise 6h   Wildcard
- Using Customers Table, create a Query
- Use all Fields - Base the Query on the Wildcards: *o* set up under "Last Name"
- Sort on Date of Birth: Ascending Order
- Save as: "Exceptional Sales"

Exercise 7a
- Create a Query based on the Table: "Social33", created above - use all Field Names and Save as "Social Circuit"

Exercise 7b
- Create a Query on the Table: "Social33" again, but base Query on the Fields: Name/Address & Amount only
- Save as "Good Contacts"

Exercise 7c
- Using Social33 Table, create a Query
- Set up the Criteria: Type of Entertainment = Lunch
- Save as: "People that Lunch"

Exercise 7d
- Using Customers Table, create a Query
- Set up the Criteria: Amount: <60
- Save as: "Cost Effective"

Exercise 7e   OR
- Using Social33 Table, create a Query
- Use both the Criteria: "Date" <1 March 1997 OR Type of Entertainment = Lunch
- Sort on Amount
- Save as: "Sustaining Food"

Exercise 7f   AND
- Using Social33 Table, create a Query
- Use both the Criteria: "Date" = 15/6/97 AND Business Purpose = Annual Review
- Sort on Date in Descending Order
- Save as: "Business"

Exercise 7g   Wildcard
- Using Social33 Table, create a Query
- Use the Fields: Date, Type of Entertainment and Amount only - Base the Query on the Wildcard: *C* set up under "Company Name"
- Save as: "Entertainment"

Exercise 7h   Show
- Using Social33 Table, create a Query
- Use all Fields but don't Show Fields: Date and Amount when you run the Query
- Save as: "Drink Reception"

Exercise 8a
- Create a Query based on the Table: "Golfers", created above - use all Field Names and Save as "Golfers"

Exercise 8b
- Create a Query on the Table: "Golfers" again, but base Query on the Fields: Member's Number, Member's Name and Member Since
- Save as "Talented Youth"

Exercise 8c
- Using Golfers Table, create a Query
- Set up the Criteria: Member Since >01/06/1998
- Save as: "Very Keen Golfer"

Exercise 8d
- Using Golfers Table, create a Query
- Set up the Criteria: Last Competition >= = Yes
- Save as: "Members Only"

Exercise 8e   OR
- Using Golfers Table, create a Query
- Use both the Criteria: "Last Competition Played" >1st August 2001 OR "Type of Membership" = 2
- Sort on Type of Member
- Save as: "High Handicappers"

Exercise 8f   AND
- Using Golfers Table, create a Query
- Use both the Criteria: "Type of Member" = 1 AND Second Line of Address = "Dungourney"
- Sort on Member Number
- Save as: "Dungourney"

Exercise 8g   Wildcard
- Using Golfers Table, create a Query
- Use all Fields - Base the Query on the Wildcard: M* set up under "Member's Name"
- Save as: "Early Birds"

Exercise 8h   Wildcard
- Using Golfers Table, create a Query
- Use all Fields - Base the Query on the Wildcards: *W* set up under "Member's Name"
- Save as: "Eastern Allegiance"

Forms

Forms are based on Tables. Most data entry is done in forms because appropriate designed forms facilitate data entry and guarantee data validity.

Creating a Form

- Select **Forms New**

- ..**New Form** dialog box opens, select **AutoForm Columnar** (because this provides facility for setting up Header & Footer in Design View):

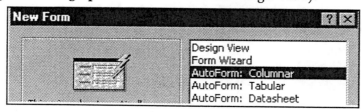

- Select **Table** on which your Form is to be based - **Employees details:**

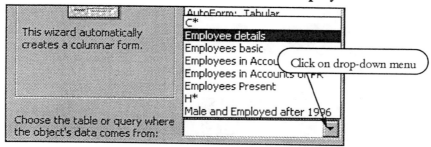

- Click **OK:**

- .. Form opens in **Design View** displaying Record 1:

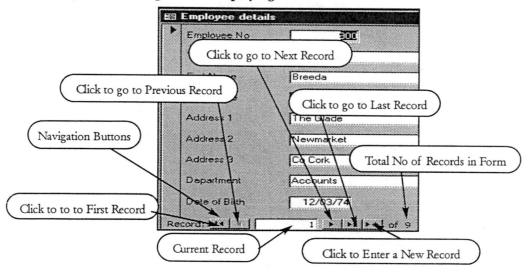

Add the following records in Form View

- Click Navigation Button: **New Record** for each Record before you key in:

909	Mr	Mark	Foley	Leeside	Midleton	Co Cork	Rentals	12 March 1970	Yes	M	1990
910	Ms	Rena	Dixon	Riversedge	Gort	Co Galway	Sales	23 June 1972	No	F	1995
911	Mr	Mike	Roche	Pea Green	Schull	Co Cork	Sales	28 May 1969	Yes	M	1988

Sort Records in Form View

- We will sort in **Descending Order** on the **Last Name**
- In **Form View**, Click in **Last Name**; click **Sorting** icon:

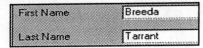

- ..the records are sorted in **reverse order** based on the **Last Name** field:

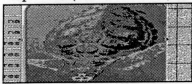

First Name   Breeda

Last Name   Tarrant

Adding a Picture to a Form in Design View

- Switch to **Form Design** View, select **Insert Picture** from Menu:
- **Insert Picture** dialog box opens; select **folder** containing picture
- Click **OK** - selected picture (ours is a Turtle) is inserted into Design View of Form:

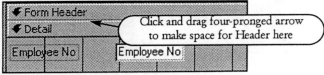

- **Move** picture by **selecting, & clicking** (a full hand displays) & **dragging** to location
- Picture can **resized** as the Picture within Word was resized - by selecting selection points and dragging in the desired direction.

Adding a Header & Footer to a Form

- Switch to **Design View** of Form:

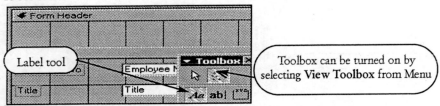

Form Header
Detail
Employee No   Employee No

Click and drag four-pronged arrow to make space for Header here

- ..it will then look like:

Form Header

Label tool

Toolbox

Employee N

Title   Title

Toolbox can be turned on by selecting **View Toolbox** from Menu

- In **Header** section, draw a box using the **Label Tool**; key in **Header**:

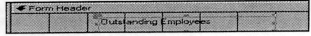

Form Header

Outstanding Employees

Inserting a Footer in Form Design View:

- Switch to **Footer** section - it is based down at the bottom of **Design View** screen
- Using the **label** tool as before, draw a **box** and type the **footer**:

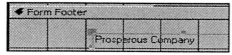

Changing Design of Form

- In **Form Design View**, select **Format AutoFormat** from Menu:

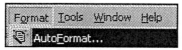

- - **AutoFormat** dialog box opens:

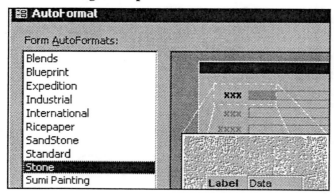

- Select from the range of **Formats**, for example: **Stone**, click **OK**
  ..new Design is applied to **each** record in the current Form - switch for **Form View** to see the effect:

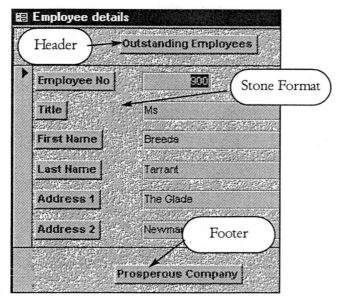

- **Save** Form as:

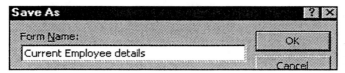

Reports

A report is an effective way of presenting data in a **printed format**. You have control over its **size** and **appearance** and you can display the information the way you want to see it. You can create reports using **AutoReport** icon or **Report Wizard**.

Create a Report using Report Wizard

- Select **Reports New, Report Wizard**, select **Employee Details** as **Table**, click **OK**

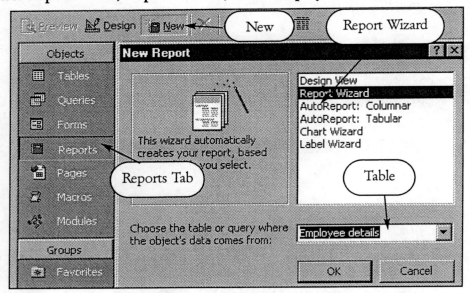

..a **new** screen opens asking you to select **fields** required for **Report**:

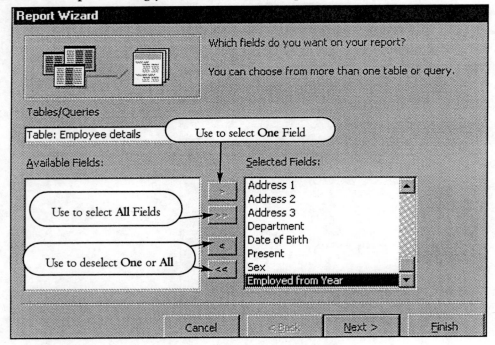

..our example: select **all** fields

- Click **Next twice** (as we are not interested at the moment in the **Grouping** Option):

- **Sorting Screen** opens, select **Sex** for Sorting purposes:

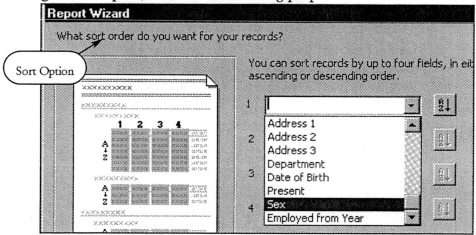

- Click **Next twice** - we don't want to modify either the default **Layout** or **Style**
- Set up the **Title**:

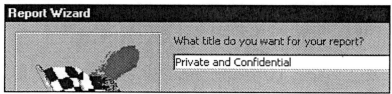

- Click **Finish**..

..Report opens in **PreView**:

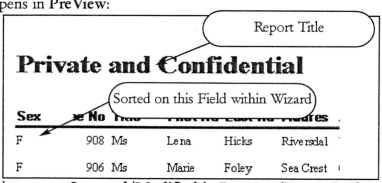

Note: Pictures are **Inserted/Modified** in **Reports** (Report Design View) as Pictures are Inserted/Modified in **Forms** -

Exercise 9

- Create a form based on the "Books" Table above
- Add the following records in Form View:
- Sort on "Publisher"

Publisher	Year of Publica	Author	Numk	Cost	Title of Book
Hillcrest	1998	James Cagney	340	€15.67	The Rise and Fall of Gondola
Langlet	1999	Jill Waters	400	€18.00	The Sea Dragon

- Add the Header: "The best of Irish Literature"
- Add the Footer: " "The Sea Dragon" has been nominated "
- Change the design of the form to "International"
- Create a Report based on the Books "Books" - use all Fields in the Report excluding "Number of Pages" and "Cost"
- Sort on "Year of Publication"
- Set up the Report Title as: "Some Titles included in Book Sale".   Save.

Exercise 10

- Create a form based on the "Customers" Table above
- Add the following records in Form View:

Last Name	First N	Company Nan	Partn	Phone Nu	Mem	Date of A	Year of Birth
Carter	Noel	Fresco Ltd	Kate	2345432	☑	04/08/98	1970
Walton	Tessa	Lipton & Co	Ger	987789	☐	01/07/98	1972

- Sort on "Company Name"
- Add the Header: "Eligible for Doheny Discount"
- Add the Footer: " 10% Vouchers to Everybody "
- Change the design of the form to "Rice paper"
- Create a Report based on the "Customers" Table - use all Fields in the Report excluding "Partner" and "Year of Birth"
- Sort on "Last Name"
- Set up the Report Title as: "Invitations extended to All"
- Save

Exercise 11:

- Create a form based on the "Business Marketing" Table above

Date	Name/Address	Type of Entert	Amount	Business F
01/07/98	Jack Miller The Crescent Co Cork	Brunch	€35.00	Promotion
02/02/96	Kit Mack The Glade Youghal Co Cork	Morning Coffee	€20.00	Discussion

- Add the following records in Form View:
- Sort on "Business"
- Add the Header: "Bank Holiday: May 28"
- Add the Footer: " John Carter, MD, retires on June 30 "
- Change the design of the form to "Expedition"
- Add a picture of your choice to the Form - position in a free area of the form
- Create a Report based on the "Business Marketing" Table - use all Fields in the Report excluding "Date" and "Amount"
- Sort on "Type of Entertainment"
- Set up the Report Title as: "Additions to MD List". Save

Exercise 12:

- Create a form based on the "Golfers" Table above
- Add the following records in Form View:

Member	Ty	Member's	First Line c	Second line	Third Li	Phone Nu	Member S	Last Competit
HY789	2	Lia Farrell	Main St	Rosscarbery	Co Cork	2134356	23/07/97	02/09/01
LO098	3	Joe Haven	The Square	Clonakilty	Co Cork	21321321	17/08/99	19/06/99

- Sort on "Member Since"
- Add the Header: "Mixed Foursomes: July 23"
- Add the Footer: " President's Prize: Aug 4"
- Change the design of the form to "Sumi Painting"
- Create a Report based on the "Golfers" Table - use all Fields in the Report excluding "Third Line of Address" and "Phone Number"
- Sort on "Type of Membership"
- Insert an appropriate Golf Picture in the Report - Position effectively
- Set up the Report Title as: "Additions to Handicap List". Save.

Consolidation

Reinforce the Access studies outlined to this point by completing the Practice Exercises below

- Set up the Table below and use it for reinforcing Queries etc
- Save the Table as: "Students"

	Field Name	Data Type
🔑	Student Number	Number
	First Name	Text
	Last Name	Text
	Address	Text
	Course	Text
▶	Course Fee	Currency
	Date of Birth	Date/Time

- Field Width is 12
- 0 Decimal Places
- Short Field Format

- The records for "Students" are:

Student N	First Nam	Last Name	Address	Course	Course Fee	Date of Birth
69876	Barbara	Lee	Galway	Science	IR£35,800	12-Mar-75
87965	John	Sinclair	Galway	Commerce	IR£3,000	03-Jul-77
98709	Marie	Walker	Cork	Law	IR£4,500	08-Aug-76
876908	Cora	Lysaght	Wicklow	Commerce	IR£3,000	12-Sep-78
987987	Lisa	Miller	Dublin	Arts	IR£2,500	11-Oct-74
9875430	Dick	Francis	Mayo	Arts	IR£2,500	01-Aug-78

Practice 1a:

- Create a new Table named: Products Inventory
- The Field Names for the Design are:

Field Name	Data Type
Product No	AutoNumber
Product Name	Text
Product Description	Text
Supplier No	Number
Units In Stock	Number
Units On Order	Number
Unit Price	Currency

- Use the "Product No" as the Primary Key
- In Datasheet View, fill in three records
- Sort the Products on "Products Name"
- Create a Form
- Create a Form Header: "Fresh Produce is our Trademark!"
- Create a Form Footer: "Serving the People of Munster"
- Insert a suitable picture in Form design - Position effectively

Practice 1b:

- Recall the "Students" Table; Save as: "Semester MW"
- Extract from this table all records of Students studying "Commerce" and whose date of Birth is greater than 1 September 1978; Name as "Commerce Students"
- Amend the Table by adding another Field Name: PIN (Data Type: Number) - create an Index key also on this Field Name - no Duplicates Allowed
- Delete the record relating to "Law"; Sort Table on "Course": Ascending Order
- Extract all records relating to Fees Greater than £3,000 (note currency sign is not typed in Criteria Row); Save as: "Fees"
- Create a Form; Add a Picture of your choice to the Form
- Create a Report; use all Fields; Sort on "Address". Use Title: "Students: 2001/2"; Save.

Practice 2a:

- Create a new Table named: Employees
- The Field Names for the Design are:

Field Name	Data Type
Employee ID	AutoNumber
Department	Text
Social Security Number	Text
First Name	Text
Last Name	Text
Title	Text
Date of Birth	Date/Time
Salary	Currency

- Use the "Employee ID" as the Primary Key
- In Datasheet View, fill in the three records:

JH786	Accounts	KJ8765	Ms	Marie Wall	7 Oct '78	£40,000
KL987	Sales	LK9876	Mr	Tom Draper	2 Dec '79	£35,000
HY789	PR	GT675	Ms	Alice Walsh	1 Nov '80	£25,000

- Sort the Records on "Department"
- Create a Form - use the Dusk design for the Form
- Create a Header for Form: "Recent Recruits"
- Create a Footer for the Form: "Listed for Training"
- Insert a suitable picture in Form design

Practice 2b:

- Recall the "Students" Table; Save under a new Table name: "Students 87"
- Extract from this table all the records of Students whose Last Name begins with "L" - Save as "L Candidates"
- Edit the Course Fee for Science - this should read: £3,500
- Extract the records of all students living in "Galway" OR whose Date of Birth is greater than 1 July 1977 - Save as "Galway Mature"
- Add another Field Name: "Course ID" - this is the new Primary Key; Attach an Index key to the "Student Number" Field Name - no Duplicates Allowed
- Delete record relating to "Science"; Sort Table on "Date of Birth": Descending Order
- Create a Form; Add a Picture of your choice to the Form
- Add a new Student through the Form:

   Joan Hanover of Wexford is studying Science - Fees as above;
   Date of Birth: 23 March 1977 - Student No: HY6543

- Create Report; use all Fields
- Sort on "Address"
- Add a Picture to the Report - Centre across Page
- Use Title: "Academic Year: 2002"
- Save

Practice 3a:

- Create a new Table named: Employees
- The Field Name for the Design are:

Field Name	Data Type
First Name	Text
Last Name	Text
Town Of Birth	Text
ID Code	Text
Year of Birth	Number
Interests	Text
Fee Paid: Yes or No	Yes/No

- In Datasheet View, fill in the records below:

First Nam	Last Name	Town Of Bi	ID Code	Year of B	Interests	Fee Paid
Rita W	Peale	Youghal	D6	1945	Badminton	☑
Mike	Tanner	Fermoy	G566	1934	Football	☐
Philip	Fuller	Cork	H11	1950	Football	☑
John	Sweeney	Fermoy	H1986	1934	Cycling	☑
John	Murphy	Cork	H5	1950	Golf	☐
Kit	Rice	Fermoy	H78	1966	Golf	☐
Rita	Farris	Mallow	P198	1963	Tennis	☐
John	Collins	Fermoy	P8	1950	Golf	☑
Dick	Philpott	Arklow	PT78	1934	Soccer	☑
Mary	Roberts	Youghal	W13	1945	Hockey	☐
John	Sorenson	Mallow	W135	1978	Soccer	☑

- Save; Sort the Records on "Department"
- Create a Query (use all Fields) extracting all the Employees whose Town of Birth is "Youghal"; Save as "Town: Youghal"
- Modify Query to Display only the Fields: Year of Birth, Interests, First and Last Name - Save this modified Query as: "Distinguished Employees"
- Create a Form
- Create a Header for Form: "Recent Recruits"
- Create a Footer for the Form: "Listed for Training"
- Insert a suitable picture in Form design. Save - Close Database.

Practice 3b:

- Start Database - Recall the "Employees" Table above
- Extract from this table all the records of Employees whose Last Name begins with "F" AND who come from "Cork" - Save as "Cork Staff"
- Extract employees' records relating to ID Codes starting with "H" and who like to play "Golf" - Save as: "Golfers"
- Extract records of employees whose Year of Birth is Less than "1940" and whose Fees are Paid (Remember to type Criteria for Yes in full, i.e. Yes
- Create a Form - Apply International Design to the Form
- Add a new record via the Form:
    Leo Dowling of Arklow has an ID Code of P876; Born on 23 Feb 1965; is very interested in Soccer and has his Fees Paid
- Add an appropriate sporting Picture to the Form
- Create Report using all Fields; Sort on Interests; Title: "Wide Range of Interests"
- Save and Close Database

Practice 4a:

- Create a new Table named: Employees
- The Field Name for the Design are:

Field Name	Data Type
Code	Number
Purchaser	Text
Sales Person	Text
Product	Text
Date of Purchase	Date/Time
Paid	Yes/No
Cost	Currency

- Save as: "Misc Goods MW"; Fill in the following records:

Code	Purchaser	Sales Person	Product	Date of Purchase	Paid	Cost
908	Sam Holt	Ber	Video	12/03/00	☑	IR£150.00
909	Jim Ryan	Jack	Dishwasher	19/03/00	☐	IR£340.00
910	Hilda Curtis	Liz	Microwave	20/03/00	☑	IR£160.00
911	Kim Barry	Ber	Video	21/03/00	☑	IR£200.00
912	Alice Cooke	Jack	Dishwasher	12/03/00	☐	IR£365.00
913	Vera King	Ber	VCRs	14/03/00	☑	IR£140.00
914	Sean Hewitt	Liz	Microwave	17/03/00	☑	IR£180.00

- Sort on Product
- Edit the purchase made on the 19 March by Jim Ryan - he bought a Microwave
- Delete Kim Barry's Purchase - the Video was returned
- Create a Form with Industrial Design; add an appropriate Picture

Practice 4b:

- Create Table below:

Field Name	Data Type
Employee Number	Number
Surname	Text
Sex	Text
Age	Number
Date of Registration	Date/Time
Department	Text
For Promotion	Yes/No
Salary	Currency

- Save as: "Register 2002". Input the following records:

loye	Surname	Sex	Age	Date of Registration	Department	For Promot	Salary
789	Willis	F	30	12/03/00	Accounts	☑	IR£30,000.00
890	Barton	F	34	19/07/00	PR	☐	IR£34,000.00
900	Curtis	M	40	12/09/99	Sales	☑	IR£40,000.00
876	Allis	F	23	19/08/00	Media	☑	IR£17,000.00
654	Evans	M	27	17/07/00	Salaries	☐	IR£27,000.00
908	Ellis	F	29	19/08/00	PR	☑	IR£29,000.00
910	Burton	F	39	12/08/00	Sales	☐	IR£34,000.00

- Create a Query to Extract all "Female" "Sales" employees - Save as "Female Sales"
- Extract Employees listed "For Promotion" who are 30 years or over: Save - "30's"
- Create a Query called "Registered Males" showing all Male employees who registered before the 15/09/00
- Extract employees who earn more than £25,000 and whose surname begins with "E" - Save as "E Earners"
- Add a Report - use all Fields except the "Employee Number"
- Sort on "Department" and use the Title: "Established Employees". Save as "Departmental Listings" and close Access.

Microsoft PowerPoint 2000

Presentation Graphics

PowerPoint is Presentation Graphic software, which translates data from a database or spreadsheet into a chart or graph, as well as being able to integrate text, titles, art, sound and even multimedia activities. The end result is a high-tech slide show that can be viewed on a monitor or projected onto a screen from slides.

Getting Started

- Turn on computer: **Windows98** (our example) is loaded into memory; Desktop appears.

Loading PowerPoint for Windows

- Start **PowerPoint** by clicking on **Start Menu, Programs** and selecting **Microsoft PowerPoint.**

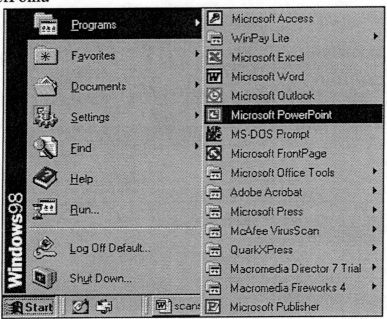

..the **PowerPoint Dialog Box** screen appears offering four choices for creating or modifying a presentation. This screen displays only once in every usage - immediately after PowerPoint loads. Thereafter, other methods are used to access the **four** options here:

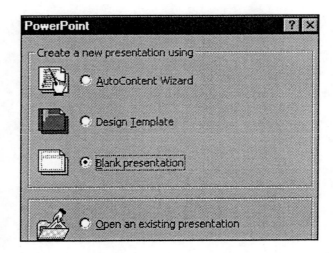

Other methods of accessing Opening Screen options:

- Each time, you select **File New** from drop-down menu in PowerPoint, the **New Presentation** dialog box with four tabs opens:
  - General
  - Design Templates
  - Presentations
  - Office 97 Templates

1. *General tab*

- Under this tab. a **Blank Presentation** can be selected (other choice is AutoContent Wizard) - the equivalent of selecting the **Blank Presentation Option** button on Opening screen:

2. *Design Templates*

- Under this option, choose from a wide variety of professionally designed templates containing **color schemes, styled fonts,** all designed to create a particular look. After you apply a design template, each slide you add has the same **custom** look:

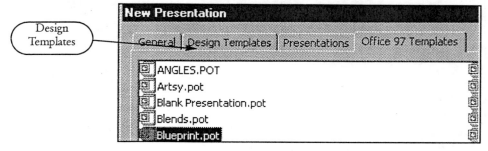

3. *Presentations*

- **24 Pre-designed** presentation which can be modified to suit your needs.

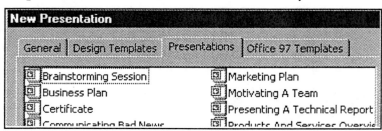

4. Office 97 Templates

- Under this Tab are listed a range from the previously described Tabs: Design Templates and Presentations.

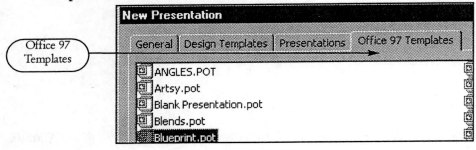

Open an Existing Presentation (Last option on Opening Screen)

- Selecting the **Open** icon from the Standard **Toolbar** or selecting **File Open** from the drop-down menu is the equivalent of selecting this **Opening** option from the Opening PowerPoint screen.

Example: Modifying a presentation within AutoContent Wizard

- From **File** menu, select **New** and **General** tab. .Double-click **AutoContent** Wizard: .. the first screen displays:

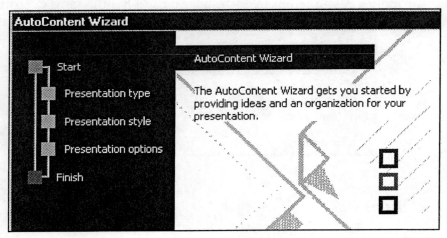

- Click **Next** to move to next screen: **Presentation type:**

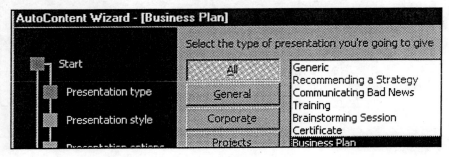

- Select Tab: **All**; Select Presentation: **Business Plan:**

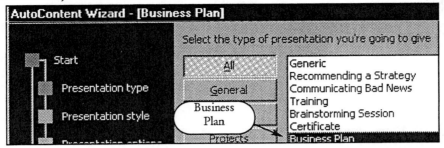

- Click **Next** - to go to **Type of Output** screen, select **Color Overheads**

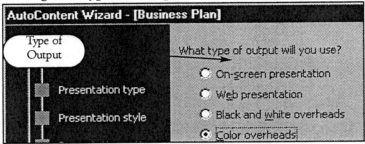

- Click **Next** - to go to **Presentation Title** etc screen:

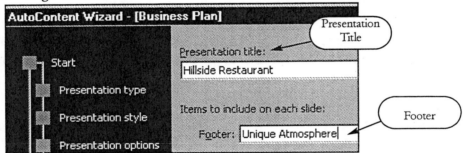

- Key in text as above opposite **Presentation Title**, and **Footer.**
- Click **Finish** - PowerPoint opens a **12-Page** presentation in **Normal View** based on the Business Plan **pre-set presentation** chosen above
- **Status Bar** shows the **current** position:

  Slide 1 of 12

- The new text typed in the AutoContent Wizard is shown as Slide 1:

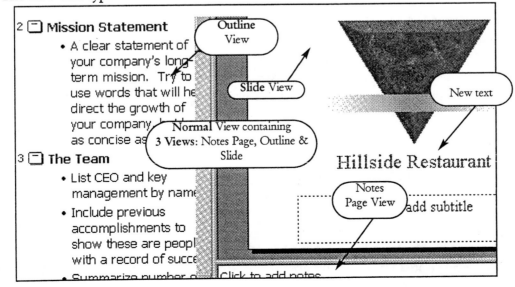

Saving:

- Create a **new Folder** called **Presentation Practice**
- Save **current** Presentation as: "Hillside Restaurant MW" - substitute your initials for "MW"

PowerPoint Views

Microsoft PowerPoint comes with different views to help you while you are creating a presentation. The two main views you use in PowerPoint are **normal** view and **slide sorter** view. To easily switch between views, you click the buttons at the lower **left** of the PowerPoint window.

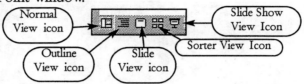

Normal view

Normal view contains three panes: the **outline** pane, the **slide** pane, and the **notes** pane. These panes let you work on all aspects of your presentation in one place.

Outline pane

Use the outline pane to organize and develop the content of your presentation. You can type all of the text of your presentation and rearrange bullet points, paragraphs, and slides.

Slide pane

In the slide pane, you can see how your text looks on each slide. You can add graphics, movies, and sounds, create hyperlinks, and add animations to individual slides.

Notes pane

The notes pane lets you add your speaker notes or information you want to share with the audience. If you want to have graphics in your notes, you must add the notes in notes page view.

Slide sorter view

In slide sorter view, you see all the slides in your presentation on screen at the same time, displayed in miniature. This makes it easy to add, delete, and move slides, add timings, and select animated transitions for moving from slide to slide.

Slide show view

At any time while you are creating your presentation, you can start your slide show and preview your presentation by clicking Slide Show.

Slide View

- The newly created Presentation currently in **Normal** View, Double-click **Slide** icon to switch to **Slide** view.

Slide 1 in Slide View: Add sub-title:

- Click in **subholder** and **type** as below:

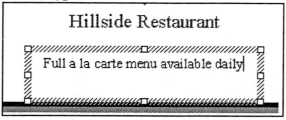

- Press **Page Down Key** to move to **Slide 2**: Slide 2 Slide View:

Replacing default Text in Slide

- In **Slide 2,** replace the **default** text included with the Business Plan Presentation Wizard created above as below:

Slide Show View

- To see how your slides show will look, click **Slide Show** icon
- Press **Page Down** or **Page Up** buttons to **move** from one slide to the next
- Press **Esc** key to cancel **Slide Show View**

Closing Presentation:

- Select **File Close** from Menu

Changing Design of Slides:

- Change the **design** of the slides from "Dad's Tie" to "Contemporary Portrait":
- Click **Apply Design** Template icon on Toolbar:
- Select "Nature" from **Apply Design Template** dialog box:

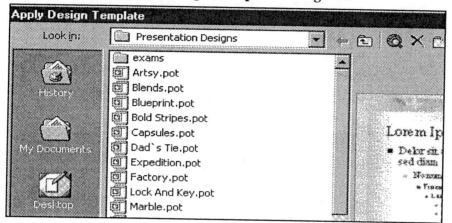

- Click **Apply** - "Nature" Design has now been applied to the Slides:

Add a new Slide with Text & Chart AutoLayout

- Insert a **new** Slide
- Select **Chart AutoLayout** - there are a choice of 3 Chart AutoLayout:
  Text & Chart, **Chart & Text** and **Chart** only:

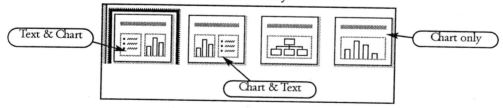

- **Select** Text and **Chart type** - Key in the **Chart Title** text and **Bullet Point** text but **remove** Bullet from emboldened Heading: "Other Restaurants"
- Apply **Shadow** to "Other Restaurants" text

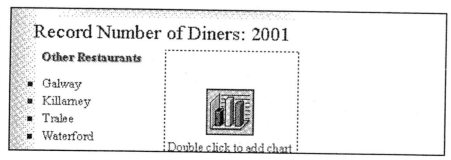

- Double click **Chart** icon - a Chart Toolbar **replaces** default Standard Toolbar and a **Datasheet** containing **default data** displays - Datasheet can be **hidden** by clicking Datasheet **icon** on Toolbar:

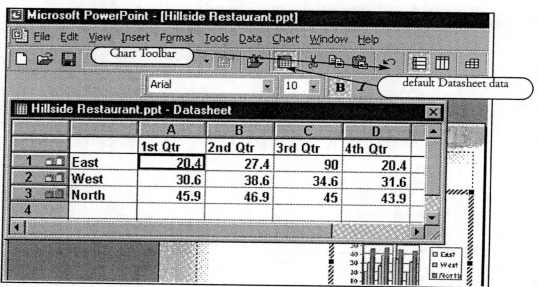

- **Chart Toolbar** looks like:

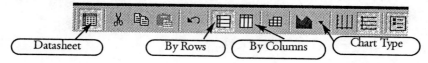

- **Key** in data for the Datasheet:

		A	B	C	D
		1st Qtr	2nd Qtr	3rd Qtr	4th Qtr
1	Galway	4506	4567	4568	6689
2	Killarney	5647	7654	8760	7689
3	Tralee	3456	5678	4567	5567
4	Waterford	6548	8795	7689	4587

- Click the Datasheet **icon** to display Chart only

Change Chart Type:

- **Select** Chart - Select Chart **Type** icon on Toolbar, click **drop-down** menu:

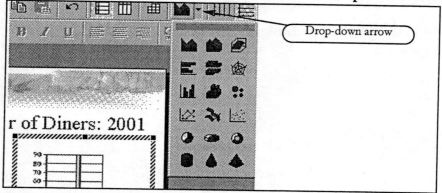

- Select **3-D** Column Chart Type

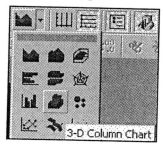

- Chart **changes**:

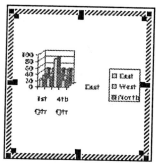

Add a new Slide with Text & Organization Chart AutoLayout

Organizational Charts are used to demonstrate the structure of seniority within a work situation

- Insert a **new Slide**
- Select **Organization Chart** AutoLayout:

- **Type** in "Banqueting Personnel" and **centre** in Title Placeholder

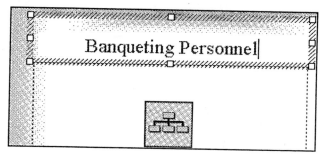

- **Double click** the Organizational chart icon - **new** screen opens with Toolbar:

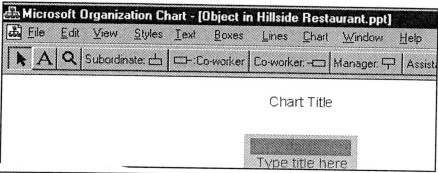

- **Key** in the names of the following **Personnel** in the **Org Chart** boxes:

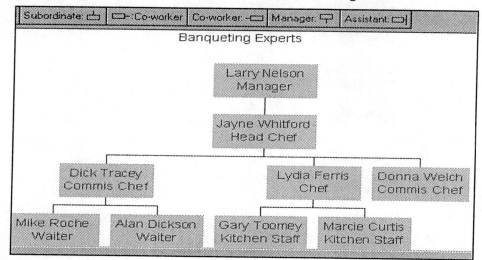

- Chart **boxes** can be **added** to your Organization chart by clicking a chart box type on the **Standard** toolbar of the Organizational chart and then selecting the **chart box** you want to attach it to, for example, Click the **subordinate** button and then click **Dick Tracey** box, a box will display at a **lower** level.
- The box **titles** as such are self-explanatory - the stem protruding from each box indicates the point at which the box will **connect** to a selected box

Add Clip Art to Slide 1
(Clip Art icon is part of the Drawing Toolbar)

- The **Drawing** tool bar has tools you can use to **draw, manipulate** and **format** all kinds of objects as well as **adding** Clip Art.
- Turn on **Drawing Toolbar** with **View Toolbars** from drop-down menu, and click on **Drawing** to select::

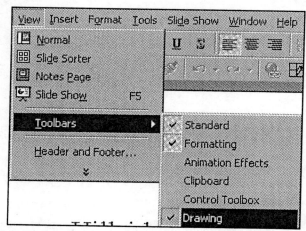

- .. Drawing Toolbar displays at bottom of screen above Status Bar:

- Press **Page Up** key until **Status Bar** reads **Slide 1:**

Slide 1 of 17

- Click **Clip Art** icon on Toolbar:
  ..Clip Art **Gallery** screen showing a **range of categories** displays - double click **Food & Dining** Category icon:

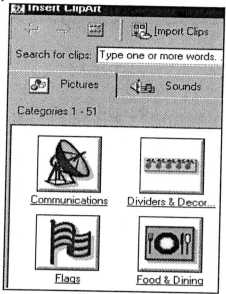

- Select appropriate clip, as below, click on **Insert Clip** icon

- ..Clip, surrounded by **8 Selection Handles**, is inserted into **Slide1**:

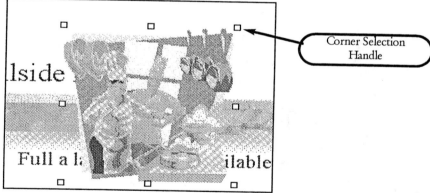

Corner Selection Handle

- Adjust both **vertically** & **horizontally** simultaneously by **selecting** & **dragging** corner selection handle until clip is required **size:**

Moving Clip Art:

- **Move** Clip to a central position in Slide 1:
- Select, **click** and **hold** on **clip** and **move** as required:

- **Centre** the **Main Title:** Hillside Restaurant - **Slide** 1 now looks like:

Using Clip Art AutoLayout

Rather than using the **Clip** icon form the **Drawing Toolbar,** you may use one of the **2 choices** of **Clip** in AutoLayout: **Text & Clip Art** or **Clip Art & Text::**

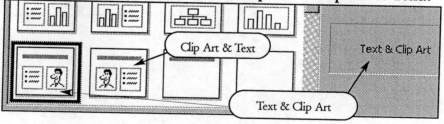

- Insert a **New Slide** after current Slide 5 and select the **AutoLayout: Text & Clip Art:** screen will look like:

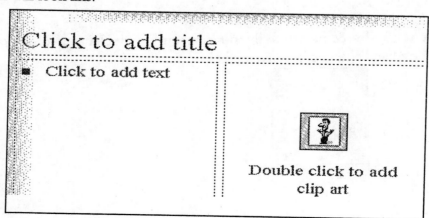

Text & Clip Art AutoLayout detail:

- **Type** in **Main Title**. In the **bulleted** text area, **type** in as follows:

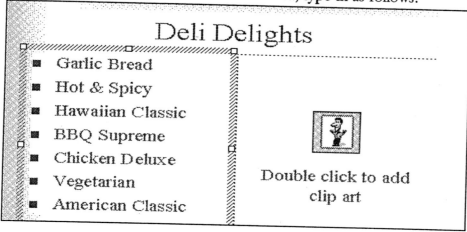

- Double click **Clip** icon to **add Clip Art**:
- From **Food & Dining** Category within the Clip Art range, select the **Clip**:

- .. the clip is **automatically** inserted into the placeholder in the **current** slide, which now looks like:

To add Border to Clip

- **Select** Clip, Select **Line Style** from Toolbar:
- Select Border Thickness of your choice, Border is **added** to Clip:

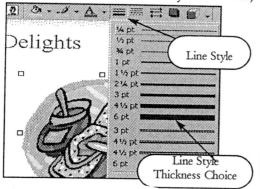

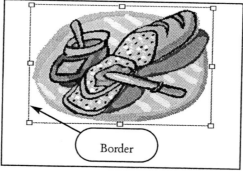

Add a Picture from File

Pictures can be added to a Slide in a similar way to the **Insertion of Clip Art** Pictures can be graphics that were created in another file, scanned photographs etc.

Insert a picture

- **Display** the slide you want to add a picture to.

- On the **Insert** menu, point to **Picture**, and then click **From File:**

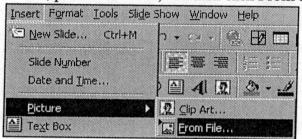

- Locate the **folder** that contains the picture you want to **insert**.

- **Select** the picture, click **Insert** - the **selected Picture** is added to the Slide - our example shows a photo **scanned** into Microsoft Paint:

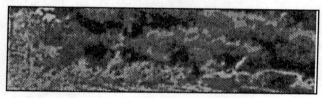

- Pictures can be **selected, stretched** or **reduced** in size in the same way as **Clip Art** objects are.

Text Box

Use the **Text Box icon** from the Drawing Toolbar to input **Pizza info**

- Create a **New Slide & Title Only** AutoLayout:

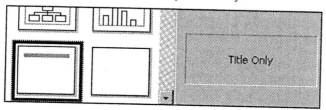

- **Key** in Centered Title in placeholder:

- Select the **Text Box** icon on Drawing Toolbar

- **Click** and **drag/draw** a Box:

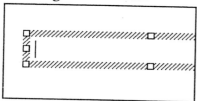

- **Type** in details of Pizzas, enhance as indicated:

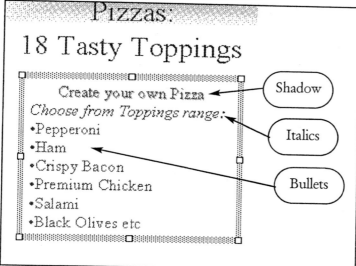

Deleting Slides

Our initial Presentation created by modifying Business Plan had 12 Slides
We have added several slides ourselves. We can see on the Status bar the number of
the current Slide and the total number of slides in the Presentation:

We now only require the first eight, so we will delete the remaining slides.

Deleting Slides in Outline View:

• Switch to **Outline** View by clicking on Outline **icon**:

• Highlight **Slides 9-19**:

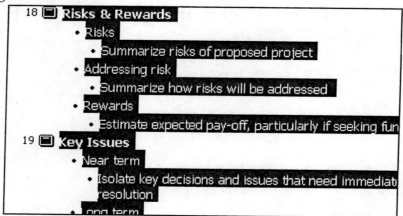

• Press **Delete** key
• ..Slides are deleted - Status Bar in Slide View now reflects **adjusted** number of slides:

Moving Slides In Slide Sorter View:
Move Slide 5 to Slide 8 position:
• **Switch** to Slide **Sorter** View by clicking on Slide **Sorter** icon

• **8 Slides** display - **Slide 5** is currently selected (indicated by heavy Frame):

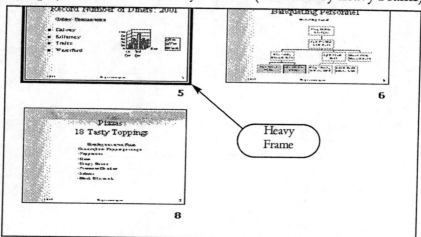

- **Click** and hold **down** mouse button with **Slide 5 selected**, and drag to **new** position: Slide 8 - as you drag slide, before you release mouse button, an **icon** and a **line** will display as you move:

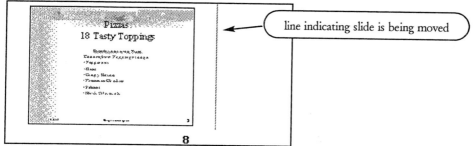

- When mouse button is **released** - slide displays in its **new** position:

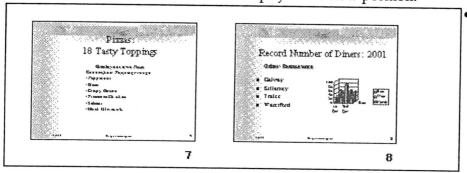

Changing Layout of Slide:

- **Slide 3** (currently Bulleted Slide Layout) might look better with a **Title** only Layout

- Select **Slide 3,** and select Slide **Layout** icon from Toolbar:

- Select **Title** Slide from the **Slide Layout** dialog box

- Click **Apply** - **Title Slide Layout** is applied to Slide 3:

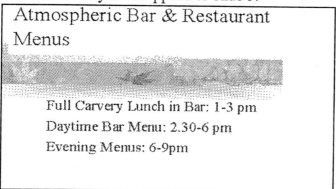

- It looked better the way it was; also the last line has been lost

Undo icon

- To revert to the **original layout**, click the **Undo** button:

- ..the Slide layout is altered to its **original form**.

Page Setup

To see the **default** settings in **Page Setup** for PowerPoint, select **File Page Setup** from Menu:

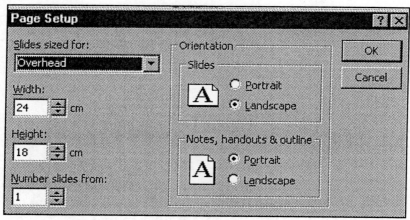

To Change Slide Size to A4 Paper (other Sizes are selected by same method)

- Select **A4 Paper** from the drop-down choices under **Slides sized for:**

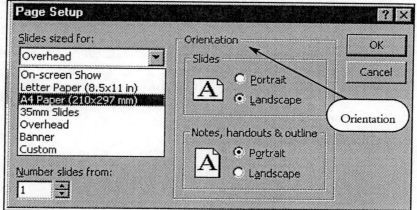

Orientation:

- Similarly, Orientation of Slides can be changed between **Portrait** and **Landscape** under **Slides Orientation** options.
- Choice of Orientation for **Notes, handouts & outline** can also be made.
- Click **OK** button when choices have been finalised.

Printing

- To print the **whole** of the **current** presentation with the default settings **once**, click on the **Print** icon on the Toolbar:

- To Print with **modified** settings, select **File Print** from Menu:
- Print dialog box opens:

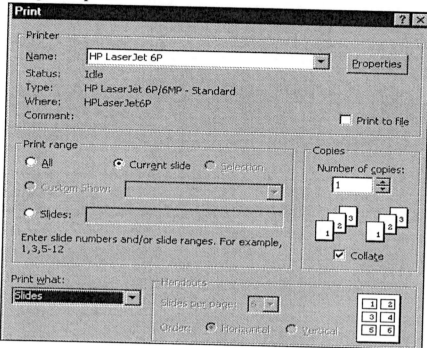

Print Range:

- Under this option, select **All** to print each Slide, select **Current** Slide to print the Slide currently on display or select **Selection to Print** the data currently selected:

- Select **Slides** to print a **range** of slides other than **All** or **Current Slide**.
- We have **8 slides** in the current presentation; to print **Slide 2, Slides 4-5,** and **Slide 8,** *excluding:* **Slides: 1, 3, 6** and **7,** key in requirements in the **Slides** box like:

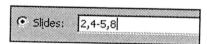

Copies:

- Under this option, accept the **default:** 1 copy, or **key** in the number of copies you require to print:

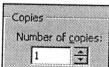

Print What

- The **default** is **Slides**
- To **change**, click the **arrow** next to the **Print what** box. and choose from: **Slides. Handouts, Notes Pages** or **Outline** View:

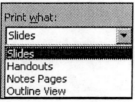

Handouts:

- Change **option** to **Handouts** under **Print What** and options under **Handouts** becomes accessible. You can set settings for: **Slides per page** & **Order** Orientation:

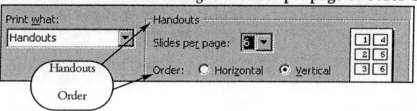

Print to File:

- To print at a later date, the **Print to File** option may be selected:

- Click **OK** - the **Print to File** dialog box opens:

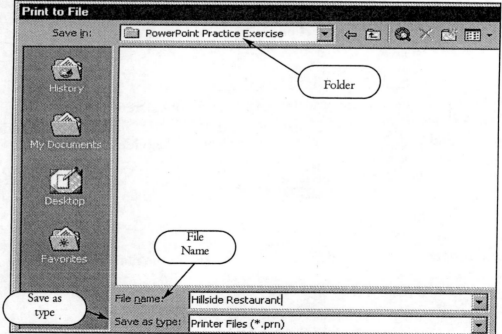

- Type in an appropriate **file name**, e.g. Hillside Restaurant
- Select an appropriate **Folder**, e.g. PowerPoint Practice Exercise
- Accept **Save as type** default: Printer Files (*.prn); Click **OK**.

Create Speaker's Notes Pages:

- Click the **Notes Pane,** and then type your **notes** for the **current** slide.

- To see more of the notes pane, point to the **top border** of the notes pane until the pointer becomes a **double-headed arrow,** and then **drag** until the **pane** is the size you want.
- Use the **outline pane** to move to **other slides** you want to **add notes** to.

Add Notes to Slide 2:

- With **Slide 2** displayed. switch to **Speaker's Notes Pages View:**
- Select 100% View from **Zoom** icon display:

- ...and **Type Notes** below:

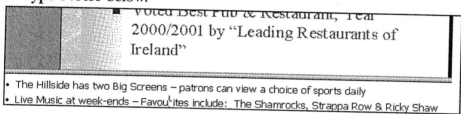

Headers & Footers:

(Our **current** presentation: "Hillside Restaurant.." - has a **Footer** already set up in **Slide View** keyed in when we were working through the initial Wizard)

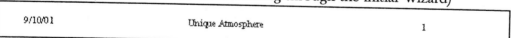

Adding a Header & Footer:

We will now set up a **Header and Footer** for Notes & Handouts:

- Select **Header & Footer** from **View** Menu:
..dialog box now opens showing Header & Footer settings for Slides

Header & Footer dialog box:

Slides: Header and Footer Settings:

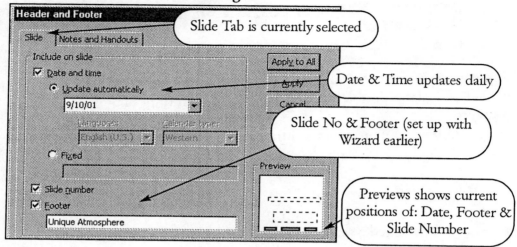

Notes & Handouts - Header and Footer Settings:

- Select **Tab** for **Notes and Handouts**
- ..dialog box opens showing **current** settings for **Header & Footer** for **Notes & Handouts** - key in **Header & Footer** below (**Date & Number** are already selected)

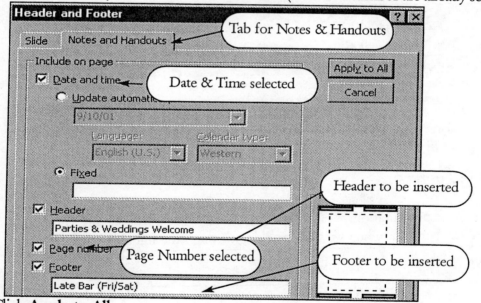

- Click **Apply to All**

Viewing:

- To **View** Select **View Notes Page** from Menu:

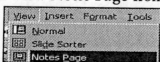

- **Header** in **Notes & Handouts Page View** will look like:

  | Parties & Weddings Welcome |

- **Footer** in **Notes & Handouts Page View** will look like:

  | Late Bar (Fri/Sat) | 1 |

Adding a Background:

A **shaded** background gives the effect of a **solid colour** gradually changing from light to dark or dark to light PowerPoint has one and two colour shaded backgrounds with six styles: vertical, horizontal, diagonal right, diagonal left from corner and from title.

• From the **Format** menu, click **Background** - the background dialog box opens
• Click on the **drop-down** background fill box:

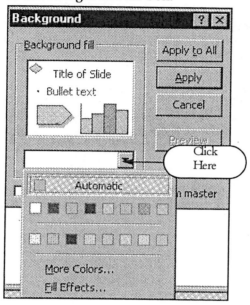

• You can choose between "**More Colors**" and "**Fill Effects**" - we will choose "More Colours" - we select "Yellow"

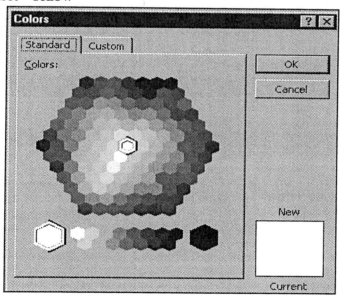

• Click **OK** - **Background** dialog redisplays - Click **Apply to All** - **Colour Background:** Yellow is applied to **all** Slides in the Presentation:

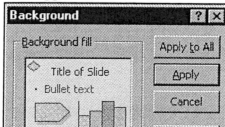

Slide Shows

- Create a Slide Show by selecting **Slide Show, Set Up Show...** from drop-down Menu

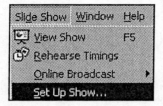

- **Set Up Show** dialog box opens:
.• Under **Slides**, Select **All**

- Under **Advance slides**, choose **Manually** - this means that the user will move from slide to slide within the Slide Show by pressing **Page Down** or **Page Up** key

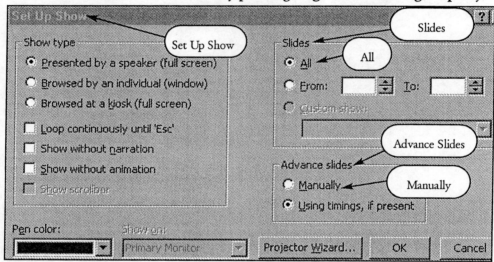

- Click **OK**

Animation

- You can animate - add a visual or sound **effect** text, graphics, sounds, movies, and other objects on your slides. You can have each main **bullet** point appear independently of others, or you can have objects appear **progressively**, one after another. You can set up the way you want each bullet point or object to **appear** on your slide: to fly in from the left, for example or to dissolve on the screen.

- To set up Animation, switch to **Sorter** View

- **Select** each Slide in turn or Select All with Control A (if you want same Animation for all Slides)

- Select preferred **Preset Animation** from Slide Show Menu

Selecting an Animation Type:

- **Select** required Animation type from the **Range** for each Slide, e.g. Flying:

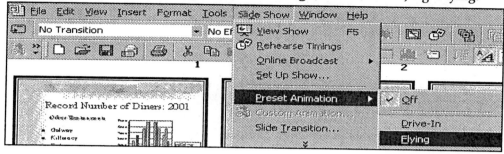

Viewing Animation:

- **Select** View Slide Show to see same Slide Show seen above with Animation added

Slide Transition

Adding transitions to a Slide Show:

Transition is a special **effect** used to introduce a slide during a slide show. For example, you can fade in from black or dissolve from one slide to another. You can choose the transitions you want, and you can vary the **speed** of each.
- In slide or slide sorter view, **select** slide or slides you want to add a transition to.
- On the **Slide Show** menu, click **Slide Transition**:

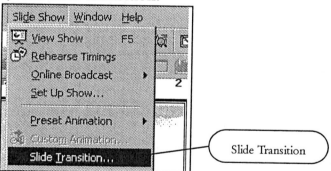

- ..Slide Transition dialog box opens:

- Select **Cover Down**; click **Apply to All**
- To **apply** the transition to **all** the slides, click **Apply to All** or **Apply** to apply transition to **one** slide.

Drawing with tools from Drawing Toolbar :

Creating Lines

- Create a **line** by selecting **Line Tool** from Drawing Toolbar

Line Examples:

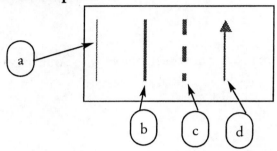

Basic Line:
- **Click** and **Drag** to draw the line - see (**a**)
- To **constrain** the line to draw at **15-degree angles** from its starting point hold down **SHIFT** and **drag**
- To **lengthen** the line in opposite directions from the first end point hold down **CTRL** as you **drag**

Line Style: an object must be selected for the range of styles to display:
- **Select** Line at (**a**):

- Click on **Line Style** icon on Toolbar:

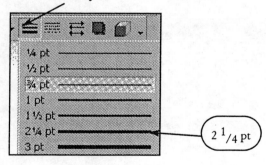

- ..range of **Line thicknesses** set in varying points displays as above

Change Thickness of Line:
- **Copy** the line at (**a**) and **Paste** at (**b**) location
- Select 2 $^1/_4$ pt line **thickness** from **Line style range**
- Line changes to new style - see (**b**)

Change Line to Dash Style:
(an object must be selected for the range of dash styles to display)

- **Copy** the line at (a) and **Paste** at (c) location
- Select line at (c); click on **Dash** style icon - range of dash styles displays:

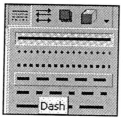

- Line changes to selected dash style - see (c)

Creating an arrow in 1.5 Line style

- Select **arrow icon** on Toolbar and draw an arrow - see (d)

- Select **arrow**; select **Line** style: **1.5 pt** from Toolbar - arrow will now look like (d)

Rotation icon used to rotate arrow:

- Select arrow at (d); select **Rotation** icon on Toolbar - note selection squares at either end of arrow:

- Click and hold **Rotation** icon and rotate until arrow is pointing in **direction** required:

Drawing a Rectangle with Rectangular Tool from Drawing Toolbar:

Rectangular Examples:

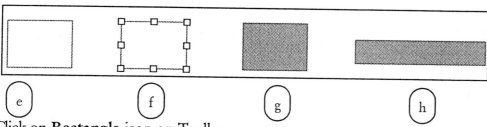

e   f   g   h

- Click on **Rectangle** icon on Toolbar:

- Click and drag - rectangle is created - see (e) above:

Changing the Colour of a Rectangle - Fill colour
(Object must be selected before fill range will display)

- You can use the **Fill colour** icon on the Drawing toolbar to fill objects with

  solid colours, a gradient, a pattern, or a texture

- To **remove** the fill or **create** a transparent object, click the arrow next to Fill Colour and then click **No Fill**

  To fill:
- **Select** the Rectangle - see (f) above
- Select the **Fill colour** icon on Toolbar:
- **Range** of colours display - select one - our example: green:
- ..selected rectangle fills with selected colour - see (g) above:

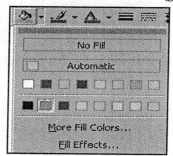

Changing Horizontal & Vertical Size of Rectangle

- Select rectangle at (g) - 8 selection handles display:

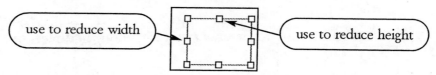

- To **change size** Horizontally, click on selection handle indicated at drag to required width - see (h)

- To **change size** Vertically, click on selection handle indicated at drag to required height - see (h)

Changing Fills, Borders, Shadows etc of Rectangle

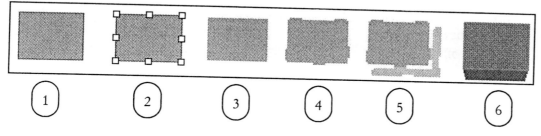

- Select rectangle at (2)
- Change **Line style** to **3 pt**

- Select **Line Colour** icon on Toolbar:

- ..range of line colours display:

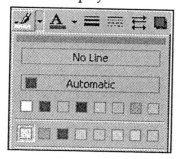

- our example, select **yellow** - 3 pt border surrounding rectangle changes to yellow - see (3) above
- Change selected rectangle to **Long dash** style - see (4) above

Applying a Shadow to a selected rectangle

- Select **Rectangle** at (4)
- Select **Shadow** icon on Toolbar:

- ..range of **Shadow options** display:

- Select **Shadow Style 6** for our example - selected rectangle now displays in chosen shadow - see (5) above:

Applying a 3D Dimension to a selected rectangle:

- Select rectangle at (4)
- Select 3D icon on Toolbar:

- ..range of options under 3D display:

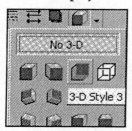

- our example, select 3-D Style 3 - chosen 3D is applied to selected rectangle - see (6) above

Drawing a Circle with Oval Tool from Drawing Toolbar:

Oval Examples:

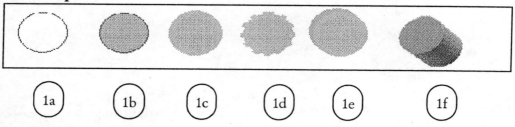

- Click on **Oval** icon on Toolbar to create the Circle at (1a):

- Same features illustrated above for the rectangle can be applied using the Oval icon - see **Examples:**
  - (1b) shows a circle **filled** with **blue**
  - (1c) shows a circle enclosed in a **4.5 pt orange border**
  - (1d) shows a circle with a **square dot dash style**
  - (1e) shows a circle with a **Shadow Style 13**
  - (1f) shows a circle with a **3-D Style 5**

Add text by using the Text Box tool

- On the Drawing toolbar, click **Text Box** icon:

- To add text that **doesn't wrap,** click where you want to add the text, and start typing:

Cork City Sports

- To add text that **does wrap,** drag to where you want to add text, and then start typing:

International
Athletics
Meeting

AutoShapes:

- PowerPoint comes with a set of ready-made shapes that can be used in presentations.
- The shapes can be resized, rotated, flipped, coloured etc.
- The AutoShapes menu on the Drawing toolbar contains several categories of shapes, including lines, basic shapes, stars and banners, and callouts.

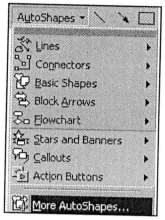

- To use, click **AutoShapes**, point to a **category**, and then click the **shape** you want.
- To maintain the shape's **width-to-height ratio**, hold down **SHIFT** as you drag the shape.
- The **More AutoShapes** category displays AutoShapes located in the **Clip Gallery**. Just drag the AutoShape you want from the Clip Gallery onto your slide:

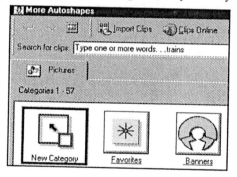

- You can **add text to AutoShapes** by just clicking in the shape and typing. Text you add becomes part of the shape - if you rotate or flip the shape, the text rotates or flips with it.
- Example: Select **AutoShapes, Basic Shapes** - range will display:

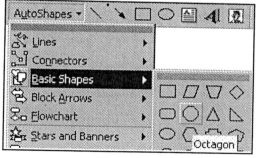

- Select **Octagon** icon and click on the slide. **Type** as below:

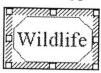

Change Shape

- Select the AutoShape to be changed - use Wildlife example above.
- On the Drawing toolbar, click **Draw**, point to **Change AutoShape,** select a **category: Basic Shapes,** and then click the shape you want - **can:**

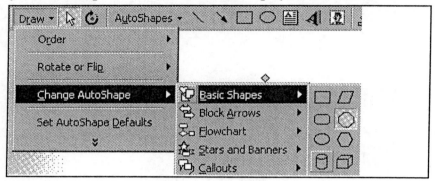

- ..Shape changes to **can** shape:

Using Stars and Banners Category

- Select **AutoShapes, Stars and Banners,** select **Star** shape

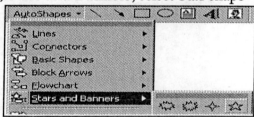

- Create a **Star** shape on slide

- Create a **Vertical Scroll** Shape:

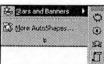

- Combine two shapes by selecting the Star shape and placing it on top of Scroll Shape:

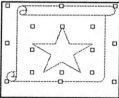

- **Group** Shapes by selecting one shape, holding down **Shift,** selecting the second before selecting **Group** fro m **Draw** menu:

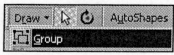

- ..combined shapes may now be moved, resized, etc simultaneously.

Practice: When you have satisfactorily completed our study of PowerPoint up to this point in the manual, attempt the varied exercises below

Exercise 1:

- Create a 3-Page Presentation - Use the Icons: New and Insert New Slide as required -use your initiative in your choice of **Font** type and sizes - Use Bold Strips as Design

- Slide 1: Title Slide AutoLayout:
    Main Title: Lisdoran Golf Course -
    Repeat this Title on Slides 2 & 3 - use Copy and Paste to copy to other Slides

    Sub-Title: Spectacular Development
    Place a suitable Clip Art on this Slide
- Slide 2: Bulleted List AutoLayout:
    Bullet Points:
        - Breathtaking Views
        - Friendly Atmosphere
        - Unique Water Features
- Slide 3: Title Only AutoLayout:
    Insert a Clip Art - Centre under Main Title on this Slide
- Change the Background Colour to Green and Save as: "Lisdoran Golf "
- Close Presentation
- Open "Lisdoran Golf " again - Add an additional Slide - Bulleted List AutoLayout
    Main Title as above
    Bullet Points: Mid-week Fourball & Special Offers: Early Birds!
    Remove Bullet Points
- Change Design to: Artsy
- ReSave and Close Presentation

Exercise 2:
- Create a 4-Page Presentation - use Notebook Design
- Main Title - Slide 1: Title Slide AutoLayout - "AquaPark Tenerife"
  Sub-Title: "Water Park-Dolphinarium"
  Insert and Centre an appropriate Clip Art below Main Title
- Slide 2: Bulleted List AutoLayout: Main Title: AquaPark
- First Bullet Point: "Attractions" (Large Font) -
  Remove Bullet Point, Centre and Embolden Title
- Other Bullet Points:
  - Children Slides
  - Twister
  - Diving Board
  - Lazy River
  - Children Area
- Slide 3: Bulleted List AutoLayout: Main Title: Tenerife
  Centre and Italicise, Remove Bullet from first entry: Well Worth Seeing!
    Bullet Points:
    - Santa Cruz
    - Golf del Sur
    - Puerto de la Cruz
    - Los Cristianos
  Replace Bullet Points with Numbering - Highlight points, and click Numbering icon
- Slide 4: Bulleted List AutoLayout - Main Title AquaPark Extra Services
    Bullet Points - replace with Numbering and type points:
    1. Restaurants
    2. Souvenir Shop
    3. Photo Shop
    4. Sunbeds
  Insert a suitable Clip Art in top right-hand corner - Insert a 1 pt Border to Clip
  Using Cut and Paste relocate Point 4 to Point 2 position and vice versa
- Change Layout of Slide 3 to Title Only
- Change Design to: Mountain
- Number Slides and Save as "AquaPark MW"; Print to File

Exercise 3:
- Create a 3-Page Presentation
- Main Title - Slide 1: Title Slide AutoLayout - "Great Southern Hotel" - apply a
    Shadow - Repeat on Slides: 2-3
  Sub-Title: "Killarney" - Font Size for Sub-Title: Arial (12)
  Insert an appropriate Clip Art in Bottom Right-hand corner
- Slide 2: Bulleted List AutoLayout: - Edit Main Title to include: Party Nights 2000
- First Bullet Point: "Christmas Party Night" - Remove Bullet Point, Centre and
  Italicise Title - Change Font Colour to Yellow
- Other Bullet Points:
  - Mulled Wine Reception
  - 4-Course Christmas Banquet with Wine
  - Disco with Fantastic Spot Prizes
- Slide 3: Title Only with Clip Art (with thick border) centered
- Add a Footer to all Slides: "Traditional Christmas Fare!"
- Set up Print screen to Print Handouts - 6 per Page - Landscape Orientation
- Spell Check and Save as: "XMas Celebrations" - close Presentation

Exercise 4:

- Slide 1: Main Title: Horace's Bistro - Font: Algerian (24) also include Shadow
  Insert Clip Art relating to Food - Stretch Clip to fill width of Printing area of Slide
- Add a second Slide: Table AutoLayout:
  Main Title: Full Bar - Beer Wine & Spirits - Font: Arial Black (20) with Shadow
  Table: 2 Columns & 5 Rows - Table Content: (Italicise Prices)

Food Choice	Cost from
Seafood	£20
Prime Steak	£18
Lamb	£15
Italian	£12

- Add a suitable Picture from file (or Clip Art) to Slide 2 - Apply a 2 pt Border
- Add a New Slide with Chart AutoLayout:
  Datasheet contents are:

Sales	Beer	Wine	Spirits	Minerals
Jan	600	300	400	600
Feb	700	250	450	700
Mar	450	320	560	560

  Graph Type should be: Bar
  Title for this Slide is: "Average Consumption: First Quarter"
- Set up a Slide Show - Add Flying Animation
- Apply Yellow Background to Slides; Move Slide 3 so that it will display as Slide 2
- Number Slides; Set up a Footer for Slides: "Great Service & Great Value!"
- Use Spell Check, Save as: "Beverages"; Print Slide 1 only
- Delete Slide 2 and ReSave; Close File

Exercise 5:

- Create a New Presentation - use your initiative on AutoLayout choice
- Slide 1 Content: Philips Entertainment (repeated on Slide 2)
                       Presented by: Dick Lee
- Slide 2 contains: Sale starts in our branches in:
                       Finglas
                       Rathfarnham
                       Templeogue
                       Sutton
                       on May 10 - 10% with this Voucher
- Slide 3:   Text and Chart Layout - details is
               Main Title: "Special Offers on:"
- Text for body of Slide:
  Superflat TV
  Nicam VCR
  Philips "Pronto"
  Toshiba Stereo
- Content of Datasheet for Graph: Bar is:

- Final Slide: Same Main Title as Slide 1
  Add Text Box to contain:
  Philips: The Ultimate Remote Control!
- Add "Box In" Animation;   Save as
  "Entertainment";
  Print Slides: 3 Slides to Page; Close Presentation

	Cost	Colour
Superflat TV	£700	Black
Nicam VCR	£450	Brown
Philips "Pronto"	£900	Silver
Toshiba Stereo	£350	Brown

Exercise 6:

- Create a 4-Slide Presentation - add a Clip of a Car to the First Slide in Top-Left Corner - copy and position this Clip in the same way for the Slides 2-4
- Slide 1 Title(s): Cranesley Motor Company Ltd - Font Times New Roman (32)
  New Cars available for immediate delivery - Italics & Shadow
- Draw a line of 1.5 pt thickness and position evenly across the Slide
- Draw a Star, fill with yellow, and position directly below line
- Create a Column Graph Slide for the data:

Models	Cost
Audi S3 1.8Lt	£30,000
Mitsubishi Evolution	£48000
BMW 323	£35,000
Mazda Tribute	£30000

- An Organizational Chart should be set up to display: Main Title from Slide 1 and:

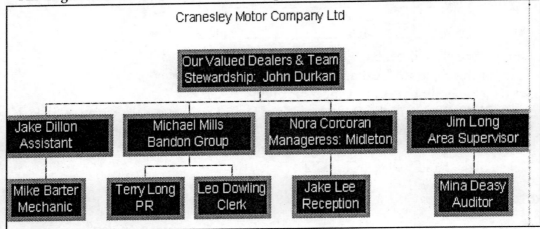

- Final Chart - Main Title as on first Slide
  Key in the text: "Opel makes a bold statement"
- In Notes Page enter:

  It is a car of contradictions, the Opel Speedster. Dramatic in looks with an invigorating performance there's no power steering, the interior is bare aluminum and spartan and getting in or out is a test of human agility, especially with the roof in place. It isn't cheap at £35000!

- Set up a Slide Show, apply both Animation and Transition of your choice
- Move the Organizational Chart to 2nd position in Slide Show
- In the Notes and Handouts, set up both a Header and Footer:
  Header: "A car you can believe in!"
  Footer: "Covered by a comprehensive warranty"

- Print to File

Consolidation

To consolidate the PowerPoint data introduced above, please complete the 4 Practice Exercise below

Practice 1:

- Create a 3-Page Presentation with effective use of varied Font Types and Size
- Slide 1 In Title Slide AutoLayout set u the text below & include suitable ClipArt

> # Blarney Park Hotel Conference Brochure 2002
>
> Blarney Co Cork Ireland
>
> Telephone: 021 385281   Fax: 021 381506
>
> eMail: blarney@iol.ie

- Slide 2 will have a Table Slide AutoLayout - this will read as follows:

Blarney Park Hotel
Room Capacity

	Banquet Style	Theatre Style	Classroom Style	Board Room	U-Shaped Room
Park Suite	340	350	130	80	50
Bard Room	56	50	30	26	20

- Slide 3 will have a **2-Column Text AutoLayout:**
- The 3rd Slide will read: (Include Formatting as displayed:

Blarney Park Hotel

Day Delegate Rate	24-Hour Delegate Rate
£25 per Day	**£75 per Day**
To include:	• Extensive Leisure Facilities
• Tea/Coffee on Arrival	• Evening Dinner
• Four-Course Lunch	• Full Irish Breakfast
• Afternoon Tea & Biscuits	

- Set up a **Footer** on each Slide - Use Blue Font Colour:

> Blarney Co Cork Ireland   Telephone: 021 385281 Fax: 021 381506

- Position a centered suitable **Clip Art** at the bottom of Slide 1
- Copy this Clip Art to Slide 2 - place in top right-hand corner - **reduce** in size
- Number each Slide; Change Paper Orientation to Landscape
- Set up a **Slide Show;** Apply **Dissolve Animation** to **All Slides**
- Apply **Box In Transition** to **All Slides; Print** - 3 Slides per Page - **Save** Presentation as **"Blarney Show";** Close PowerPoint.

Practice 2:

- Create a 3-page presentation for the **Cork Law Society**
- Include a **template** of your choice
- Use "**Cork Law Society**" as the **title** on all three pages of the presentation
- **Type** the following text in the first page:
    "**34 Hawke's Rd**", **Cork** - email **info@indigo.ie**
- Vary **font type** and **size**
- **Type** the following in **Slide two:**
    "The Law Society offers:
        1. Education
        2. Social Evenings
        3. Seminars
        4. Leisure Centre
        5. Other in-house benefits"
- **Type** the following in **page 3**
    "This is a great year for the Law Society.
    It now has 340 members in Cork alone" - use **Yellow Font Colour**
- Insert a suitable **Picture** or **Clip Art** from file - position in bottom left-hand corner
- Use **Typewriter** Animation and **Cover Left** Transition on All Slides
- Number all Slides
- Create a **slide show**
- **Print to File**
- **Close Presentation**
- **Open Presentation** above again
- **Save** it under a new **Name: "Society 3"**
- **Delete Slide 3**
- Change **AutoLayout** of **First Slide** to: **Bulleted**
- **Add Bullet Points:**
    In-house Extra: **10% Discount** to all Members at Waterstones
    Musical Evenings resume on November 30
- Add a **new Slide: Organizational AutoLayout:**

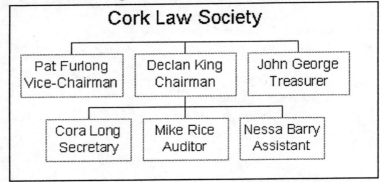

- **Save** and **Close Presentation**

Practice 3:

Create a 2-page presentation about the Au Bon Pain Cafe

- Select an appropriate template for the presentation
- Type the following first page title: "Au Bon Cafe Guarantees Freshness and Quality"
- Type the following text below the title on the first page:
  "We're **concerned** about your Health
  We're *Committed* to <u>Giving</u>
  We're Committed to Quality service

- Number each point
- Slide 2 will include a graph (bar chart) and text.
- Type the following title for the page:
  "The number of Sandwiches being munched daily continue to rise
  Judge for yourself - Sales for this Year Returns:

	Q1	Q2	Q3	Q4
Muffins	5000	5500	5600	6000
Croissants	6000	6100	6300	6900
Cookies	7000	7800	7900	8000
Scones	6600	6700	6800	6900

- Type the following text at the bottom of the page:
  "Our breads, bagels, pastries and cookies are baked fresh every day, all day long, so you can count on their freshness and flavour"

- **Centre** the text and use a different **font** to highlight the different breads.

- Insert an appropriate clip art - Centre below Graph

- Apply a Light-coloured Background to All Slides

- Apply **Animation** to all Slides: **Drop-In** and **Blinds Horizontal Transition**

- Create a slide show and save it with an appropriate name

- Use Landscape Paper Layout and Print to file

- Save all files and close application

Practice 4:

- Create a **3-page presentation**
- Create a **title slide** on slide 1:
  "Bounty new tempo plus" and copy to Slide 2
- On slide 1, insert the following text:
  Bounty Classic White
  Bounty Stronger soaker upper
  Choice of imaginative designs
- **Bullet** these points
- Adjust the **line spacing** to 1.3
- Apply a **shadow** effect to the word "Bounty"
- Add a suitable **clip art** and resize it on the top right hand corner
- On slide 2 set up a datasheet for the graph as follows: (Graph and Title)

City Sales	Jan	Feb	Mar
Cork	2300	4500	4590
Dublin	2349	4600	4600
Waterford	3400	4560	4800
Limerick	3500	4450	4600

- Choose a **3D Area Chart** for the chart type
- Set up a **third** slide and add the **title:**
  Bounty - All the softness you want, all the strength you need

- Adjust the **font** to **Arial** , size **14** and **colour blue**
- Insert the following **autoshape** in slide 3

- **Type** in the text, as displayed, in the **AutoShape** and Add a **Clip Art**
- **Fill** Shape with the **colour blue**
- Set the **line width** of the autoshape to **3 point**
- Insert **slide numbers** on all slides
- Apply a **light coloured design** to the slides; Apply **animation** to slide 2
- Apply a **slide transition** to the presentation and set up a **slide show**
- **Print** the presentation: three slides to a page
- Save as "Bounty Sales "

Internet

The Internet

The Internet is a vast international network of Computers linked together to share information and resources. The word Internet itself is made up from a combination of the two words: "**inter**national" and "**net**work",

Origins

The Internet originated in the 60's with the design of a computer network by the US Defence Department, resistant to nuclear attack; was used for exchanging scientific information and intelligence. There was no central control so if part of the network was destroyed, the information could be transmitted by alternative routes to its destination. This network was known as Advanced Research Projects Agency NETwork or ARPANET.

> **Networks**
> *Are two or more computers joined together by telephone so they can communicate with one another*

In the 70's Supercomputers in research agencies and universities in England as well as in America were linked to exchange research information. In 1986, the National Science Foundation Network established NSFNET network, linking together five university supercomputers which enabled external universities to tap into superior processing power and share resources. Over the next few years many more countries joined this network

> **Supercomputer**
> *This is a main frame sized computer that operates much faster than a normal desktop or laptop computer, and is used for special science and military projects.*

In 1990, Tim Berners-Lee of CERN, a Swiss physics institute, initiated the design of a network for the consistent exchange of physics research that could be accessed by users on any type of computer using the same software - this lay the basis for the World Wide Web as we know it today. The first graphical Web browser was released - Mosaic - which made using the Internet as simple as pointing and clicking a mouse.

> **Mosaic**
> *The first point and click Web browser*

World Wide Web

The popularity of the Internet grew with the development of World Wide Web(WWW). The WWW is made up of millions of linked Web pages like pages in a picture book stored on computers (called hosts or servers) all over the world which can include video clips, sound samples, animations and interactive elements as well as texts and pictures

> *World Wide Web*
> *Graphic and text documents published on the Internet that are interconnected through clickable "hypertext" links*
>
> *Web Page is a single document*
> *Web Sites are a collection of Web pages, created by the same designers - are usually stored on the same computer*

HTML

- Web pages are written in HTML (HyperText Markup Language) ie links to other documents can be **embedded** within text. **Hypertext links** are usually **highlighted** in another colour and/or underlined

Clicking on HyperText

- To activate a link on a Web Page, click on highlighted text or image - a new document or image will display in a page which might be e.g. in England. This English Web page might contain links to a page in Moscow which in turn might have links to a page in Washington etc - these links thus establish a network of connections around the world, from which comes the term: "World Wide Web"

Web Browsers

- In order to look at or "Browse" Web pages, you need software known as a "Web browser". It enables you to search for, download documents, photos, sound and video clips from all computers that are linked to the Web. The two most popular browsers today are: Microsoft Internet Explorer and Netscape. As well as enabling you to view pages on the WWW, the latest versions of these browsers include accessories to enable you to send e-mail, access newsgroups, edit home pages and use multimedia etc.

> **Hypertext links**
> *The links on a Web page are clicked on to connect to other pages on the Web*

Getting Connected: *what you need*

- A **computer** e.g. a PC running Windows 98, with a fast processor, 32MB of RAM (Memory), up to 100 MB of free hard disk

- A **Modem** (stands for **modulator-dem**odulator) internal or external: the most commonly used and cheapest method of connecting to the Internet is by installing a modem and dialing via the standard telephone network.

> **Web Browsers**
> *These are software programs that let you navigate through the WWW and see graphics & text on your computer screen and allow you to make leaps to other Web sites*

- The **speed** (data transfer speed) of your modem will determine how quickly you can browse the World Wide Web: usual speed is **56K**.

- A **Telephone** line

- An **Internet Service Provider (ISP)** - such as Indigo or Ireland-on-Line. Your modem via the telephone line will link you to the Internet through the computer system of the service provider, which is permanently linked to a vast number of modems.

- **Connection Software:** provided by the Service Provider to enable you to establish a connection through their company to the Internet

Getting connected to the Internet

- Before you run your Web Browser and access the Internet for the first time, you must install the special connection software provided by your Service Provider. This software persuades your modem to connect your computer to the Internet. This is done by running a small program called a 'winsock' - also known as a 'dialler' which will control your modem.

- The winsock not only handles the connection, but also establishes a TCP/IP interface, enabling other programs to send and receive data, TCP/IP stands for **Transmission Control Protocol/Internet Protocol** language converter that allows different computers on the Net to speak the same language. Every Computer on the Internet has a unique address, or 'IP number'. TCP/IP tells each computer how to send and receive packets of data, that often have to travel through multiple networks in order to reach their destinations. TCP/IP also checks that the information gets delivered in one piece without errors

Installing Service Provider Software (winsock)

- Follow the instructions given with the software and it will create a working winsock.
- Once the winsock has been installed and configured, you can use it to connect to your service provider's computer. You then leave the winsock program running in the background while you use Internet Explorer.

Sound
A sound card must be installed in your computer with speakers attached if your computer is to produce sound

Signals
Information is sent across telephone networks in the form of sound waves - analog signals. Computers produce data in *digital* form (**digital** signals) To communicate over analog telephone lines, a modem is needed, which converts *digital* signals into *analog* signals and back again

Video
A powerful graphics card must be installed to enjoy quality animation and videos on the Net

Password
This is the secret name chosen by you in consultation with ISP and used initially when installing ISP connection software

User Name
This is the name you use to log on to a network as agreed with your service provider and recorded in the network's databank

---

Searching the Internet with:

- **Web Browser:** Microsoft Internet Explorer

- **Service Provider:** Indigo

To run Internet Explorer:

- Double click on its **icon** on the Desktop:

  or select **Internet Explorer** from the **Programs**, Internet Explorer, section of your **Start** menu -

- ..the **Home Page** of the Microsoft Internet Explorer Web site appears

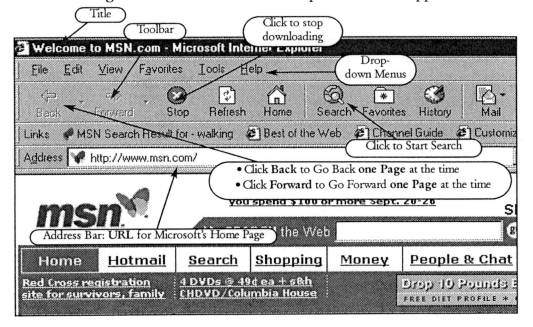

URLs

- Every Web page has a unique **address** - known as an **URL** - this stands for Uniform Resource Locator
- The **URL** of our Web site is:

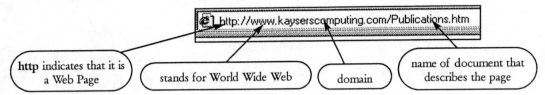

- **http://** is optional - Microsoft Internet Explorer assumes you are looking for a Web Page anyway
- If you are looking for the **main page** of a Web site, don't type anything after the first forward slash, i.e. after the "/" in ".com/", i.e. our **Home Page** is: **www.kayserscomputing.com**
- **Domain Name** is the name given to a **host computer** on the Internet
- The host computer is the one that is **connected directly** to the Internet

Home Page

This term has **two** meanings in World Wide Web:
- It can refer to the page that appears when you **start your Browser** and acts as your **home** base for exploring the Web.
- It can mean the **Introductory** page of the Web page of a client. It details information on what your site contains; it may also give such detail as when the page was built or modified
- When **surfing** the Net, you can always press the **Home** key to take you back to beginning:

Searching the Net:

Options are: 1. Keying in URL, or
                   2. Searching with "key words"

1. Keying in URL:

If you **know** the URL of the Web Page you want, **type** the address directly into the **Address Bar** - our example - the URL for the Irish Times: **www.ireland.com/** When **Return** is hit, the required Web Page opens:

2. Searching with "Key words" in Search Box

The most efficient way of searching the Net is by using a Web Search Tool called a Search Engine. The Search Engines are programs which allow you to search or query the text on millions of Web pages for "key words". The "key words" of a Web page generally sum up the page's contents.

- Type in key word to Web Page in **Search Box**, click **Go**:

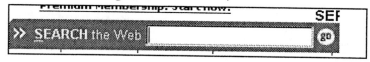

..the Net will be searched using the Search Engines selected in the background

To View Search Engines

- Click **Search** on Toolbar, Click **Customise**:

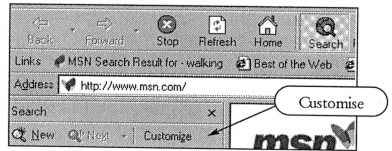

- ..dialog box opens with names of **Search Engines** displayed - to select a **Search Engine** click on **check** box - our example show **all** Search Engines are selected:

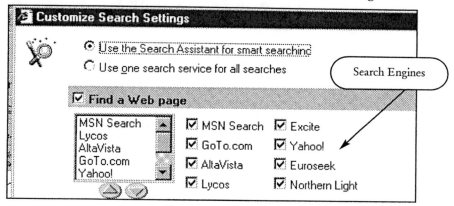

Example: Search using "Key words" - we will look for any Web sites relating to "soccer":

- Type in **key word**:

- Click Go

- - the resulting Web sites relating to this search was:

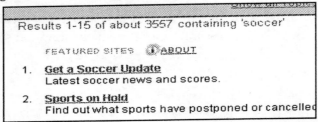

Results 1-15 of about 3557 containing 'soccer'

FEATURED SITES ⓘABOUT

1. **Get a Soccer Update**
   Latest soccer news and scores.

2. **Sports on Hold**
   Find out what sports have postponed or cancelled

- the key word "soccer" is too general a term - to pinpoint web sites containing "soccer" but more specifically the web sites relating to **Soccer** and **Roy Keane**, we will use the operator: " +"

Using Operators: + or -

These operators can be used with key words to make the result of the search more specific

Example:

   "soccer + Roy Keane" will **confine** display to Web pages relating to Roy Keane, *whereas*

   "soccer" - Roy Keane" would display web sites on soccer **excluding** Roy Keane

First Example: "Soccer + Roy Keane" results in:

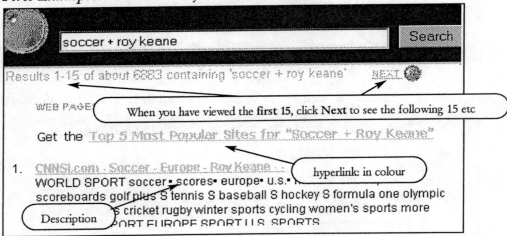

soccer + roy keane   Search

Results 1-15 of about 6683 containing 'soccer + roy keane'   NEXT

WEB PAGE   When you have viewed the first 15, click **Next** to see the following 15 etc

Get the Top 5 Most Popular Sites for "Soccer + Roy Keane"

1. CNNSI.com - Soccer - Europe - Roy Keane ...
   WORLD SPORT soccer · scores· europe· u.s.·   hyperlink: in colour
   scoreboards golf plus S tennis S baseball S hockey S formula one olympic
   cricket rugby winter sports cycling women's sports more
   Description   PORT EUROPE SPORT U.S. SPORTS

- Each Web site in the list includes a **hyperlink** to a Web page which contains the key words "soccer" & "Roy Keane" and a **description** of that page.
- When you see a hyperlink matching what you are looking for, click on on it and the Web Page will **download**.

> *Download*
> *Means to copy a file from a computer on the Net to your own computer*

Copying data from a Web Site and Pasting into Word:

- We found an interesting site on "Roy Keane" - we will copy a selection into Word

> ◎ **BBC News | Football | Keane**
> **could face surgery**

- **Double click** to open site; **highlight** area to be copied, select **Edit Copy** from Menu:

> **Keane could face surgery**
> Manchester United skipper Roy Keane is waiting to find out if he
> needs surgery on his problematic knee.

- **Open** Word; **Paste** in the normal way into a document and **Save**

Directories:

- A Web Search Tool known as "Directories" differ from the Search Engine. Directories list sites by **topic** and **subtopic**.

- **Yahoo** is the most popular and can be found at address: **http://www. yahoo.com**

- Other popular directories are: **America on Line, Cool Tools**, and **BigFoot** - search for the key word **"directories"** to see the full range of directories on the net.

- Directories usually **sort** sites into **categories** and sometimes include **reviews** or **comments**.

- Sites are sorted by **subject, date, platform,** or even their level of "coolness".

- Yahoo directory covers a **broad range** of subjects.

Find Yahoo Directory

- Key in the address: **http://www.yahoo.com** - the Yahoo Home Page with numerous categories (topics) looks like:

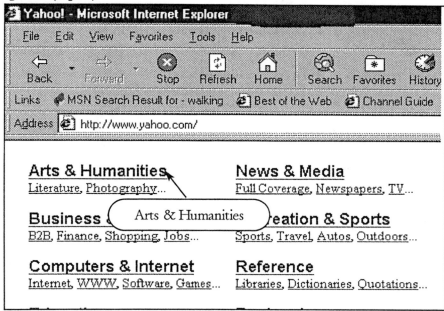

Selecting a Category

- Select the **Category: Arts & Humanities** by double clicking on the name - our favourite fictional author is "John Grisham" so we will type the name and click Search:

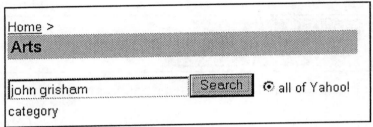

- this will result in two "hits":

- The first site looks interesting so we will double click to open:

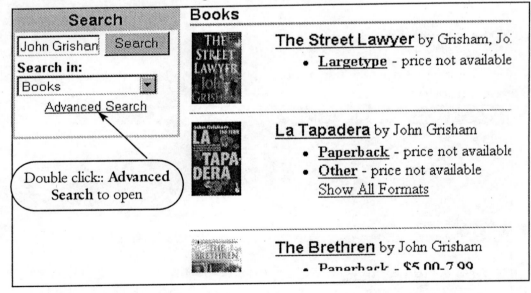

- this is the correct site but rather than undergoing a long laborious search for the book we are interested in: "The Chamber", we will use the hypertext entitled: **Advanced Search:**

- Key in the name: "the chamber" in the **exact phrase** box:

- Click **Search Shopping** - the result will be:

- The **International Edition** looks like the one we want, so we double click:

Chamber: International Edition / Grisham, John

ISBN: 0440295335   **List Price: $6.99**
Dell Publishing

User Rating:
★★★★★
(Unrated)

This Product Is Currently Not Available on Yahoo! Shopping

Use Yahoo! Shopping Alerts to notify you when this product becomes available.

Alert Me When Available

- It looks like it is not currently available to buy through Yahoo Shopping so we will let it to another day!

Another Searching Category Example:

- We are great fans of **Sean Connery, the actor.** We saw a great film: "Finding Forrester" earlier in the year; we now want to know is it available on Video - we will use the Entertainment Category, sub-category "Movies" to establish this fact:

- Select **Entertainment** Category and double click Moves to open:

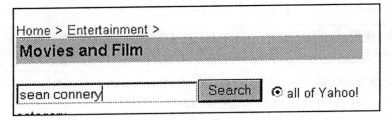

- Type in his name and click Search:

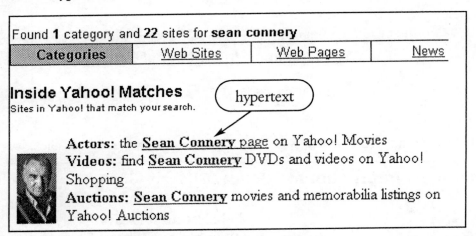

- Click the hypertext: **Videos** and **Sean Connery:**

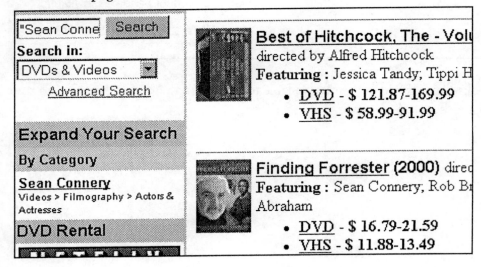

- We need look no further (no need for Advanced Search) - the video we are interested in is in the first page:

![Search page showing results]

"Sean Conne   Search

Search in:
DVDs & Videos
Advanced Search

Expand Your Search

By Category

Sean Connery
Videos > Filmography > Actors & Actresses

DVD Rental

Best of Hitchcock, The - Volu
directed by Alfred Hitchcock
Featuring : Jessica Tandy; Tippi H
- DVD - $ 121.87-169.99
- VHS - $ 58.99-91.99

Finding Forrester (2000) direc
Featuring : Sean Connery; Rob Br
Abraham
- DVD - $ 16.79-21.59
- VHS - $ 11.88-13.49

- Double click the hypertext: **Finding Forrester** for further information:

Finding Forrester (2000)

User Rating: ★★★★☆ (4.8 out of 5)
See User Reviews (6) - Write a Review - Email this page

DVD
Other Formats...

Available: 04/24/2001
MPAA Rating: PG-13

e-Mail

E-Mail is short for **electronic mail** and it's the Internet equivalent of letters and faxes. It's better than either though - not only because it's quick and cheap, but also because you can attach files to an e-mail message. This means you can send text documents, pictures, sound samples and program files as well as simple messages.

Composition of an email address?

- You can send e-mail to anyone on the Internet: you just need to know their address, which will look something like our e-mail address:

kaysers@indigo.ie

| part *before* the @ is the recipient's **user name** | part *after* the @ is the recipient's **service provider (ISP)** | **country** code: Ireland |

Country Codes:

- Every country has its own unique code. Some country codes are:

tw	Taiwan
ca	Canada
uk	United Kingdom
se	Sweden
jp	Japan

- If the e-mail address doesn't include a country, it usually means that it is **American**.

Domain types:

Domain types include the following:

ac	Academic (UK)
com	Company or commercial organization
co	Company or commercial organization (UK)
edu	Educational institution
gov	Government body
mil	Military site
org	Non-profit organisation

Sending e-mail:

- When you send an e-mail message, it is delivered to the recipient's service provider very quickly - usually within a few minutes. It is then sorted in the recipient's mailbox until he or she next logs on and checks for new e-mail.

Getting started with e-Mail

- With the Internet loaded on the screen, click the **Mail** button on the **Toolbar:**

- From the drop-down menu, select **Read Mail:**

- ..a screen similar to the one below (containing folders for incoming, outgoing, sent, deleted and draft) displays (Inbox is selected):

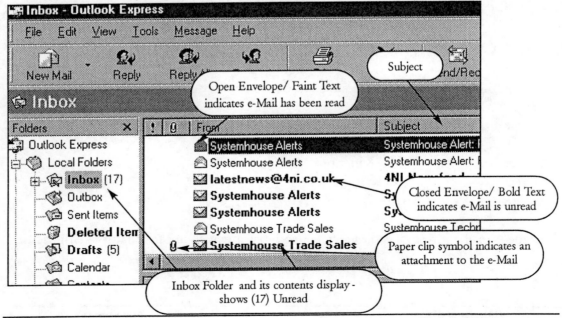

Sending a Message

- To **compose** a message, click the New Message button:

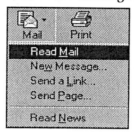

..a **New Message** window appears:

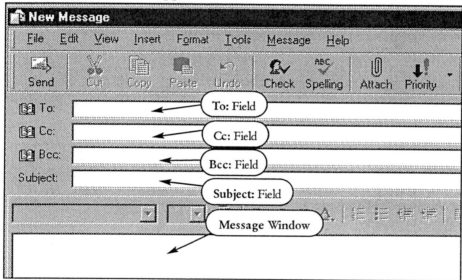

Example of an e-Mail:

You enter recipients' details in the To, Cc and Bcc fields. You can enter as many names as you like in each field separated by commas or semi-colons (;)

Fields:

To: The main recipients should go in the 'To' field

Cc: Anyone to whom you would like a 'carbon copy' sent should go in the 'Cc' field. When the message is received, all the recipients will be able to see to whom it was addressed and who received 'Cc' copies.

Bcc: The 'Bcc' field (blind carbon copy) is used to send copies to extra recipients, just as 'Cc' does, but hides their names from other recipients, so that no one else knows who has received a 'Bcc' copy.

Subject line: As the name suggests, you enter a general description in the Subject line of the e-mail content. Your recipients will first see it in a list of messages in the Inbox listing:

Message text: Type in Message window - messages up to 65,000 letters in length are permissible - but generally, e-mail messages tend to be short. Attachment facility can be used for fuller detail.

e-Mail Example:

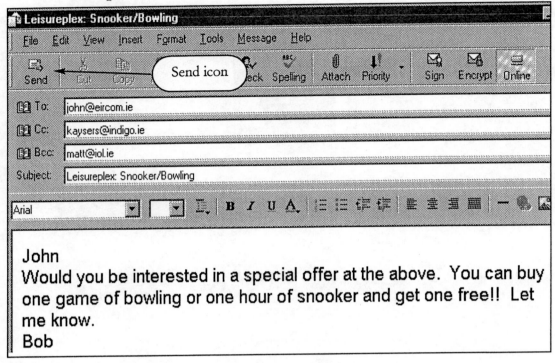

- Key in the e-Mail above; use your own e-mail address so that it will be sent back to you.

Send icon:

- Click the **Send** icon :
  ..this transfers the e-mail to the **Outbox**. A warning message reminds you still have to dispatch your e-mail:

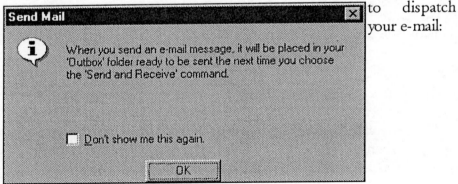

Outbox:

- The Outbox up to now was empty - once you click **OK** above, the **Outbox** will register that it now contains [1] message:

- When you're ready to send all of your message, click **Send and Receive** icon:

File Attachments

If you want to send a long message via e-mail, it is recommended that you use the attachment facility. You create the document in an application - the only requirement is, you must make sure the recipient also has the application or a suitable 'viewer' program. To attach a document, you click the **paper clip** symbol on the toolbar, and select the **file** you want to attach:

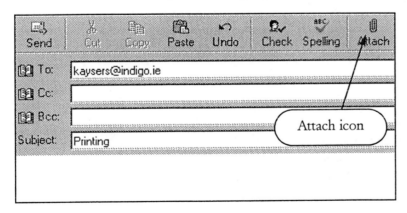

- Attachments generally turn up in the recipient's mail as clickable icons to open or save the file.

Example of a File Attachment:

- We will send an e-mail to ourselves enclosing an attachment created in Word on Commercial Printing

Create the file for the Attachment:

- In Word, the following text is keyed in:

> Commercial Printing
>
> We will now analyse the effect on the Commercial Printing option an additional colour is added to a publication.

- We will save under the **file name:** "Printing Commercial" on the Desktop - therefore, as you see, you create a file for attaching in an application: Word etc. You save in the normal way; as usual, you note the folder where it is saved so that you will be able to locate it.

Creating the e-Mail for the Attachment:

- E-mail is created in the normal way: our example just contains: **To** and **Subject**:

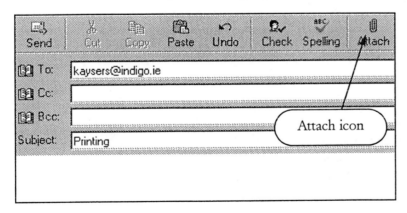

Attaching File to e-Mail:

- We now click **Attach** icon to add attachment - Attachment dialog box opens - we switch to the Desktop, we find file: "Printing Commercial" and click **Attach** button:

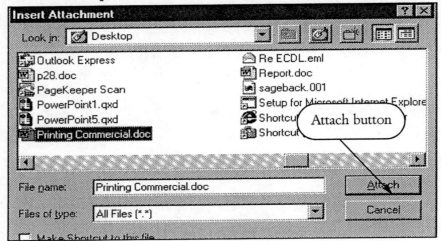

- ..the File for attachment: Printing Commercial is now listed in a new Row in e-Mail:

- Click **Send** to send the e-mail
- When the e-mail is received in the Inbox, it will look like:

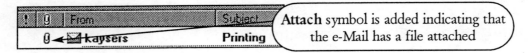

- Double click the e-Mail to open - it will look like:

- As you see the Word symbol is included with the file name in the Attach box telling us that the attachment was created in Word - as we have Word on our PC we will have no trouble opening this file - to do so, double click and the result will be:

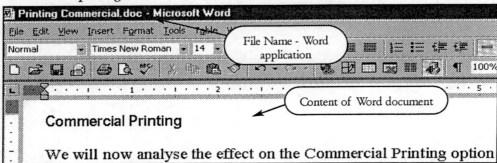

Replying and Forwarding

When you receive messages, you'll need to reply to them, or to send them on to other people.

- To reply, you use the icons: **Reply** or **Reply All** or if you are forwarding an e-mail on to somebody else, use the **Forward** button.
- After selecting one of these options - Outlook Express will create a new message based on the original.
- The subject will be a copy of the original subject, but prefixed with Re: or Fwd:.
- The original message will be copied into the new message body, headed with ' **Original Message** '.

Reply:

- If you selected **Reply icon** , original sender's name is automatically entered in 'To' field:

- Key in the Message below:

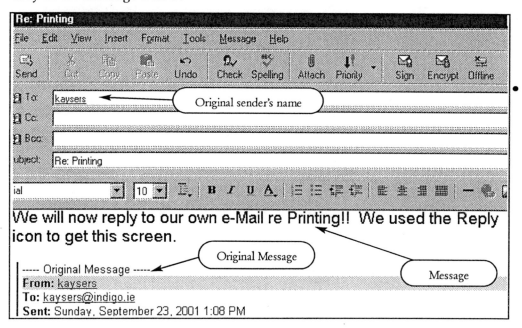

- Click **Send**

Reply to All:

- If you clicked **Reply to All,** then the original sender will be entered in the 'To' field and all other recipients of the original message (except Bccs) will be entered as Cc addresses, so they receive a copy of your reply.

Forward:

- If you click **Forward,** the recipient fields are left blank.
- You can then add any additional recipients, and then complete the message to be sent.
- You can add extra text before the original message, or edit it.
- You can also edit the subject, although it is often a good idea to retain its original identity if you are either sending a reply or forwarding the original message:

- Key in our Message below:

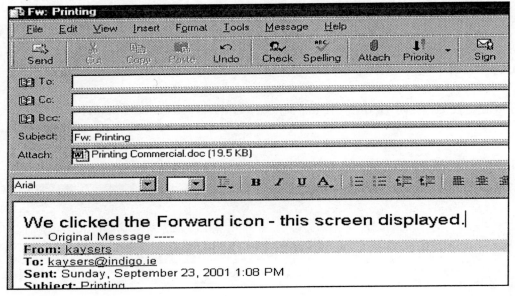

Offline:

- It is economical to Work Offline for many e-Mail activities
- Switch Offline by selecting **File Work Offline** from Menu:

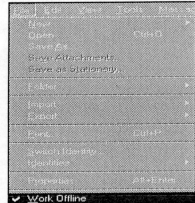

- When you create or reply to a message offline, and then press **Send,** the message is not sent immediately, but is stored in the **Outbox** folder until you are ready to go online.
- If there are messages in your Outbox, you will see a number in brackets after the folder name, indicating how many messages are waiting to be sent.
- You can go online again by repeating **File Work Offline** to send eMails, preferably in a batch.
- When you are ready to send and receive messages, just click **Send and Receive** button. Outlook Express will dial-up your e-mail provider, send any messages waiting in your Outbox, check for new incoming messages, and transfer them to your Inbox.

Sending and Receiving:

Receiving e-mail

- When somebody sends you an e-mail, it's delivered to your service provider's mail server, which puts into your personal mail box. You must then log on and collect it.

To check your mail:

- Run **Outlook Express** and click **Send and Receive:**

..it will connect to the Internet, send any message which is waiting in your Outbox and fetch any new mail:

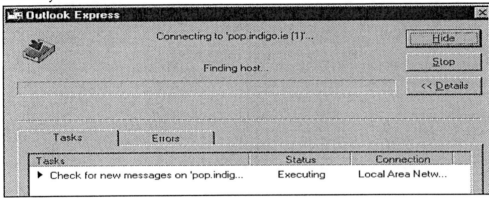

..the new messages are placed in your **Inbox:**

- You can then log off and read them at your leisure.
- Select the **Inbox folder** to see a list of the messages you have received:

- Click once on a message to select it and display the text in the **Preview pane** at the bottom of the window:

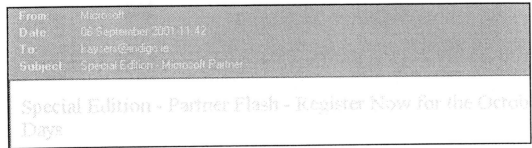

- Click twice to display message in a separate window:

Address Book

- The address Book enables you to store all the e-mail addresses you use regularly. You can then add them to messages more easily.
- To open the Address Book, click the **Addresses** button on Toolbar:

- The Address Book provides a convenient place to store contact information for easy retrieval by programs such as Microsoft Outlook Express. It also features access to Internet directory services, which you can use to look up people and businesses on the Internet.
- You can store important information about people & groups important to you
- With your address book, you have a place to store e-mail addresses, home and work addresses, phone and fax numbers, digital IDs, conferencing information, instant messaging addresses, and personal information such as birthdays, anniversaries, and family members.
- You can also store individual and business Internet addresses, and link directly to them from your address book

Adding an address

- To add an address, click the **New Contact** button:

- Fill in the **person's name**
- Enter a short but easy to remember **nickname**
- Enter the **e-mail address** and click **Add** to add it to the list - the result will be:

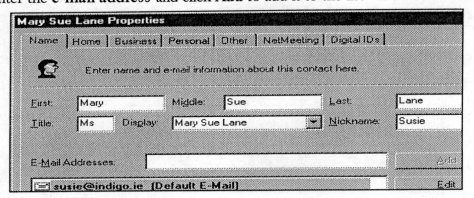

- Click **OK** to finish - this new contact is now added to the Address Book:

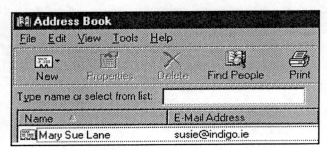

- Outlook Express will look up the address whenever you send a message.

CONSOLIDATION

To consolidate the Internet knowledge acquired in this unit, complete the exercises below:

Practice 1:

- Search the Internet for Web sites on "Rembrandt" - see how many "hits" there are
- Reduce Search by including "National Gallery" with "Rembrandt";
  i.e. "Rembrandt + National Gallery"
- Open one site and copy a portion to Word for Windows; Save File

- Type in the URL for Phoenix Park in Dublin, i.e.
  http://www.dublin tourist.com/regional/castleknock/phoenixpark.shtml
- Copy the section relating to "Dublin Zoo" to Word and Save appropriately

- Find "Brian Kennedy, song writer" - narrow search by including his album:
  "A better Man" - see are the lyrics printed in a site - if so, copy to a Word document;
  otherwise copy details of the Album to Word

- Send an e-mail to Lena - use your own e-mail address so that you can Send it to yourself

- The **Subject** of the e-mail will be: "AGM of Hockey Club"

- The **Text** of the e-mail will be:
  "Lena: I hereby give notice that I intend letting my name go forward at the next AGM for the position of Hon Secretary - I am relying on you for your support.
  Regards, Sheila"

- **Send** e-mail

- **Reply** to this e-mail when it comes back to you

- Your Reply will be:
  "Sheila - delighted to hear of your ambitions within the Hockey Club for the coming year - you can be assured of my vote. I will let Kit know also. Regards. Lena"

- Lena **Forwards** Sheila's e-mail to Kit

- Include with the forwarded e-mail, the following note:
  "Kit:: I am forwarding Sheila's e-mail to you - Sheila would certainly make a welcome addition to the club's officers. Regards: Lena"
- Kit will now send an **attachment** to Lena - set up attachment in Word under the file name: "Hockey 2002" - the said text will be:

  > Two Ladies have applied for Membership of Clondoyle Hockey club - they are:
  >
  > Ms Joan Collins The Mardyke Cork
  > Ms Sue Collins Lee Road Cork

- Kit **replies** to Lena:
  "Thanks for your e-mail - I will certainly support Sheila. I enclose details of two applicants for membership. 'Bye for now - Kit"

Practice 2:

- Go into the **Yahoo.com;** Find the **Entertainment** Category. Find the **Humor,** followed by the **Comedy** section; thereafter keep searching through **Humor, Jokes** - until you find the **Joke of the Day** section - copy a joke relating to a sport into Word

- Within the **Yahoo.com** site, go to the **Science** Category; Select **Deep Sky** within **Astronomy;** find **Stellar Clusters** and copy the **Definition** to a Word Document

- Staying with **Yahoo Directory,** select the **Photograph** section within the **Arts and Humanities** category; from within **Holographic Art** go to the Titantic **Holography Project** and **copy** two paragraphs of its **Home Page** to Word

- Key in the URL: **http://www.geog.nau.edu//tg/contents/v3/index.html**

  Find the text: "TOURISM GEOGRAPHIES - VOLUME 3 - 2001"
  Table of Contents and Links to Editorials & Abstracts/Résumé/Inhaltsangabe/Resumen (not available until 2002)" and copy to a new document within Word - Save as: "Tourism Geographies"

- Create an e-mail, send, reply, forward and attach as below - use your own e-mail address so that you can practice on your own incoming mail etc

- The text of the e-mail Jim **sends** will be:
  John: If you are serious about strengthening your natural defences this Winter, make sure to take an Actimel from Danone every morning. Jim".
  Send
  The **Subject** here is: **Enduring the Winter**
- John **Replies** as follows:
  "Jim: Thanks for the tip Hibernian - I will remember your advice on my next shopping trip. John"
- John **Forwards** Jim's e-mail to Robert: with the comment:
  "Robert, see the advice Jim gave me - do you know that it's a delicious probiotic yogurt drink available in both Original and Orange flavours. John"

- Set up a file in Word now - Save as: "Defence Plan"
  Content of File:

  > Danone Actimel contains L.Casei Imunitass so it helps protect you and your family against what lies ahead. See Web site at: www.actimel.com

- Robert e-mails Dara: **Subject:** Actimel Web Site
  E-mail text: "Dara: See **attached** info entitled: "Defence Plan" - Site is well worth looking at. Robert"

- Dara opens the attachment and **copies** the web site address - he e-mails Jim - he pastes the web address into the e-mail **Subject** line and before **Sending** includes the comment - "John: As you are responsible for starting this whole new debate, delve deeper at this web site! Dara"

Practice 3:

- Search the Internet for Web sites on "Irish Times"
- Narrow search to include "Kevin Myers"
- You are interested in buying his book: "an Irishmam's Diary" - Extend search to include this title
- When you find the relevant site - copy details of the correct title of this book plus the cost price and paste into a file in Word - Save this File as: "Irish Fiction"

- Search the 'net for "Australian Wine"; you are interested in information on the Award winning wine: "Rosemount's Shiraz" - the bottle looks like:

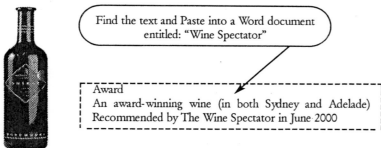

Find the text and Paste into a Word document entitled: "Wine Spectator"

Award
An award-winning wine (in both Sydney and Adelaide)
Recommended by The Wine Spectator in June 2000

- You are researching Irish Presidents particularly Douglas Hyde. Find a site on his biography including the text: "Hyde, Douglas (1860-1949), Irish statesman and scholar, born in Frenchpark, county Roscommon, and educated at Trinity College, Dublin." and Paste into Word; Save this File under "President of Ireland"

- Go to Yahoo Home Page
- Follow systematically through the categories: Society & Culture and Environment, Climate Change, Global Warming, Sea Level Change Category, until you get to the site on: **Rising Sea Levels**

  Copy the quote: "My command stands firm like the mountains and my falcon rises high into all eternity" by Hatshepsut, fl 1503 - 1483 BC
- Paste into Word - Save as: "Hatshepsut 2002"

- Practice e-mail features - use your own e-mail address as before:

- Alice **Sent** this e-mail: "**Subject:** Mary McAleese: August 1998
    Abby: Did you know that our President was not present at the RDS Horse Show to present the Aga Khan trophy in 1998 as she was learning Irish in Donegal."
- Abby **Replies** as follows:
    "Alice: That's right, Abby - she also impressed republicans that September in Australia - one anti-royal activist said that a woman like her would give Queen Elizabeth a run for her money!!"
- Alice **Forwards** Abby's e-mail to Kate: with the comment:
    "Kate, I know you are a fan of our President - so I am forwarding Abby's anecdote. Alice"
- Set up a file in Word now - Save as: "Irish Heroes" - Content of File is:

    Mrs McAleese wins more fans when she joins with the Queen in remembering Irish war dead at Messines in Belgium

- Abby e-mails Alice also with the comment: "Alice: Did you know that Mary McAleese was in Belgium in November 1998 - see attached file. Abby"